TABLE OF CONTENTS ON PAGE 9

2022 Anunnaki Code: End of The World Or Their Return To Earth ?

Ulema Book of Parallel Dimension, Extraterrestrials and Akashic Records

Maximillien de Lafayette

A PUBLICATION OF TIMES SQUARE PRESS AND ELITE ASSOCIATES
NEW YORK   CALIFORNIA   LONDON   PARIS   TOKYO

PUBLISHED AND DISTRIBUTED BY AMAZON.COM COMPANY

PRINTED IN THE UNITED STATES OF AMERICA

2008

***   ***   ***

IN THIS SERIES: 22 PUBLISHED BOOKS, WRITTEN BY MAXIMILLIEN de LAFAYETTE

Read more at

1-ufozetareticuli.com 2-anunnakibooks.com 3-maximilliendelafayettebibliography.com

Probing and analyzing the secret events, chronicles, files and dossiers of governments, organizations, societies, and powerful people. A collection of the most important theories, concepts, essays and analyses by top scientists, theologians, investigators, philosophers, media, believers and skeptics. From UFO, and the assassination of President Kennedy to time/space travel, parallel universes, Jesus Christ, Maria Magdalena, immortality, quantum physics, and the hidden world of the occult.

The series is a prism of the reflections and opinions of highly regarded scientists, philosophers and investigators.

The author presents summaries of their theories and opinions. It should please both the believers and the skeptics. This series is an essential reference tool and guide to the secret world of UFOS, extraterrestrials, the greatest conspiracies, cover-ups and controversies of our time.

Available worldwide and at www.amazon.com

Published (December 20, 2007- April 25, 2008):

- **1-**From Zeta Reticuli to Earth: Time, Space and the UFO Technology. (400 Pages)
- **2-**The Biggest Controversies, Conspiracies, Theories and Coverups of our Time: From the Secret Files of Science, Politics, The Occult and Religion. (400 Pages)
- **3-**Inside A UFO: Alien Abduction, Hypnosis, Psychiatry, Quantum Physics and Religions Face to Face. (400 Pages)
- **4-**UFOs and the Alien Agenda. The Complete Book of UFOs, Encounters, Abduction And Aliens Bases On Earth. (400 Pages)
- **5-**Extraterrestrials Agenda: Aliens' Origin, Species, Societies, Intentions and Plan for Humanity. (400 Pages)
- **6-**The Anunnaki's Genetic Creation of the Human Race: UFOs, Aliens and Gods, Then and Now. (400 Pages)
- **7-**Extraterrestrials-US Government Treaty and Agreements: Alien Technology, Abduction, and Military Alliance. (400 Pages)
- **8-**Biographical Encyclopedia of People in Ufology and Scientific Extraterrestrial Research: People Who Matter. (740 Pages)
- **9-**Zeta Reticuli and Anunnaki Descendants Among Us: Who Are They? (400 Pages)
- **10-**UFO-USO and Extraterrestrials of the Sea: Flying Saucers and Aliens Civilizations, Life and Bases Underwater (400 Pages)

***   ***   ***

8 NEW BOOKS BY MAXIMILLIEN DE LAFAYETTE EN ROUTE

Pre-Order Your Copies Now From Amazon.com
Libraries and Booksellers/Distributors: Place Your Standing Orders Right Now

En route: (May 25, 2008):

- **1**-Ulema: Code and Language of the World Beyond (400 Pages)
- **2**-Zeta Reticuli and Greys Encyclopedia (550 Pages)

En route: (June 25, 2008):

- **3**-UFOs And Extraterrestrials Meet Astronauts, US Presidents and USAF: Sightings, Encounters, Aliens-US Secret Bases and Black Projects (300 Pages)
- **4**-The Book of Ra-Dosh: Anunnaki, Creation of the Genetic Man, and DNA of our Future (300 Pages)

En route: (July 25, 2008):

- **5**- Anunnaki Map of the After-Life: Where And How You Continue Your Life After Death (300 Pages)
- **6**-World Who's Who in Ufology and Study of Extraterrestrial Civilizations (400 Pages)

En route: (August 25, 2008):

- **7**-Thematic Encyclopedia of Ufology and Extraterrestrial Research (740 Pages)
- **8**-Anunnaki Return To Earth And The Future Of The Human Race (300 Pages)

Note: Titles and dates subject to change

*** *** ***

Acknowledgments and Gratitude

For their enormous contributions, articles, comments, and generosity, I am deeply grateful to:

Dr. Ilil Arbel, London's Natural History Museum, American University in Yerevan, UNESCO, University of Ain Shams, University of Munich, Kaslik University, American University in Beirut (AUB), La Sagesse University, University of Pennsylvania, Peter Farley, L.C. Geerts, University of Chicago, Oriental Institute of the University of Chicago, Roc Hatfield, Dr. Robert F. Harper, Richard C. Haines, McGuire Gibson, John Chambers, Amitakh Stanford, Dr. Noel Huntley, Dr. Malachi York, John Carpenter, John Jaeger, Dr. Sasha Lessin, Boyd RiceChristopher B. Siren; Stasonorg; Tularc: Special thanks for their data on Sumerian deities), John Strickland, John Lear, University of Cairo, The British Museum, Staff of the Library of the Vatican, Lebanon National Museum, Syrian Ministry of Education, Egyptian Ministry of Education, University of Cairo, American University of Beirut, Harvard, Oxford, New York University, Iraqi Ministry of Culture and Education, Lebanese Directorate General of Antiquities, Sherry Shriner, Rabbi Mordachai, University of Paris, The Smithonian Institution, Monsignor Maroon, Cheik Ahmad Al Huseini, Joy Elliot, Dr. Steven Greer, Dr. Richard Boylan, Dr. William Birnes, Dr. Michael E. Salla, Dr. Zecharia Sitchin, John Stokes, late Dr. Carl Sagan, Prof. Sam Chang, Dr. John Chen, Dr. Kurt Rosenstadt, Dr. Gisele von Guntenbergersen, Lyssa Royal Holt, Alex Collier, Dr. David Jacobs, Branton, Nick Pope, Dr. Lynne Kitei, Helen Littrell, Jean Bilodeaux, Pamela Stonebrooke, Louise Compton, Nigel Watson, Barbara Tandory, Chris Rutkowski, Dr. John Dreher, Shoshanna Rosenstein, Dr. Carol Lexter, Michele Bugliaro Goggia, Victor Martinez, Richard Nolan, Bill Ryan, Michael Lindemann, Len Kasten, Tim Swartz, Linda Moulton-Howe, Mark Pilkington, Dee Finey, Sal Rachel, Estelle Nora Harwit Amrani, Dr. Al Mutawalli, Dr. Erica Soderholm, Indiadaily, M.D., Forbes Magazine, Woodruff T. Sullivan III, Dr. Albert A. Harrison, Dr. Joel T. Johnson, Dr. Seth Shostak, Elie Crystal, Vj enterprises ufologists group, geosites group, Dr. Wolf, David Icke, Marcus LiBrizzi, James Donahue, PUFFON, John Jaeger, Alienmonstruous, watchersfiles, bibliotecapeleyades, geosites, thothweb, Sherry Shriner, G. Sandow, Charles Plemmons III, Dirk Vander Ploeg, Steven Mizrach, Texfiles, Michael Lindemann, Nigel Watson, Barbara Tandory, Michelle Guerin, Filip Coppens, Marcia Jedd, Alienabduction.com, Angela Hind, BBC, Dr. Naomi Wolfberg,Melonda Leslie, Mark Williams, The Library of Congress, Staff of the National Archives, New York Times, The Washington Post, World Jewish News Agency, The International Herald Daily News, London Monthly Herald, The New York Monthly Herald, Art and Style Magazine, Paris Match, Bibliotheque Nationale, Showbiz Time Magazine, Peter R. Farley, Katharina Wilson, Dr. Donald A. Johnson, Neil Freer, Giorgio de Santillana, Ph.D., Hertha von Dechend, Ph.D., David Hudson, Richard C. Hoagland, Dr. Malachi York, Erol O. Torun, KeelyNet, Lance Oliver, The Daily Mirror, The Los Angeles Times, The Washington Post, CNN, Professor G. Gordon Broadbent, Rense.com, The Daily Telegraph, Leslie Watkins, David Ambrose, Christopher Miles, Gerry Neugebauer, US News World Report, IndiaDaily, The Astronomical Journal, R. Harrington, Vince Johnson, Long Island UFO Network, Martin Cannon, Jenny Randles, Robert Durant. John Keel, Ed Conroy, Dr. Helmut Lammer, Carl Feindt, Dr. Stuart Mackay, John Vincent Sanders, Bordeland Science, CSETI, Monte Leach, Share International, John Lear, Art Bell, Dan Sewell Ward,Laurence Gardner, Bantam Books, Ashayana Deane, NOVA, PBS, Joe Morton, Budd Hopkins, Fancy Living Magazine, BlackVault, Brandon. SETI, NASA, United States Air Force, The Pentagon, The FBI, RRR Group. The Author

Table of Contents

*** *** ***

FROM ZETA RETICULI TO EARTH
Time, Space And The UFO Technology

About the book: Anyone who thinks that our universe is a simple one, where two and two always add to four, and where all we needed to know we had learned in the proverbial kindergarten, lives in denial. This is a very complex universe and just a glimpse into the works of such greats as Albert Einstein, Niels Bohr, or even the early visionaries like Leonardo da Vinci or Emanuel Kant, will shake anyone's complacent world view after a few minutes of reading.

As human beings, we seek comfort. Perhaps we are finding it in religion; perhaps we look for it in the teachings of Kabbalah or New Age. We feel the need to know, to understand, because if we do not we cannot be comfortable and may even be scared. And the factions of conservative religions, atheism, science, spirituality, evolution supporters, creationists, etc., clash and fight, each honestly convinced that their own views are the only correct ones, and the rest of the world must be persuaded to follow that path.

But to read, understand, and enjoy this book, try to adopt the one and only state of mind that would allow it: *for a few hours, try to be an agnostic.* Adopt the one tenet of the true agnostic, which is, very simply, the admission that you simply don't know. That you cannot know, because you are three-dimensional while the universe is multi-dimensional. That you are willing to open your mind to the possibilities – and perhaps enjoy the freedom and liberation that such attitude can bring.

This book has everything, and it does not take a judgemental stand. It reports, discusses, and engages the reader in fruitful lines of investigation and independent thought. From time travel to UFO phenomena, from modern physics and the role of the astronauts and the military to blatant cover-ups and controversies, from the views of the most distinguished scientists and thinkers of our time to sceptics and scoffers, it simply covers the field in the most complete way one can hope to find in a single volume.

The book can be read from beginning to end and be greatly enjoyed by any intelligent reader. However, some of us may have a pet topic. Perhaps you are fond of cover-ups? Perhaps, specifically, presidential involvement? You will find a chapter about it. Eisenhower, Bush, Clinton, Truman? They are there. Interested in Element115? Hard to find, right? Well, here you will find it in detail. Travel exceeding the speed of light? Of course. Relationship with Zeta Reticuli? Right here. And you don't have to be a believer. Part III will support the opposition. This is a spectacular book, written in a language that all of us can understand, but never talks down. It will enlighten and entertain and give you food for thought and reflection for years to come. And if I may indulge in a cliché – it may change your life!

HYBRID HUMANS AND ABDUCTIONS:
Aliens-Government Experiments
An Explosive Book!

The author explores the hidden world of alien-human genetic programs and genetic experiments on abductees.
An astonishing variety of topics such as:

- A hybrid race? Is it possible?
- How does alien/human hybridization tie into all of this?
- How do aliens possess human bodies?
- Who are the Illuminati? Children and bloodlines?
- Why are bloodlines so important to these people?
- Why do you think the late conspiracy theorist William Cooper went back on his claims of UFOs and aliens later on in his life?
- Who are the human grey hybrid?
- Summary: Height, weight, skin, eyes, head, hair, language, speech, habitat, emotions and feelings, amusement, family ties, etc...
- Some theories...
- **1**-Theory: Extraterrestrial cross breeding
- **2**-Theory: Hutchinson-Gilford syndrome

Those Who Claim To Be Alien-Human Hybrids
The Hybrid Program

- Theories of the alien-human-hybrid program
- Hybrids surpass us in intellectual and psychic abilities
- How will this hybrid race be created?
- What is the actual process used in the creation of hybrids?
- Successful hybrids are those who can indefinitely survive in a densely physical environment
- What is the soul nature of these hybrids?
- Why can't aliens stay in our physical environment for prolonged periods of time?

What about military abductions?

- It is now possible to discern at least four specific programs that the aliens have put into effect to achieve their goal
- The abduction program
- Breeding program
- The hybridization program
- The integration program

*** *** ***

THE BIGGEST CONTROVERSIES, CONSPIRACIES, THEORIES AND COVERUPS OF OUR TIME

From the secret files of science, politics, the occult and religion

- "To dare to write such a book is a risky affair. Maximillien de Lafayette who wrote it got to be exceptionally brave, an idealistic or totally crazy. This book could jeopardize his life. This is not the first time Mr. De Lafayette writes about a delicate and dangerous subject. He did it once before when he authored "Extraterrestrials-US Government Treaty and Agreements." But he must be protected by some powerful organizations to come forward and present those facts about secret and influential people and governments who control the world and our life. Once you start to read this book you will not be able to put it down. An amazing, revealing and explosive book. Get your copy. It will take you to the world of conspiracies, greed, power, and world domination. Probing and analyzing the secrets, events, chronicles, files and dossiers of governments, organizations, societies, and powerful people."- New York Monthly Herald

- A collection of the most important theories, concepts, essays and analyses by top scientists, theologians, investigators, philosophers, media, believers and skeptics.

- From UFO, the assassination of President Kennedy to time/space travel, parallel universes, Jesus Christ, Maria Magdalena, immortality and hidden world of the occult. The book is a prism of the reflections and opinions of highly regarded scientists, philosophers and investigators.

- The author presents summaries of their theories and opinions. It should please both, the believers and the skeptics. This book is an essential reference tool and guide to the secret world of the greatest conspiracies, cover-ups and controversies of our time.

*** *** ***

15

INSIDE A UFO

Alien Abduction, Hypnosis, Psychiatry, Quantum Physics and Religions Face to Face

This book is a prism of the opinions and theories of the most brilliant minds of our times, and an expose of the thoughts and findings of skeptics, believers, therapists, psychiatrists, psychologists, UFOlogists, scientists, astronauts, governments' officials, and the abductees. It contains an astonishing variety of topics, including but not limited to:

- Alien abduction.
- Portraits and profiles of alien abductees and their experiences.
- Sleep paralysis, false memories, trauma and regression hypnosis.
- Aliens' telepathy, intentions and agenda.
- UFO technology; space/time travel possibilities and paradoxes.
- Description of the aliens' societies, families, physiognomy.
- Surgical operations performed on abductees.
- Interviews with leading authorities in the field.
- Types, categories and origin of aliens.
- Conspiracies, cover-ups, alleged governments contacts and treaties with aliens.

*** *** ***

UFOs and Extraterrestrials Day by Day from the 1900 to the Present

Chronicles of everything that happened from 1900 to the present. Including but not limited to:

- All the crashes
- Most important sightings
- Major events in contemporary ufology
- Documented encounters
- Major alien abductions
- Governments' secret projects
- Government secret memoranda
- New facts, findings and discoveries
- Secret military-aliens bases on earth, underground and underwater
- All the leading theories

UFOS AND THE ALIEN AGENDA

The Complete Book of UFOs, Encounters, Abduction And Aliens Bases On Earth

The book includes multi-varied topics and in-depth articles including but not limited to:

- UFOs: Complete history, conspiracies, cover-ups, security threat, defense, and government secrecy
- National Security and UFOs
- What the U.S. government knows about unidentified flying objects
- UFOs as a threat and the evidence
- The reasons why the government might have chosen not to disclose the ET reality: The 65 reasons
- A correlation between nuclear devices and UFOs
- Reverse engineering alien technology at United States government facilities
- Extraterrestrials' agenda. Cosmic top secret
- The plot thickens at Area 51 and Hangar 18
- Seeing UFOs at Area 51
- United States acquisition of advanced technology and interaction with alien cultures
- Report on the motivations and activities of extraterrestrial races
- A typology of the most significant extraterrestrial races interacting with humanity
- 57 extraterrestrial races known to the U.S. military
- Very first communication between aliens and the United States
- Setting up the first written protocol and the signing of a treaty between aliens and the United States government
- First set of the treaty and a know-how technical book given by aliens to Eisenhower and American scientists.
- The first alien hostage at Holloman AFB;
- "KRILL": The first book on aliens' technology written by aliens and given to the US military and US space program.

EXTRATERRESTRIALS AGENDA

Aliens' Origin, Species, Societies, Intentions and Plan for Humanity

An explosive book! Everything about the aliens' agenda, including in-depth articles about (to name a few):

- Historical chronology: The era of "modern" interaction with non-human terrestrial and non-terrestrial entities
- The United States air force and the central intelligence agency exercised complete control over the 'alien secret
- Plans were formulated to defend the earth in case of invasion
- The impact of UFOs and their occupants on religion
- Given their technological superiority, why don't hostile alien forces just take over the planet?
- What about military abductions?
- Can anything be done to stop the alien agenda?
- There are artificial humans who are manufactured by alien forces
- Alien threat response security
- Earth may be a combined multi-alien race
- The symbols of nature and evolution and ETs

*** *** ***

THE ANUNNAKI'S GENETIC CREATION OF THE HUMAN RACE

UFOs, Aliens and Gods, Then and Now

The most comprehensive published work on the Anunnaki and their impact on the human race. Wealth of information and in-depth articles on so many topics, including, but not limited to:

1-ETs' role in human development
2-God and the extraterrestrials
3-The mystery surrounding Jesus and the Sons of God
4-The extraterrestrials are responsible for genetic intervention in the modern era
5-The 'God' of the Old Testament, Yahweh/Jehovah, is in fact an "intermediary god" or extraterrestrial
6-How the Anunnaki created us genetically
7-The real story of Nibiru (Planet X)
8-We created you. We came from space
9-The truth behind human origins
10-The alien gods were genetic engineers
11-The Nephilim an ancient race of half-breed humans... And much much more...

*** *** ***

EXTRATERRESTRIALS-US GOVERNMENT TREATY AND AGREEMENTS
ALIEN TECHNOLOGY, ABDUCTION, AND MILITARY ALLIANCE

A must read book!

It details all the agreements and treaty signed between the United States and Aliens from Zeta Reticuli and other planets. Complete disclosure of the articles of the SECRET TREATY.

The book discusses a wide variety of fascinating subjects, including:

- What aliens wanted from us, and what the US Government gave them?
- What did we receive in return?
- How secretly NASA and US astronauts dealt with UFOS,
- President Eisenhower 1954 meeting with extraterrestrials, the first United States contact, and treaty with extraterrestrials, points and agreements of the treaty,
- The formulated plans by the United States and Russia to defend the earth in case of invasion,
- The whole story of MJ-12
- Aliens agenda and purposes on earth.

*** *** ***

Biographical Encyclopedia of People in Ufology and Scientific Extraterrestrial Research: People Who Matter (740 Pages)

Who Are the World's Best Ufologists?

Here they are in alphabetical order!

- The world's largest and first biographical encyclopedia of the most important people, ufologists, scientists, researchers, writers, believers and skeptics of all time.
- Their life, times, career highlights, theories, opinions, work, books and contributions.
- Including interviews and historical analyses of ufology from its dawn to the present.
- Followed by Volume 2 (740 pages) and the Yearbook (400 pages).
- A total of 1,880 pages!

*** *** ***

UFO-USO And Extraterrestrials Of The Sea

Flying Saucers and Aliens Civilizations, Life and Bases Underwater

*** *** ***

Everything you needed to know about USOs/UFOs and extraterrestrials who live here on earth, underwater;
1-Their lives,
2-Occupations,
3-Families,
4-Communities,
5-Habitat
6-Technology,
7-Flying saucers,
8-Agenda,
9-Military bases in the United States and worldwide,
9-Contacts between the US Navy, CIA and Aliens.

Fascinating book detailing locations, maps, and addresses. of all aliens underwater bases and communities. Some of the discussed topics:

- Comprehensive list of sightings and encounters, including dates and charts.
- List of all known bases, locations, description, roles and functions.
- Extraterrestrial civilizations and aliens living and operating underwater.
- USO and the United State Navy face to face: Secret reports, sightings and encounters.
- How USOs operate, fly and hide.
- Why USOs are there? Purpose and agenda.

*** *** ***

REVELATION OF AN ANUNNAKI'S WIFE
Christianity, The White House, And Victoria's Hybrid Congressman Son.

Co authored by Maximillien de Lafayette and Ilil Arbel, Ph.D.

THE WORLD'S FIRST AUTO-BIOGRAPHY OF AN EXTRATERRESTRIAL

The amazing autobiography of Victoria, an Anunnaki wife in her own words...no channeling, no trances, no séances. Direct data by and rapport with Victoria in person. Including explosive revelations about:

- Major UFOs-Extraterrestrials incidents and threats inside secret military bases,
- Governments' involvement with 2 particular alien races,
- Description of the world of extraterrestrials,
- The Anunnaki's community, societies and families
- Description of life on Zeta Reticuli,
- Description of the habitat on Planet X,
- Victoria-Alien husband love story, and wedding ceremony,
- Victoria's voyage to Zeta Reticuli,
- Victoria's personal involvement with her alien in-laws, and the leader of the Anunnaki,
- Victoria's hybrid congressman son and the major role he will be playing on the arena of world politics,
- Dwight Eisenhower's direct contact with extraterrestrials,
- The Vatican's secret files on UFOS, extraterrestrials, Christianity-Alien entities connection,
- Jesus Christ's life after the crucifixion; his trip to Marseille, his family, children and their bloodlines, and his wife Mary Magdalene,
- Victoria's take on channelers, contactees, abductees, ufologists, and charlatans,
- Earth's future, multiple universes, interdimensional beings,
- Anunnaki's existence and civilization on earth: Past, present and future.

Times Square Press is pleased to announce a historical and literary event in the field of Ufology: The publication of the book *Revelation of an Anunnaki's Wife* by Maximillien de Lafayette and Ilil Arbel

For the first time in history, the wife of a high-rank Anunnaki, an earth woman who is a direct descendant of the Phoenician/Anunnaki race, has come forward to reveal new and astounding information about many subjects that have, until now, been top secret. The woman, who is known only by her first name, Victoria, was born on earth and adopted by a prominent family. A brilliant and beautiful woman, Victoria attended one of the best universities in the Northeast and became a successful business woman, but through unforeseen events had been approached by a high ranking Anunnaki with the request to bear a child, who is now a prominent U.S. senator, and instrumental to the future of the human race. Eventually, Victoria became the ambassador of the planet Nibiru, the home of the Anunnaki, to various governments on earth, was involved with top security missions, and at a certain time in her career, hunted by the CIA.

At age sixty, when Victoria was ready to return to Nibiru to be rejuvenated and prepared for a lifespan of hundreds of thousands of years, she decided to give the benefit of her experience to humanity. Victoria approached two authors with her request to publish her story, choosing them carefully. Maximillien de Lafayette is a well-known authority on UFOs, extraterrestrial issues, and particularly the Anunnaki. His latest book, The Anunnaki Encyclopedia, has just been published. But Mr. de Lafayette is not a Ufologist – he is a historian, an academic, and the author of over a hundred books and encyclopedias on many other subjects. He has made it a point to let the public know that he is not affiliated with any Ufology group, and maintains his objectivity and independence. Ilil Arbel is also far from being a Ufologist. She has published biographies and memoirs, and is a contributor to a noted online Encyclopedia, and to a literary society. After pursuing the work of many authors, Victoria found them most appropriate for her publication plan.

The book is highly newsworthy not only for these reasons, but for the subject matter and the revelations. It includes such explosive subjects as earth governments cooperating with alien abductions for their own gain; high-ranking officials adopting hybrids and allowing them to merge with society, thus contaminating our genetic material; the current acceleration of alien atrocities; the Anunnaki's creation of the human race – in their image – starting with the first woman; the truth about Jesus and Mary Magdalene, and some mistaken beliefs of Christians, Jews, and Muslims; alien technology; immortality and life after death; and much, much more. The reader follows Victoria for forty years, as she gives birth to her Anunnaki son, studies at the Nibiru Academy, views the horrors of alien experiments, works on an earth base of aliens as part of her mission, learns to use telepathy, attends the Akashic library, marries a most attractive, high-ranking Anunnaki, and escapes those who wish to kill her, be it government officials or ancient, evil spirits. The book combines high suspense with scholarly explanations, and will appeal to a variety of readers – historians, Ufologists, readers of biographies and memoirs, and anyone else who loves a good adventure.

ULEMA

CODE AND LANGUAGE OF THE WORLD BEYOND

About the book: This is NOT a book on magic, occultism, channeling, spirits, and communicating with the dead! Simply because the author does not believe in "such things" as he put it bluntly.

The book is far deeper and more complex. It has roots in science, power of the mind, and transmutation of thoughts and visions into mental rapport with Ulemas who communicate with terrestrial beings through codes and secret language known to very few. It is hard to categorize the content of this book, since it does not belong to the commonly known aspects and teachings of "new age", Eastern philosophy, mind-body concepts, meditation, Zen, Yoga, spirituality, "energy", and similar disciplines.

For years, the author was reluctant to put in writing what he has discovered and learned from a secret group of scientists, philosophers and inquisitive minds who believe in a parallel world, and the scientifico-mental powers of the mind.

They are the ULEMAS; they do not teach religion, nor impose any moral doctrine.

The ULEMA hold a secret; the ultimate knowledge of at least one world beyond the one we know. In this book, the author tries to explain their thoughts, and attempts to introduce us to some codes and techniques they use to communicate with far more advanced "cosmic presence."

No! They are not UFO, extra-terrestrials, or the spirits of the dead.

They are the manifestation of an "intelligence" the human race can benefit from.

This book can change the way you understand the world you live in, and open your eyes to "unseen powerful and positive intelligence" that surrounds you, lives around you, and could change your whole life.

*** *** ***

WHAT EXTRATERRESTRIALS AND ANUNNAKI WANT YOU TO KNOW

Their true identities, origins, Nibiru, Zeta Reticuli, Plans, Abductions and humanity future

This is the book that will turn the world of ufology, extraterrestrials and paranormal upside down.

The most powerful, revealing and unique book ever written in the field. New information, secrets and ultimate knowledge revealed for the first time in history directly by Victoria, A Human-Hybrid Annunaki Wife, her Husband, Sinharmarduchk, An Anunnaki Leader, and The Ulema Masters. Among the topics: the 7 different genetic human races, the habitat and life on Nibiru, Zeta Reticuli and dozens of other planets, how they live, what they do, the origin of humanity, predictions about our future and all the military cooperations with governments worldwide.

Partial listings of discussed topics:

On Religions:
1-The Immaculate Conception: An Anunnaki pattern
2-The Exodus as we know it, never happened
3-The Origin of the Ten Commandments
4-The real Moses
5-Ufology's major theories about the Anunnaki, extraterrestrials, Greys and how they fit in the scenario of the creation and the origin of the human race

Communicating with extraterrestrials via channeling and telepathically:
1-Communication with aliens is done through artificial spatial structures in fifth or higher dimension
2-What is the best way to communicate with extraterrestrials?

Real physiognomy, faculties and senses of extraterrestrials:
1-Description of all the extraterrestrial races

From metaphysical to bio-electro-plasma and to physical:
1-Some aliens are from our future
2-What is an "Alien's Manifestation"? What is an "Alien's Apparition"?
3-You can interpret it as "Metaphysical Energy" before it fully materializes
What is an "Alien's Teleportation"?

UFOs, Aliens' Impregnated Women, Extraterrestrials And God:

Sex with Reptilians, Alien Motherhood, The Bible, Abductions and Hybrids

The author probes and analyzes the most mind-boggling aspects and darkest mysteries of UFOs: Alien motherhood and impregnation of women by extraterrestrials. A most explosive and informative book in the genre. The book includes all the theories, facts, reports, stories and experts opinions in the field.

- Read the stories of raped women
- And people victimized by extraterrestrials.
- Hear the voices of their hybrid babies.

A powerful book that will turn the world of ufology and paranormal phenomena upside down. No other compendium can match the abundance of information and in-depth articles you will find in this work. Here is a list of some of the discussed topics:

- Aliens who abduct humans are from far into the future, anywhere from 1000 to 3000 years in the future,
- Aliens abducting women, impregnating them, and later abducting them again,
- How do they get the sperm samples out of male abductees?
- Concerns over the coming of "outsiders" carrying off women and breeding with them,
- Some women abductees have suffered from a various internal complications, including a high incidence of ovarian cysts,
- Presentation of events which occur during an alien abduction,
- There are still today genes of the hybrid species product of the "Fallen Ones" and "Daughters of men" on the earth,
- The Immaculate Conception concept, impregnated women by "something" or "somebody" other than their husbands, and how all these pregnancy mysteries and extra-marital affairs are related to extraterrestrials,
- All these women conceived without having an intercourse with their husbands,
- According to Freud's logic, "Jesus may have had no biological father". Was Jesus a bastard? An Extraterrestrial? God? How about his DNA?
- Almost all the founders of the world's greatest religions could be considered bastards, because they did not have a terrestrial and/or a known father!

460,000 Years of UFO-Extraterrestrials Biggest Events and Secrets

Contacts, Anunnaki Language, Cover-Ups, Discoveries From Phoenicia to Area 51

Partial listing of discussed topics:

1-From 460,000 to the Present

2-Man was created from the clay which is found in abundance in the region and, so that he would look like the Igigi

3-The DNA imprint is carried over after death

4-Sixteen males and sixteen females who comprised a married family traveled to Earth from Sirius

5- All lifeforms generate their own bioenergetic grids

6- The theory of the ORME (The Tree of Life and Ha Qabala). From levitation to zero point energy

7-The traditions of the Anunnaki in raising their own from the dead

8-The Alphabet: Phoenicians take letters and words from the Anunnaki's language

9-Secret extraterrestrial words that can create wealth, fortune and power

10-Ulema: God is Not the creator of the universe. The universe per se is the logical reason of its very self-existence

11-The Nephilim, Anakim, Elohim, Baalshalimroot, and the Shtaroout-Hxall Ain

12-Anunnaki live on three planets: Ashtari (Nibiru), Zeta 1 and Ashartartun- ra

13-Birth of the explosive theory of the direct link of Phoenicia, extraterrestrials, Roswell's UFOs, the Illuminati, and the Freemasons to the government of the United States

14-Phoenicia was the land of descent of the "Sons of God" described in Genesis 6

15-The amazing story of Helen and Betty Mitchell and their encounters with aliens

16-Dancing and playing games with aliens inside a UFO

17-The birth of explosive theories, claims and allegations

In brief: The whole history of UFOs and Extraterrestrials from DAY ONE to the present!

***   ***   ***

EXTRATERRESTRIALS, UFO, NASA-CIA-ALIENS MIND BOGGLING THEORIES, STORIES AND REPORTS

Anunnaki, Zeta Reticuli, Area 51, Abductees, Whistleblowers, Conspirators. The Real & THE FAKE

The world's most mind-boggling theories about UFOs, extraterrestrials, contacts with the human race, revelations by alien-hybrid-human people living among us, United States astronauts encounters with UFO on the moon and around the earth orbit, messages from aliens received by NASA, SETI and the United States Air Force, MJ12 documents, accounts by abductees taken to military bases...in brief all the theories from the most realistic ones to the strangest and most explosive as publicly stated by Ufology's leading figures, scientists, channelers and contactees.

Some of the discussed topics:

1-Theory of "Null Hypothesis"
2-Theory of "Subjective/Psychological"
3-Theory of "Subjective Projections"
4-Theory of "Psychosocial/Folklore"
5-Theory of "Natural/Fortean Phenomenon"
6-Theory of "Human Origin"
7-Theory of "Extraterrestrial Origin"
8-Theory of "Ultraterrestrial Origin"
9-Theory of "Ultraterrestrials, Fairies and UFOs"
10-Theory of "Deception"
11-Theory of" Occult/Magical/Supernatural"
12-Theory of "USO (Water UFO; Unidentified Submerged Objects)
13-Theory of "UFO's Underground Bases and Origin"
14-Theory of "UFO/USO Underground Bases and Origin"
15-Theory of "UFOs are time travelers from future human and alien civilizations"
16-Theory of "UFOs come from Wormholes and Hyperspace"
17-Theory of "UFOs Come from a Parallel Universe of Anti-Matter"
18-Theory of Dr. Carl Jung
19-Theory of "Demoniac Origin"
20-Theory of "UFOs are a Nazi Technology"
21. Theory of the Asian Vimanas (Tibetan and Indian Origin)
22-Theory of "UFOs are the Technology of an Advanced Subterranean Civilization"
23-Theory of "Erroneous observations, mass hysteria and some outright charlatanism"
24-The "Synthetic Theory"
25-The Theory of "UFOs are paraphysical phenomena"
26-The Theory of "UFOs are an affair of the mind"
27-The Theory of the "UFO phenomenon is a psychological aberration as much as it is an observable phenomenon."
28-The Theory of "UFOs are quantum manifestations"
29-Theory of the "UFOS do not exist"

ANUNNAKI ENCYCLOPEDIA

ORIGIN, HISTORY, SOCIETY, NIBIRU, SUPERNATURAL POWERS, HOW THEY CREATED US, EXTRATERRESTRIAL UFO

In Two Formats
Two Volumes Set; Each 400 Pages
One Volume, Condensed Edition Of 740 Pages

This encyclopedia is unique, much needed, and "genetically correct" for various reasons, including but not limited to:

- 1-This is the world's first massive encyclopedic work on the Anunnaki.
- 2-The book is a rarity in that it uses the authentic ancient languages, such as Aramaic, Hebrew, Arabic, Greek, Latin, Sunerian, Phoenician, Babylonian, Mesopotamian, Syriac, and even Anahk, the Anunnaki language.
- 3-The Anunnaki civilization is rich in literature, poetry, ethics, and rules governing societies. The author, therefore, included the Epic of Gilgamesh, and the Code of Hamurabi, as examples of this rich heritage.
- 4- New light is shed on the proven direct links of the Phoenicians to the Anunnaki, substantiated by the author's visits to their historical sites and ancient cities on the Island of Arwad, Tire, Sidon, Baalbeck, Amrit, and Byblos, to name a few.
- 5- The encyclopedia includes breakthrough theories, studies, and essays on unknown, major discoveries by leading authorities in the field.

We hope the readers will find it both enlightening and enjoyable, and an asset to their research and studies.

*** *** ***

The Author: Maximillien de Lafayette

International best-selling author, Maximillien de Lafayette wrote 127 books, 7 encyclopedias, 21 books on UFOs, and several world premiere musicals (One play was produced at the John F. Kennedy Center for the Performing Arts in Washington, D.C., USA.) De Lafayette is fluent in 7 languages, an expert linguist-historian of modern and ancient Middle/Near East languages, tribal dialects, and comparative history. He authored numerous authoritative books and encyclopedias such as, the 4 volume-"The 10 Language Universal Dictionary", the 10 volume- "Anthology and History of French Literature", "Encyclopedia of the 21st Century: Biographies and Profiles of the First Decade", "Biographical Encyclopedia of People in Ufology and Scientific Extraterrestrial Research", the 20 volume "World Who's Who in Jazz, Cabaret, Music and Entertainment", and "The Book of Nations".

For 25 years, De Lafayette has been researching subjects pertaining to space, time, gravity, multiple universes and "Space civilizations", and exchanging dialogues and rapports with scientists, and authorities in the field, from around the globe. He just finished writing a most unusual book "ULEMA: Code and Language of the World Beyond."

A multi-lingual, a syndicated columnist, a world traveler who has visited 46 countries, studied and taught comparative civilizations, international law and social systems for two decades; de Lafayette is in a privileged position to write this book. His columns, articles and books are read by more than 20 million readers in 135 countries, and his work has been translated in 17 languages. At 13, he published his first book; a collection of poems in French, hailed by members of the L'Academie Française as a masterpiece. Said book was translated in English by Dr. John Chen, Laureate of the United Nations/UNESCO, and former member of The White House Presidential Convention on Library Science and Information Services.

His latest international best-seller is "Entertainment: Divas, Cabaret, Jazz Then and Now". It hits the top chart, the world's 25 most popular items on the international market of Amazon. Uk.com on November 17, 2006. In addition, he has 3 international bestsellers, and two #1 bestsellers in Europe. Lawyer by trade, de Lafayette practiced international law for 20 years and served as legal advisor and counsel to several world organizations and governments in Europe and the Middle East. In the early eighties, he created the neo-cubism progressive movement in Europe, and was hailed as one of the pioneers of progressive abstract art in the 20th century. Visit a website dedicated to his paintings: www.maximilliendelafayette.com The author can be reached at:

delafayette@internationalnewsagency.org

Books by Maximillien de Lafayette

Read more about these books, description and reviews at your local library, Amazon.com, Barnes & Noble and other booksellers, and distributors websites worldwide.

Books on UFOs and Extraterrestrial Civilizations:

Published:

- **1-**From Zeta Reticuli to Earth: Time, Space and the UFO Technology. (400 Pages)
- **2-**The Biggest Controversies, Conspiracies, Theories and Coverups of our Time: From the Secret Files of Science, Politics, The Occult and Religion. (400 Pages)
- **3-**Inside A UFO: Alien Abduction, Hypnosis, Psychiatry, Quantum Physics and Religions Face to Face. (400 Pages)
- **4-**UFOs and the Alien Agenda. The Complete Book of UFOs, Encounters, Abduction And Aliens Bases On Earth. (400 Pages)
- **5-**Extraterrestrials Agenda: Aliens' Origin, Species, Societies, Intentions and Plan for Humanity. (400 Pages)
- **6-**The Anunnaki's Genetic Creation of the Human Race: UFOs, Aliens and Gods, Then and Now. (400 Pages)
- **7-**Extraterrestrials-US Government Treaty and Agreements: Alien Technology, Abduction, and Military Alliance. (400 Pages)
- **8-**Biographical Encyclopedia of People in Ufology and Scientific Extraterrestrial Research: People Who Matter. (740 Pages)
- **9-**Zeta Reticuli and Anunnaki Descendants Among Us: Who Are They? (400 Pages)
- **10-**UFO-USO and Extraterrestrials of the Sea: Flying Saucers and Aliens Civilizations, Life and Bases Underwater (400 Pages)
- **11-**What Extraterrestrials and Anunnaki Want You To Know: Their True Identities, Origins, Nibiru, Zeta Reticuli, Plans, Abductions and Humanity's Future (300 Pages)
- **12-**UFOs and Extraterrestrials Day By Day From 1900 To The Present: Flying Saucers and Aliens Civilizations, Life and Bases Underwater (400 Pages)
- **13-**Hybrid Humans and Abductions: Aliens-Government Experiments (400 Pages)
- **14-**UFOs, Aliens Impregnated Women, Extraterrestrials And God: Sex with Reptilians, Alien Motherhood, The Bible, Abductions and Hybrids (300 Pages)
- **15-**460,000 Years of UFO-Extraterrestrials Biggest Events and Secrets from Phoenicia to The White House: From Nibiru, Zetas, Anunnaki, Sumer To Eisenhower, MJ12, CIA, Military Abductees, Mind Control (400 Pages)
- **16-** Extraterrestrials, UFO, NASA-CIA-Aliens Mind Boggling Theories, Stories And Reports: Anunnaki, Zeta Reticuli, Area 51, Abductees, Whistleblowers, Conspirators. The Real & The Fake (400 Pages)
- **17-**Anunnaki Encyclopedia: History, Nibiru life, world, families, secret powers, how they created us, UFO , extraterrestrials. Volume I (400 Pages)
- **18-**Anunnaki Encyclopedia: History, Nibiru life, world, families, secret powers, how they created us, UFO , extraterrestrials. Volume II (400 Pages)
- **19-**Anunnaki Encyclopedia: History, Nibiru life, world, families, secret powers, how they created us, UFO, extraterrestrials. (Condensed Edition, 740 Pages)
- **20-**Revelation of an Anunnaki's Wife: Christianity, The White House, and Victoria's Hybrid Congressman Son (310 Pages) Co-authored with Ilil Arbel.
- **21-**2022 Anunnaki Code: End of The World Or Their Return To Earth? Ulema Book of Parallel Dimensions, Extraterrestrials and Akashic Records (400 Pages)

- **22**-Anunnaki Greatest Secrets Revealed By The Phoenicians And Ulema. Are We Worshiping A Fake God? Extraterrestrials Who Created Us. The Anunnaki who became the God of Jews,Christians and Muslims (310 Pages)

En route: (Books, study-guides, Who's Who, and encyclopedias on ufology, hypnotherapy, hypnosis, abduction, channeling, and aliens' cultures)

En route: (May 25, 2008):

- **1**-Ulema: Code and Language of the World Beyond (400 Pages)
- **2**-Zeta Reticuli and Greys Encyclopedia (550 Pages)

En route: (June 25, 2008):

- **3**-UFOs And Extraterrestrials Meet Astronauts, US Presidents and USAF: Sightings, Encounters, Aliens-US Secret Bases and Black Projects (300 Pages)
- **4**-The Book of Ra-Dosh: Anunnaki, Creation of the Genetic Man, and DNA of our Future (300 Pages)

En route: (July 25, 2008):

- **5**- Anunnaki Map of the After-Life: Where And How You Continue Your Life After Death (300 Pages)
- **6**-World Who's Who in Ufology and Study of Extraterrestrial Civilizations (400 Pages)

En route: (August 25, 2008):

- **7**-Thematic Encyclopedia of Ufology and Extraterrestrial Research (740 Pages)
- **8**-Anunnaki Return To Earth And The Future Of The Human Race (300 Pages)

In other fields:

1-Washington Does Not Believe in Tears: Play Their Game Or Eat The Blame!
2-What Foreigners Should Know About Liberal American Women
3-The Nine Language Universal Dictionary. (New Edition: The Ten Language Universal Dictionary
4-Anthologie De La Literature Française (Anthology & History of French Literature)
5-The Dating Phenomenon In The United States: Great Expectations or Justified Deceptions
6-Marmara the Gypsy: Biography of Baroness Myriam de Roszka (The script of the original play at the John F. Kennedy Center for the Performing Arts.)
7-One Hundred Reasons Why You Should And Should Not Marry An American Woman: Take Him to the Cleaners, Madame!
8-The United States Today: People, Society, Life from A to Z
9-Causes Celebres from 2,000 BC to Modern Times
10-The World's Best and Worst People
11-How Psychologists, Therapists and Psychiatrists Can Ruin Your Life in Court of Law in America
12-International Encyclopedia of Comparative Slang and Folkloric Expressions

13-Encyclopedia of Science of Mind: Religion, Science, and Parapsychology
14-Essay on Psychocosmoly of Man, Universe and Metalogics
15-The Social Register of the Most Prominent and Influential People in the United States
16-How to Use Easy, Fancy French & Latin to Your Advantage and Impress Others
17-How People Rule People with Words: From speechwriters and tele-evangelists to lawmakers and politicians
18-How to Protect Yourself from Your Ex-Wife Lawsuits
19-Divorces for the Highest Bidders
20-The International Book of World Etiquette, Protocol and Refined Manners
21-Bona Fide Divas & Femmes Fatales: The 700 Official Divas of the World
22-How Not To Fail In America: Are You Looking For Happiness Or Financial Success?
23-How to Understand People's Personality and Character Just by Looking at Them
24-The Art and Science of Understanding and Discovering Friends and Enemies
25-New Concise Dictionary of Law for Beginners
26-Comparative Study of Penal Codes As Applied In France and Great Britain
27-How to Understand International Law
28-La Pensee Arabe Face Au Continent Europeen
29-Beyond Mind & Body: The Passive Indo-Chinese School of Philosophy & Way of Life
30-New Approach to the Metaphysical Concept of Human Salvation in the Anthropological Psychology of Indian Religions
31-Worldwide Encyclopedia of Study and Learning Opportunities Abroad.
32-World Who's Who In Contemporary Art
33-World Who's Who in Jazz, Cabaret, Music and Entertainment
34-Thematic Encyclopedia of Cabaret Jazz
35-United States and the World Face to Face
36-Music, Showbiz and Entertainment
37-Entertainment: Divas, Cabaret, Jazz Then and Now
38-Showbiz, Pioneers, Best Singers, Entertainers & Musicians from 1606 to the Present
39-Best Musicians, Singers, Albums, and Entertainment Personalities of the 19th, 20th and 21st Centuries
40-Entertainment Greats From the 1800's to the Present: Cinema, Music, Divas, Legends
41-You, the World, and Everything Around You
42-World of Contemporary Jazz: Biographies of the Legends, the Pioneers, the Divas
43-Living Legends and Ultimate Singers, Musicians and Entertainers
44-People Who Shaped Our World
45-International Register of Events and People Who Shaped Our World
46-United States Cultural and Social Impact on Foreign Intelligentsia
47-Directory of United States Adult and Continuing Postsecondary Education
48-Comprehensive Guide to the Best Colleges and Universities in the United States
49-The Best of Washington: Its People, Society, and Establishments
50-Credentials Academic Equivalency and New Trends in Higher Education Worldwide
51-How Foreign Students Can Earn an American University Degree Without Leaving Their Country
52-Comprehensive Guide to the Best Academic Programs and Best Buys In College Education In The United States
53-How to Learn Seven Thousand French Words in Less Than Thirty Minutes

54-Comprehensive Guide to the Best Colleges and Universities in the U.S.

55-World's Best and Worst Countries: A comparative Study of Communities, Societies, Lifestyles and Their People

56-World Encyclopedia of Learning and Higher Education

57-How Much Your Degree Is Worth Today In America?

58-Worldwide Comparative Study and Evaluation of Postsecondary Education

59-Thematic Encyclopedia of Hospitality and Culinary Arts

60-Five Stars Hospitality: La Crème de la Crème in Hotel Guest Service, Food and Beverage

61-Hospitality Best & Worst: How to Succeed in the Food and Hotel Business

62-Encyclopedia of American Contemporary Art

63-Encyclopedia of Jazz: Life & Times of the 3.000 Most Prominent Singers & Musicians

64-Encyclopedia of Jazz: Life and Times of the 3.000 Most Prominent Singers and Musicians (V.2)

65-Concise Encyclopedia of American Music and Showbiz

66-The World Today: Headliners, Leaders, Lifestyles and Relationships

67-Evaluation of Personal and Professional Experiences: How to convert your knowledge and life experiences into academic degrees.

68-Contemporary Art, Culture, Politics and Modern Thought

69- Maximillien de La Croix « Mistral », Life and Times of Maximillien de La Croix de Lafayette

70-International Rating Of Countries in Higher Education And Comparative Study of Curricula, Degrees And Qualifications Worldwide

71-Alternative Higher Education

72-Dictionary of Academic Terminology Worldwide

73-Fake Titles Fake People

74-How to Use Greek, Latin and Hieroglyphic Expressions and Quotations to Your Advantage and Impress Others.

75-The Best and Worst Non-Traditional and Alternative Colleges and Universities in the United States

76-Directory of United States Traditional and Alternative Colleges and Universities

77-The Non Traditional Postsecondary Education in the United States: Its Merits, Advantages and Disastrous Consequences

78-Lafayette's Encyclopedic Dictionary of Higher Education Worldwide

79-Academic Degrees, Titles and Credentials

80-Independent Study Programs

81-America's Best Education at a Low Cost

82-Fictitious Credentials on Your Resume

83-Distance Learning

84-New Trends in American Higher Education

85-Directory of United States Postsecondary Education

86-Directory of United States Traditional and Alternative Colleges and Universities

87-National Register of Social Prestige and Academic Ratings of American Colleges and Universities

88-The Book of Nations

89-The World's Lists of Best and Worst

90-The Ultimate Book of World's Lists, Volume I
91-The Ultimate Book of World's Lists, Volume 2
92-Biographical Encyclopedia of the Greatest Minds, Talents and Personalities of our Time
93-Encyclopedia of the 21st Century. Biographies and Profile of the First Decade
94-Hospitality and Food Best and Worst: How to Succeed in the Food and Hotel Business
95-The Biggest Controversies, Conspiracies, Theories & Coverups of our Time, Vol. I
96-The Biggest Controversies, Conspiracies, Theories, & Coverups of our Time, Vol. II
97-Ulema: Code and Language of the World Beyond
98-The 1,000 Divas and Femmes Fatales of the World
99-140 Years of Cinema
100-Ulema: Code and Language of the World Beyond
101-Anunnaki Map of the After Life: Where And How You Continue Your Life After Death

Encyclopedias:

1-International Encyclopedia of Comparative Slang and Folkloric Expressions
2-Encyclopedia of Science of Mind: Religion, Science, and Parapsychology
3-World Encyclopedia of Learning and Higher Education
4-Worldwide Comparative Study and Evaluation of Postsecondary Education
5-Thematic Encyclopedia of Hospitality and Culinary Arts
6-Encyclopedia of American Contemporary Art
7-Encyclopedia of Jazz: Life & Times of 3.000 Most Prominent Singers and Musicians
8-Concise Encyclopedia of American Music and Showbiz (2 Volumes)
9-Encyclopedia of the 21st Century. Biographies and Profile of the First Decade
10-Biographical Encyclopedia of the Greatest Minds, Talents and Personalities of our time
11-Biographical Encyclopedia of People in Ufology and Scientific Extraterrestrial Research: People Who Matter and Most Important Figures
12-Thematic Encyclopedia of Ufology and Extraterrestrial Sciences (En route)
13-Anunnaki Encyclopedia (A set of 2 Volumes)
14-Maximillien de Lafayette Anunnaki Encyclopedia (1 Volume. Condensed Edition)

Dictionaries:

1-The Nine Language Universal Dictionary: How to Write It and Say It in Arabic, English, French, German, Italian, Japanese, Portuguese, Russian, Spanish (4 Volumes)
2-How to Learn 7,000 French Words in Less than Thirty Minutes
3-Lafayette's Encyclopedic Dictionary of Higher Education Worldwide
4-Dictionary of Academic Terminology Worldwide
5-How to Use Easy, Fancy French & Latin to Your Advantage and Impress Others

*** *** ***

Prologue

This remarkable book has many facets, and is so extremely rich in content that trying to introduce it is not an easy task. The material is unique, to start with. Most of it has been learned from sources that are totally out of reach for the average reader – and even for many scholars. Some of this material was hidden in the archives of museums, some written on tablets that have never been translated before, and some of it is oral knowledge that have never been given to a Westerner before. The author, Maximillien de Lafayette, have been so fortunate as to study with those who are the guardians of this knowledge in Lebanon, Egypt, Iraq, the islands of Arwad and Cyprus, and his travels even took him to the Far East, where he studied with Tibetan and Japanese teachers. This is the first time he is making use of this depot of knowledge, and we are very lucky to have access to it.

The subjects introduced in this book are explosive. Most important is the fact that it reveals the potential return of the Anunnaki in 2022, and the most frightening transformation that it would bring to the earth. If this is going to happen, a huge number of the people on earth, those grossly contaminated by Grays' DNA, will be annihilated. You know who they are – the child murderers, the rapists, those who torture, those who abuse, etc. Yes, we all know who they are. But the Anunnaki, who have no false sentimentality at all, will not tolerate even a medium level contamination. Unless they do their best to clean themselves during the grace period of the next fourteen years, those of mid level contamination will also be destroyed. Those who would manage to clean themselves to a certain degree may possibly (but without any guarantee) be able to escape the burning, smoking earth through special portals, called Ba'abs. Only those who are naturally uncontaminated and those who managed to clean themselves completely will be taken up through an antimatter bubble, with the animals and certain important buildings and inanimate art and culture objects, and kept safe until the earth would be clean again. Such a scenario is, to say the least, disconcerting. Even if you are not sure whether you are a believer or not, you should certainly consider the possibilities – and the book teaches you exactly how to save yourself.

For those of us interested in the use of esoteric codes, they are here for you to learn. Each term will teach you how to use it for your benefit, how to apply it not only to your spiritual growth, but to your business, relationships, and daily life. You will learn how to interpret the codes in many ancient languages, how to build a physical amulet/code that will protect certain aspects of your life, and how to develop your psychic and extrasensory powers by simply using these codes.

You will learn how the Anunnaki were our original creators, who else tempered with our genetic materials, and how God factors into all this. Religion, true and false, will be explored. Jesus, who never really died on the Cross, will be shown as a historical figure, with his wife, Mary Magdalene, with whom he escaped to ancient Marseille. Who were Adam and Eve? Who was the Serpent? How do the gods of Sumer signify to us?

You will be asked to consider the old theory, now discarded, that the Anunnaki came here to mine gold. You will meet the earliest civilization, and no, it was not Sumer. It was, believe it or not, Phoenicia! You will learn many secrets about the Anunnaki themselves – such as their extrasensory powers, their deep knowledge of genetics and science, and their unbelievably long lifespan. Who is their God? What kind of social classes they have? What spiritual principles do they exercise? And most important, what is their plan for humanity after the apocalyptic cleansing of the earth. Will they control our minds? Will they change our lifestyle, our monetary system, and our businesses?

Space is allowed for respectfully examining the work of pioneer Anunnaki scholars and their past achievements. Much of it is still quite valid, other material must be discarded in view of new research. Science and technology is here to examine the question of the Anunnaki in their light. And of course, the question always remains – how much science and technology has been given to earth governments already? And if they were, how much of it is given by the vicious Grays, who have contaminated us from the early days until the present, drawing our blood for their experiments, in exchange for such science and technology, all the while dealing with unscrupulous governments all over the planet, including our own?

In the end of the book, you will find the Enuma Elish, the great poem that reveals so much about our past and which has been studied by all researches in quest of answers to the question of who really created the early human race.

As I was studying the book, I asked Mr. de Lafayette if there was more to it than what he has written in this book. "Of course," he said. "This is just the tip of the iceberg. I plan to continue working with this material, with more books to follow. I think the world now needs the wisdom expressed in this material." I could not agree with him more.

And yet, despite the uniqueness of this material, the book is entirely accessible. It is important to note that both the Ulema and the Anunnaki always feel that knowledge should be imparted in the most straightforward way, with a simple and down to earth approach. The teacher is never to complicate any data with esoteric, foolish jargon. The result is a book you can both enjoy and learn from – on many subtle levels.

The book is arranged in the time-honoured tradition of questions and answers. To me, it suggests a formula that has been enthusiastically embraced by students for many, many years. You can get the most from this book by studying one question and one answer each day. Of course, some of the answers are short, some are long. But don't let the short ones deceive you into thinking that you can read two or three. Each question requires its own time, its own thinking. In this way, each question is much like a Japanese koan. The simplicity of the question does not reveal the complexity of the answer. The long answers, on the other hand, could certainly be divided into a few days of reading.

By the time you have finished the book, you will be one of those lucky individuals who really understand the Ulema teaching, and the Anunnaki Code and its implications. The return of the Anunnaki is not a new idea. It has been already announced in sacred scriptures, but of course interpreted differently. Some said Jesus is an Anunnaki, and he will return as a cosmic Messiah. A new school of religious thought in Iran suggests that Mohammed will return as a celestial being. And we should not to forget the Rapture and the Gnostics as well. But all of them have their origin in the Anunnaki texts, because these texts were written thousands of years before the Old Testament, the New Testament, and the Quran. The book will explore this topic.

The author has told me that he hopes that the religious material, some of which is avant-guard to the extreme, will not offend anyone. He is aware that much of it is different from all organized religions, but he hopes that the reader will approach this part of the book with an open mind, taking it away from Biblical context. Whether the depiction of God according to the author, contributors, the Ulema, the Sumerians, the Phoenicians, and the Anunnaki, differs from the Judeo-Christian concept, in essence, they all agree that there is a major force, a creative energy, that had created the known and unknown cosmos. In fact, it is only a semantic issue. The definition and understanding of God received many face lifts as theology adopted ancient and new beliefs and customs, and as science explored wider dimensions of knowledge and discoveries.

Dr. Etienne Leroux

1-Is It True The Anunnaki Created Man From A Germ?

THE ANSWER

- The Sumerian texts tell us that the Anunnaki tried hard to create a perfect "working human".
- The very first 7 prototypes of man the Anunnaki created were not perfect. Humans lacked intelligence. They were unable to understand the instructions of the Anunnaki.
- The original intention of the Anunnaki was to create a specie of humans capable of carrying physical tasks without questioning their origin, the nature of their creators, and the reason for being created.
- The Anunnaki wanted to produce specie that can follow orders during the early phases of their enterprise on earth.
- The Anunnaki never intended to create a very "smart" human. They just needed "primitive workers" who could understand one thing: Do the job and follow the orders as the Anunnaki ask!

The Anunnaki combined their genes with the DNA of an existing human race, and vice-versa. However, several passages from the Sumerian texts tell a different story; early humans were created from the DNA of an Anunnaki who had the rank of a king, a ruler or a "god", that was blended with clay found in abundance in Sumer (Modern day, Iraq).

Later on in history, "clay" became" Tourab", dirt in Arabic, and "clay" also became "germ". The Quran referred to it. Here is an excerpt from the Quran: "Is man not aware that We created him from a little germ?"

It is obvious that the Islamic text was written in accordance with the Sumerian-Anunnaki scriptures containing the following: "We first created man from an essence of clay; then placed him a living germ in a secure enclosure. The germ we made a clot of blood, and the clot a lump of flesh. This we fashioned into bones, then clothed the bones with flesh…"

*** *** ***

2-Did The Anunnaki Come To Earth To Mine Gold?

The Answer

No, they did not! The Anunnaki are not cowboys in the West!
The Anunnaki are a very advanced race. They can transmute metals into gold anytime they want. To their scientists, it is a piece of cake.

- Besides, Ashtari, the real name of their planet is abundant with gold.
- A race that overcame the laws of physics of so many galaxies, conquered space-time travel, participated in the creation of the cosmos, and created the brain and body of so many races and humans should be considered advanced enough to conclude a very simple scientific transaction such as changing iron or copper into gold.
- Also, it is very important to remember that gold, even in a huge quantity cannot save a planet from deterioration and adjusting its weather and climate…
- They came to Earth for other reasons.

Why did the Anunnaki originally come to earth?

The Anunnaki did more than just come to earth. They have created it, million of years ago. At that time, a group of Anunnaki scientists on Nibiru, including Inanna, Sinhar Anki (EN.KI), Anu, Enlil (Ilil) etc. decided to extend their experiments in creating biological, living forms. To do that, they needed a good plan and permission from the Council, so they worked it out and requested a meeting. The Council considered their suggestions, and agreed that such work would greatly increase Anunnaki knowledge and therefore would be an excellent idea to pursue. However, they had one condition. The scientists were welcome to start working – but their laboratory would have to be off-planet.

The Council suspected that the introduction of new life forms, even in the isolated conditions of a laboratory, might be a threat to everyone already on Nibiru. Large and small animals, and particularly people that were to be created in the image of the Anunnaki, could not be tolerated to wander freely on Nibiru.

The scientists devoted more thought to their project, and agreed that what they really needed was a planet-sized laboratory, where the creations could interact in a controlled environment without the interference of previously existing life forms. The solution, to which the Council readily agreed, was to create a planet specifically for the purpose. The Council added that they understood that it would be convenient to create the planet within the Milky Way, for easy traveling, but it had to be at some distance from Nibiru, just in case.

And so the scientists went to the edge of the galaxy, and caused a star to explode and create a solar system. The sun, which they named Shemesh (Sol) was surrounded by a few planets, and after a suitable amount of time (eons to us, but nothing to the Anunnaki who can play with time as they wish) went there to decide which planet would be the most appropriate. For a short time they considered the planet we call Mars, which at the time had plenty of water (the most important ingredient necessary for the laboratory, after oxygen) but finally settled on choosing earth.

They went to earth, started creating the life forms, fostered the evolutionary process, and managed to accumulate an enormous amount of useful knowledge, all of which they telepathically transferred to Nibiru, where it was much appreciated. Unfortunately, the knowledge leaked to the Grays at Zeta Reticuli, and they decided to use the humans, and sometimes the cattle, in their doomed experiments that were geared to save their own miserable race.

While doing this, they sadly contaminated the pure genetic material the Anunnaki so painstakingly created, and the humans that resulted were no longer suitable for the study.

That was the reason why the Anunnaki deserted their research on earth.

However, it is well known that the Anunnaki, which are a most responsible and compassionate race, did not lose interest in their creations, and have never quite deserted us to the Grays.

Most important, as a result of some additional knowledge revealed to them over the last forty years, they are planning a comeback to earth. It is not clear if they are intending to continue their research, or if their coming is merely a benevolent attempt to clean the earth from all Grays' genetic material and reclaim us as better human beings, but either way, we will be made much happier, kinder, and more comfortable by the Anunnaki return. The expectation is that they would formally announce it around 2022.

3-What Is Ay'inbet?

The Answer

- **1-Origin:** Derived from the Phoenician Ay'inbet. 1-Ayin means eye, and Bet means house. In Hebrew, ayin is ayn and bet is beth. In Arabic, ayin is 'ayn, and bet is bayt (Written Arabic), and bet (Spoken Arabic). In Anakh (Anunnaki language), it is exactly the same; ayin is Ain, and bet is bet.
- **2-Numerical value:** 3.
- **3-Meaning:** 1-The eye of the house; 2-Main entrance of a home; 3-Protection of one's home. The upper class of the Anunnaki is ruled by Baalshalimroot. His subjects are called "Shtaroout-Hxall Ain", meaning the inhabitants of the house of knowledge, or "those who see clearly." Their eyes are not similar to humans' eyes, because the Anunnaki do not have a retina. Their physical eyes are used to perceive dimensional objects. While their "inner eye" sees multi-dimensional spheres. The process is created by the mind.

The word "Ain" was later adopted by the early inhabitants of the Arab Peninsula. "Ain" in Arabic means "eye". The Badou Rouhal (Nomads) of the Arabs who lived in the Sahara considered the "eye" to be the most important feature of the face. Those who have practiced "Al Sihr" (Magic) used their eyes as a psychic conduit. In their magic rituals and séances, they close their eyes and let imageries inhabit their mind. Once, the spirit called "Rouh, Jinn, Afrit" enters the body, the eyes open up and the vision is henceforth activated by the spirit.And what they saw next was called "Rou'Yah", meaning "visions".

In the secret teachings of Sufism, visions of Al Hallaj, and of the greatest poetess of Sufism, Rabiha' Al Adawi Yah, known also as "Ha Chi katou Al Houbb Al Ilahi" (The mistress of the divine love), and in the banned book *Shams Al Maa'Ref Al Kubrah* (Book of the Sun of the Great Knowledge), the word "eye" meant the ultimate knowledge, or wisdom from above.

"Above" clearly indicates the heavens. In the pre-Islamic era, heavens meant the spheres where the creators of the universe live. This sphere was shared by good gods and evil gods. The concept of hell was unknown to the pagan Badou Rouhal. Later on in history, when Islam invaded the Arab world, the "eye" became the symbol of Allah, the god of the Muslims.

In modern times, several secret esoteric societies and cultures adopted the "eye" as an institutional symbol and caused it to appear on many edifices' pillars, bank notes, money bills (including the US Dollar), and religious texts.

In ancient times, the Anunnaki eye was a very powerful symbol of the favorite regional god. It appeared on Egyptian, Sumerian, Persian, and Phoenician pillars and tablets. The Phoenicians of the city of Amrit and the Island of Arwad, considered to be direct descendants of the Anunnaki, engraved the Anunnaki eye on altars dedicated to gods' healing powers.

- **4-Code/Use according to mythology and esoterism:** To be written three times on a piece of leather or cloth and hidden in the left pocket.
- **5-Benefits:** 1-Safe return to home-base; 2-Against forced eviction. 3-Protection of one's property. 4-Peace at home.
- **6-Geometrical presentation/Symbol:** Circle. In spiritual-mental séances, the circle becomes a triangle.

*** *** ***

4-What Is Za.Yin?

The Answer

Za.Yin

- **1-Origin:** Derived from the Phoenician Zayin. Same pronunciation in Aramaic, Syriac, Hebrew, and Arabic. In Anakh (Anunnaki language), it is Za. YIL.
- **2-Numerical value:** 7.
- **3-Meaning:** Weapon.
- **4-Code/Use according to mythology and esoterism:** To be written seven times on a small stone and placed inside the house, more precisely in the foyer of the house. On the road, it is advised to grab it in your right palm, and repeat the name of the opposition seven times. Once done, you keep it in your right pocket. During mental communication, you draw a circle and you place the stone on the left side of the circle, facing north.
- **5-Benefits:** 1-Defense against intruders; 2-To overcome or change a negative decision by a third party that can affect your well-being and/or assets; 3-Helpful in negotiations and while giving a speech, lecture or a presentation.
- **6-Geometrical presentation/Symbol:** Two adjacent triangles.

*** *** ***

5-What Is Resh-Aal?

The Answer

- **1-Origin:** Derived from the Phoenician Resh. Same pronunciation in Aramaic, Sumerian, Babylonian, and Syriac. In Arabic, it is pronounced "Ras." In Hebrew, it is pronounced "Rosh". In Anakh (Anunnaki language), it is "Rash.El." All have the same meaning.
- 2-**Numerical value:** 20.
- **3-Meaning:** Head.
- **4-Code/Use according to mythology and esoterism:** To be written with "Zaa' Fa. Ran" liquid, once in the center of your left palm.
- **5-Benefits:** 1-Will heal headaches in less than 10 minutes; 2-In official meetings, and before anybody else enters the room, write it twice on your seat.
- **6-Geometrical presentation/Symbol:** A circle inside a square.

*** *** ***

6-What Is Sam.Ekh?

The Answer

Sam Ekh

- **1-Origin**: Derived from the Phoenician Samekh. Same pronunciation in Aramaic, Syriac, and Hebrew. No equivalent in Arabic. In Anakh (Anunnaki language), it is SA.Ek'h.
- **2-Numerical value:** 15.
- **3-Meaning:** Pillar.
- **4-Code/Use according to mythology and esoterism:** To be drawn in the form of three parallel lines in any direction.
- **5-Benefits:** 1-Much needed to open an oracle.
- **6-Geometrical presentation/Symbol:** Three parallel lines of the same length.

*** *** ***

7-What Is Or Who Is ABD?

The Answer

Abd

- **1-Origin:** Derived from the Arabic Abd. In Anakh (Anunnaki language), it is SA.Ek'h.
- **2-Numerical value:** 13.
- **3-Meaning:** It was the first name given to the first genetically created human by the Anunnaki. It means the same thing in Sumerian, Babylonian, ancient and modern Arabic and Anakh (Anunnaki language). The original meaning is "Slave", later on; Enki changed it to "Servant". In contemporary Arabic, the word "Abed" means two things: 1-A black person; 2: A slave. You will find many clues in the Arabic poems of Abu Al Tib Al Mutanabbi, and in the writings of Abu Al Ala' Al Maari (died in 1057), and Al-Nabigha Al-Zoubyani (535-604), and in the story of king Dabshalim and Brahman Baydaba. (Around 175 B.C.)
- **4-Code/Use according to mythology and esoterism:** Never to be used, written, or pronounced.
- **5-Benefits:** Negative effects. Bad expectations.
- **6-Geometrical presentation/Symbol:** Reverse cross inside a triangle.

*** *** ***

8-Was Mankind Created By One Sumerian/Anunnaki God?

The Answer

Was Mankind Created By One Sumerian/Anunnaki God?

Answer: No. Mankind, including the first human proptotypes were created and recreated by several Anunnaki.

Creation of Man:

Mankind was not created by one single Sumerian god. More than one Anunnaki participated in the creation of mankind. And contrary to a common belief:

- 1-The Anunnaki were not the first extraterrestrials and gods to create a human from clay;
- 2- The Anunnaki did not first land in Sumer.

An in-depth study of the ancient civilizations of the Near East and the Middle East reveals that:

- 1-Many other deities from different pantheons created also man from clay. For instance, Khnum "Kneph" (Meaning: To build, to unify in Egyptian) was one of the oldest Egyptian gods who created mankind from clay on a potter's wheel. Khnum became a variation of Ptah;
- 2-The Anunnaki first landed in Phoenicia whre they established their first colonies, and short after, they created their first and most elaborate medical center on the Island of Arwad, then a Phoenician territory.

*** *** ***

60

However, the Anunnaki ameliorated their genetic creations, and upgraded early "human forms" and primitive humans in Sumer. They were more active in Iraq than elsewhere. In addition, the Sumerian texts and their translations in western languages gave more exposure to the Anunnaki of Sumer than to other and equally powerful Annunaki in Phoenicia and Central Africa.

The Sumerian texts include various versions of the creation of mankind by a sizable number of Anunnaki. Some passages in the Sumerian texts refer to different creators (gods and goddesses), as well as to various and multiple genetic "operations".

There is no conform-monoform description of one single genetic creation of the early human races, nor a solid certainty to the fact that mankind was genetically created by one "single" god.

For instance:

1-Ninlil

The Sumerian "Queen Breeze", also called Aruru, Ninhursag, Ninhursanga "Lady Of The Mountains", ruler of the heavens, underworld, wind, earth, and grain, wife of Enlil and the mother of Nanna/Utu. She was also the goddess of creation who created Endiku, and various early forms of mankind. In the Epic of Gilgamesh we read: "…she created mankind…so numerous … she thrust her hands into the waters and pinched off some clay, which she dropped in the wilderness, in the wilderness she made Endiku the hero…" and in another passage, it was written: "My friend Endiku whom I loved has turned to clay…died, returned to the clay that formed him…"

2-Marduk

He was the son of Ea and husband of Sarpanitu, the sun-god, and also the god of war, fire, earth and heaven, and one of the major creators of heroes, gods and humans. He waged a ravaging war against Tiamat, dismembered her, and used several parts of her body to create the world and the early races of humanity. In the Sumerian epic and scriptures, the "Enuma Elish", we read: "He opened his mouth and unto Ea he spake That which he had conceived in his heart he imparted unto him: 'My blood will I take and bone will I fashion I will make man, that man may…I will create man who shall inhabit the earth, That the service of the gods may be established, and that their shrines may be built…"

3-Inanna

She was the legendary Sumerian goddess who created the first 7 prototypes of mankind. Many other civilizations worshipped her under different names, such as: Astarte, Istar, Athtar, Asherat, Ashtoreth in Phoenician and Hebrew, Ashtaroth and Ashteroth in Canaanite, Atargatis in Greek, and as Ishtar and sister of Baal in early Phoenician.

4-Nammu

Sumerian-Anunnaki goddess Nammu "Namma" and her son Enki **created** multiple forms of humans, sometimes using clay, and some other times blood of warriors they slaughtered.

5-Ea

God Ea killed Kingu, the demon son of Tiamat, and used his blood to create mankind. Ea was the son of Anu. Sometimes he is mentioned as the son of Anshar. Ea created Zaltu as a complement to Ishtar. According to Assyro-Babylonian Mythology, Ea suggested the method of creating man, in response to the heavy workload of the Igigi.

Ea was a "good god." He advised mankind when other gods would do them harm. He granted Adapa understanding, to teach mankind. When Adapa used this knowledge to break the wing of the South Wind, he cursed him and told him to complain of Dumuzi and Gizzida's absence to Anu. While in Anu's court, he advises Adapa not to eat the bread of eternal life (lest he forfeit his life on earth). He refuses to flood mankind for Ellil (En.Lil). Eventually he acceded, but only after advising Atrahasis to build a boat in which to weather the flood.

6-Aruru "Mammi"

She was the Babylonian great mother goddess of creation. Like so many other Sumerian gods, Aruru created Enkidu from clay in the image of Anu. With the help of Enlil, she created the first man. Aruru is also called the womb goddess.

Following the advice and instruction of Ea, she mixed the blood of god Geshtu-e with clay she found on the Euphrates river bank, and created seven women and seven men. She had to create the first "set" of primitive humans to do the physical work of the Igigi. According to the AssyroBabylonian Mythology, Aruru "…also added to the creation of Gilgamesh, and, at Anu's command, made Enkidu in Anu's image by pinching off a piece of clay, throwing it into the wilderness, and birthing him there. Ea called her to offer her beloved Ninurta as the one who should hunt Anzu…"

*** *** ***

Additional investigative studies of the origin of man, the creation of the first human races, and gods who descended on earth to rule earth, create humans to serve them, and a super extraterrestrial races who traveled the galaxies with "flying birds", "spaceships" and "divine solar discs" uncovered startling discoveries leading to mind-boggling theories.

During my study of the Phoenician tablets in Lebanon, Syria and Tunis, I found out that the Anunnaki of Sumer were not the only extraterrestrial race that landed in Iraq to genetically create mankind. Long time before their descent in Sumer, the Anunnaki have already established colonies in Phoenicia and Arward and began to create humans from "Tourab", meaning dirt.

Equally stimulating and formidable are the findings of superb author Alan F. Alford who seems to share similar beliefs. He wrote: "I decided to write a book about ancient Egypt, partly because Egypt was in vogue following the publication of 'The Orion Mystery' and similar books, and partly because Sitchin had not fully covered the rich Egyptian lore in his 'Earth Chronicles' series.

I therefore began to pore over the ancient Egyptian writings, looking for evidence of extraterrestrial contact. But I did not find what I expected to find. On the contrary, I began to realise that the ancient Egyptian gods were not at all flesh-and-blood extraterrestrials.

On the contrary, the Egyptian gods were personifications of celestial powers, exemplified by Ra, the Sun-god, Thoth the Moon-god, and Nut, the Sky-goddess.

But this was only the tip of the iceberg. Eventually the veil of the mystery began to lift, and I realised that these celestial gods were merely symbolic of an even deeper celestial mystery involving a planet which had exploded millions of years in the past.

This was the Egyptian 'First Time' (*Zep Tepi*), when the gods had descended from Heaven to Earth. But they had not descended to the Earth in space-ships.
Far from it.
They had descended to Earth as meteorites and floodwaters from the exploded planet. And it soon became apparent that every single aspect of ancient Egyptian religion could be integrated within what I termed an 'exploded planet cult'. The results of this research were written up in my second book, 'The Phoenix Solution', which was published in August 1998.
Where did this leave Sitchin's theory of the Anunnaki-gods?

Mr. Alford adds: "In The Phoenix Solution, I explained that the descents of the meteorite-gods to Earth was followed by the ascents (or resurrections) of their spiritual doubles back up to Heaven. In other words, the physical gods who had come down to Earth had propagated invisible, metaphysical counterparts who had risen back up to Heaven.
I then drew a number of comparisons between Egyptian and Mesopotamian traditions, and concluded that 'these accounts are so similar to Egyptian beliefs that we must surely dismiss the idea of rockets and spacecraft, and treat all the ascents (of the gods) as metaphysical.'

On The Creation Of Man:

On the creation of man: According to Mr. Alford The basic idea underlying all Mesopotamian, Egyptian and Greek myths of the creation of man is that man was created in the Underworld, i.e. in the interior of the Earth, pending a later release onto the surface of the Earth. In the Greek myths, man was thus created from clay and fire in the womb of the goddess Gaia, who personified Mother Earth. Similarly, in the older Mesopotamian myths, man was created in the womb of Mami (alias Ninharsag, 'Lady of the Mountain'), who likewise personified the Earth
The crucial idea behind the creation of man myth was that the Earth-goddess had been impregnated by the seeds of life in the form of meteorites and floodwaters from the exploded planet.
In Greece it was believed that man had been created from fallen 'stones' or from the 'teeth' of a heavenly serpent, or from the 'seed' of the fallen meteorite-god Hephaestus.

In Mesopotamia, similarly, it was believed that man had been created from the 'flesh' and 'blood' of a sacrificed sky-god, these terms being metaphors for the meteoritic materials.

Both the gods and man had been created as offshoots from the exploded planet, and hence it was said that mankind had been created in the image of the gods.

In the course of time, ancient man depicted the fallen gods poetically in anthropomorphic forms, thus giving rise to the misleading idea that man had been created in the image of human-like gods. As for the Anunnaki-gods, who put mankind to work in the excavations, it should be noted that they were gods of the subterranean Underworld.

9-What Is Adala?
Is It Karma?

The Answer

Adala

- **1-Origin:** Derived from the Anunnaki language, Ada. LA.
- **2-Numerical value:** 100.
- **3-Meaning:** As defined in the "Anunnaki Encyclopedia"; In Anakh (Anunnaki language) term for karma. Although the Anunnaki do not believe in religions as we do on earth, their sense and understanding of ethics, justice, good and evil deeds, and merits are well developed. The Anunnaki have families, parents, children, social ethics and laws. They see the universe, the development of mind and character's evolvement quite differently from the way we do. They take into a great consideration the consequences of an act, even a thought. The Anunnaki do not have courts of law, trials, tribunals, prosecutors, judges, lawyers and corporal punishment, but they have established rules that govern behavior, merits, deeds, and social justice. However, karma is not a reward for deeds after death.

> The Anunnaki do not believe in reincarnation, a spiritual life after death, the return of one's body, character and soul to Nibiru after death. It is difficult to explain the Anunnaki's karma in terrestrial terms.
> But, basically, Anunnaki's karma is the place and function a deceased Anunnaki occupies and plays in a sphere existing beyond the one he/she left.
> In contrast with karma on earth, all Anunnaki have the ability to change their karma and their next destination before they die. Even though, death does not exist in the Anunnaki's world, as we understand death on earth, all Anunnaki reach a point when and where the last cell of energy in their body ceases to function, thus resulting in the deterioration of their bodies.

After that, the Anunnaki body fades away, and the mind of the new Anunnaki occupies one of the doubles or copies of their minds and bodies.

It is at this critical moment when the karma becomes relevant. "Adala" has 2 levels:

A-Level one is a sphere of existence, where the Anunnaki ceases to evolve, and the "Conduit" is no longer fully operational. The departed Anunnaki (some live 400,000 years) could still contact the community he/she once lived in, and communicate with parents and relatives, but the range of communication is minimal.

This happens when his/her deeds were not viewed by the Anunnaki Council as of the first order.

B-Level two is a sphere of ultimate development where the Anunnaki acquires a more developed and powerful personality. This personality will have access to a new physical body and a greater "Conduit". This happens when the Anunnaki Council has honored the good deeds of the departed Anunnaki. To fully understand this concept, refer to "Conduit" entry in "Anunnaki Encyclopedia", volume one.

- **4-Code/Use according to mythology and esoterism:** Indoor, draw the geometrical symbol on the back of your favorite cooking pan. In a court of law, draw the symbol on a piece of paper and direct it toward the jury if applicable, otherwise, toward the judge.
- **5-Benefits:** 1-Improve health condition in general; 2-Bring justice to your cause.
- **6-Geometrical presentation/Symbol:** An eye inside a triangle.

*** *** ***

10-Who Is Ahat?

The Answer

Ahat (Aqhat)

- **1-Origin:** Derived from the Phoenician Ahat and Aqhat.
- **2-Numerical:** 77.
- **3-Meaning:** As defined in the "Anunnaki Encyclopedia"; Ahat was a Phoenician hero, a descendant from the Anunnaki, and a gift from god El to King Daniel who adopted him as his son. Ahat was given a celestial bow made out of circular horns. Anat (A Syrian, Canaanite and Phoenician goddess of earth) was attracted to the bow, but Ahat refused to give her his bow. She got mad, and sent her attendant Yatpan, to kill Ahat. Ahat was killed, and his bow was lost during his struggle with Yaptan. The gods became angry, cursed humans, and the supreme god Baal punished mankind by stopping the rains from falling on the lands of Phoenicia, thus creating a drought, and causing the crops to fail, and the stored grains to rot. Ahat ascended to Ashtari (Planet Nibiru) and became a legion commander under his new Anunnaki's name "Aqhat", given to him by SinharMarduck.
- **4-Code/Use:** Early Phoenicians in Tyre, Sidon and Island of Arwad wrote Aqhat name on a piece of clay and buried underground each year before summer harvest. According to Phoenician and Akkadian legends, this nourished the earth and protected grains and crops. This sort of talisman can be used today for different purposes, such as creating new positive opportunities.
- **5-Benefits:** 1-Bringing good luck and prosperity.
- **6-Geometrical presentation/Symbol:** A green leaf.

*** *** ***

72

11-Who Is Aa.Kim.LU?
Was He The Creator And God Of The Anunnaki?

The Answer

Aa-kim-lU (Akimlu, AA.Kim.LU)

- **1-Origin:** Derived from the Anakh "Akim. LU".
- **2-Numerical value:** None. It is not allowed to assign a numerical value to his name.
- **3-Meaning:** It is the name of the creator of the Anunnaki, and seven galaxies according to "The Book of Rama-Dosh". Aa-kim-lu used "Rouh-D'ab-Sha.LIM" to create the Anunnaki, 7 billions years B.C.
- **4-Code/Use according to mythology and esoterism:** Strictly used during "Plasmic Manifestations".
- **5-Benefits:** Used for identification in the early stage of communications with superior beings.
- **6-Geometrical presentation/Symbol:** A spear with three bursting stars.

*** *** ***

74

12-What Is Al-A'kh?

The Answer

Al- A'kh (Al Hak)

- **1-Origin:** Derived from the Anakh AL. A'Kh.
- **2-Numerical value:** 1,100.
- **3-Meaning:** A system of administration and government based upon the Anunnaki social code. Later, Al-A'kh became an Arabic word for justice.
- **4-Code/Use according to mythology and esoterism:** Before you open your shop at the beginning of each month, write AL.A'Kh and the number 1,000 on the left side of the door of your shop. Write it with charcoal and wipe it at the end of the day before 6:00 PM.
- **5-Benefits:** It brings stability to your business.
- **6-Geometrical presentation/Symbol:** Two identical squares.

*** *** ***

13-What Is An?

The Answer

An

- **1-Origin:** Derived from the Anakh AN.
- **2-Numerical value:** 1,199.
- **3-Meaning:** 1-Source; 2-first breath; 3-first nourishment. In Sumerian, it means celestial father. Commonly used by the Hurrians, Phoenicians, Elamites, Subarians, Sumerians, Medes, and Kasites.
- **4-Code/Use according to mythology and esoterism:** Write the word "An" and the name of your new-born child on the leaf of a white rose and keep it in a safe place for seven days.
- **5-Benefits:** It brings health and protection to newly born children.
- **6-Geometrical presentation/Symbol:** The letter "A" and a leaf of a white rose.

*** *** ***

14-Do Anunnaki Feel And React Like Us?

The Answer

There is a major misconception about the Anunnaki's emotions and the nature of their feelings. Avalanches of erroneous theses were written about their cruelty, ferocious reptilian character, and particularly about abducting humans. Among the most considerate extraterrestrial races are: 1-The Lyrans; 2-The Nordics; 3-The Anunnaki. Unfortunately, misinformed writers, some of them are very well-known in the ufology community wrote chapters upon chapters describing how the Anunnaki and their remnants on earth control our mind and disrupt the order in our societies, because they have a malicious agenda. The truth is, the Anunnaki do not interfere in human affairs. They have left earth centuries ago. Those who are abducting humans are the "Grays".

The Anunnaki express their feelings just like we do. However, they do not shed tears, nor succumb to emotional crises. Their "sentimentality" is controlled by a "Conduit" directly linked to a community-collective-awareness. This means, that their emotions are regulated – but not controlled – by an "intellect" channel. This channel is constantly balanced scientifically.

The female Anunnaki are more affectionate than their male counterparts. For instance, at the Anunnaki Academy of Learning, male Anunnaki have developed the space-time travel, remote viewing and "cosmic projection" courses. Per contra, the female Anunnaki have developed arts and "social communication" study programs. This comparison is self-explanatory. And if we go back in history, we discover that the genetically created men by male Anunnaki looked like robots and machines, while the final "product" of the early modern men as created by the female Annunaki had more appealing physical attributes, and more developed sense for aesthetics and artistic creativity.

Do The Anunnaki react and feel like us? They do not react like humans, but they do express emotions and feelings. Because their society is matriarchal in essence, the Anunnaki are deeply influenced by the female nature and element which translate into compassion, and devotion for their families. Many of the Anunnaki look like us. They share with humans many physical properties, and to a certain degree, a "partial" DNA!

15-Who Was Gb'r (Angel Gabriel)?

The Answer

Angel, Gabriel

- **1-Origin:** Derived from the Anakh Gb'r.
- **2-Numerical value:** Delta 1000
- **3-Meaning:** As defined in the "Anunnaki Encyclopedia"; An Anunnaki personage with mighty powers and major influence on the creation of the human race. Angel Gabriel is not totally and exactly what the Judeo-Christian tradition portrays. The original name is "Gib-ra-il"; the guardian of Janat Adan or Edin (Garden of Eden), in Sumerian and in Anakh is Nin-il, or Nin-Lil. Gabriel is also called "Gab" and "Gab-r-il". Gab means a female guardian, a governor or a protector. This explains why Angel Gabriel was represented to us as the guardian of the Garden of Eden. In the ancient texts of the Sumerians, Acadians and civilizations of the neighboring regions, "Gab-r" was the governor of "Janat Adan." In various Semitic languages, "Janat" means paradise, and Eden is Idin or Adan. This is how we got Garden of Eden. Angel Gabriel, the Sumerian is more than a guardian, because he was called Nin-Ti which means verbatim: Life-Woman.

In other words, Angel Gabriel was three things:

1-Governor of the Garden of Eden;

2-A woman, NOT a man, because she was described as "the female who created life";

3-A geneticist who worked on the human DNA/creation of the human race. The word "Gab-r" was phonetically pronounced as: Gab'er. The early Arabs adopted it as "Al Jaber" meaning many things including: force, authority, might, and governing. From "Al Jaber" important words, nouns and adjectives were derived. For instance, the word "Jabbar" means: mighty, powerful, capable, huge, giant, like the giants in the Bible and Sumerian/Anunnaki epics. "Jababira" is the plural of "Al Jabbar".

After the Arabs were converted to Islam, "Al Jaber" became "Al Jabbar"; one of the attributes and names of Allah (God). In the Anakh (Anunnaki language), the word "Jabba-r-oout" means exactly the same thing in early Aramaic and modern Arabic: Authority, power, rule, reign.

It is obvious that the Anakh language deeply influenced Eastern and Western languages. One more surprise for the readers. We find striking similarity in our Western vocabularies (Latin, Anglo-Saxon, French and Romance languages); Gab'r became gouverneur in French, governor in English, and gubernator in Latin.

- The Sumerian Gabriel was also known under different names according to the Sumerian texts, such as "Nin-Hour-sagh", meaning the lady governess of the mountain; an elevated region of the Garden of Eden. Gabriel as a female Anunnaki was the first to experiment with copies of a human, later to be called Adam. But first, Gabriel created 7 different types of Homo Sapiens by using the DNA of primitive beings and the DNA of an Anunnaki. Gabriel's original creations were not very successful. Later on, Gabriel used a most unexpected genetic source to create the final copy of the modern man. There are plenty of evidence and historical statements to prove this point. And all starts with her name "Nin-il", some times referred to as "Nin-ti". In Anakh, Sumerian and Babylonian languages, the word "Ti" means "rib". In later versions of the ancient texts, "Nin-ti" became the "lady of the rib", also the "lady of life", and the "lady of creation". Consequently, Adam, the man, was created from the rib of Gabriel, the female Anunnaki; the "lady of the rib". This contradicts the story of the creation of Adam and Eve as told in the Judeo-Christian tradition. According to the Sumerians and the Anakh, a woman created man; it was NOT a man who created a woman (Eve). And the female Anunnaki (Gabriel) used her rib to create Adam. The early translators - and possibly, intentionally misleading scribes and usurpers of the truth - of the ancient texts and epics of Sumer got it wrong, and their fake story of the creation of Adam and Eve invaded the Hebraic, Christian and Islamic holy scriptures.
- **4-Code/Use:** Write the word "Gb'r" seven times on a water cup and drink it in three steps.
- **5-Benefits:** It eliminates shoulder pains caused by fatigue and office work.
- **6-Geometrical presentation/Symbol:** The letter "V".

*** *** ***

16-What Is Bab (Ba'ab)?
Is It The Anunnaki Star Gate?

The Answer

Bab (Ba'ab):

- **1-Origin:** Derived from the Anakh Ba'ab.
- **2-Numerical value:** 700
- **3-Meaning:** As defined in the "Anunnaki Encyclopedia";
- An Anunnaki's stargate, from which an Anunnaki earth remnant leaves earth to reach Nibiru. The Bab opens only from the earth side and closes behind the traveling Anunnaki. It means door in several Middle Eastern and Anatolian languages, including Arabic and Turkish with identical pronunciation.
- **4-Code/Use according to mythology and esoterism:** Write the words "Bab" in capital letters on the frame of a window in your house.
- **5-Benefits:** It rejuvenates positive energy inside your home.
- **6-Geometrical presentation/Symbol:** Two parallel triangles.

*** *** ***

17-What Is Fik'r?
Is It Mind Or Soul?

The Answer

Fik'r:

- **1-Origin:** Derived from the Anakh Fik-R'r, and Fik.Ra.Sa. The esoteric Arabic word "Firasa" is derived from Fik.Ra.Sa. It means in Arabic the ability to read thoughts, understand the psyche of a person just by looking at him/her. The Ulema used Fik'r to read the mind, learn about the intentions of others, and assess the level of intelligence of people. Almost all rulers in ancient Persia, Phoenicia and later in Egypt employed in their royal courts, "People of Firasa". They consulted with them during visits of dignitaries and officials from foreign countries. It was the secret science of learning about the personality of people through the study of physiognomy. This science was called "Firasa". One of the greatest Ulema masters and experts in the field was Fakher Addīn Al- Rāzī. His noted treatise on Firasa; The Science of psycho-physiognomy was inspired by the teachings of the Ulema. In the unpublished original edition of his treatise, several Anunnaki syllables and geometric forms were included in "Al Moukamma" the introduction of the book dedicated to the "true believers of the higher knowledge".
- **2-Numerical value:** Aleph 7.
- **3-Meaning:** As defined in the "Anunnaki Encyclopedia"; Soul is an invention of early humans who needed to believe in a next life. It was through the soul that mortals could and would hope to continue to live after death. Soul as an element or a substance does not exist anywhere inside the human body. Instead, there is a non-physical substance called "Fik'r" that makes the brain function, and it is the brain that keeps the body working, not the soul. The "Fik'r" was the primordial element used by the Anunnaki at the time they created the final form of the human race. Fik'r was NOT used in the early seven prototypes of the creation of mankind according to the Sumerian texts. The "Fik'r", although it is the primordial source of life for our physical body, it is not to be considered as DNA, because DNA is a part of "Fik'r"; DNA is the physical description of our genes, a sort of a series of formulas, numbers and sequences of what there in our body, the data and history of our genes, genetic origin, ethnicity, race, so on.

- Consider "Fik'r" as a cosmic-sub-atomic-intellectual-extraterrestrial (Meaning non-physical, non-earthy) depot of all what it constituted, constitutes and shall continue to constitute everything about you. And it is infinitesimally small. But it can expand to an imaginable dimension, size and proportions. It stays alive and continues to grow after we pass away if it is still linked to the origin of its creation, in our case the Anunnaki. The "Fik'r" is linked to the Anunnaki our creators through a "Conduit" found in the cells of the brain. For now, consider "Fik'r" as a small molecule, a bubble.
- **4-Code/Use according to mythology and esoterism:** It is the most important vehicle for the mind "intellect". Through Fik'r, a person can enter higher dimensions.
- **5-Benefits:** It is of a major importance to train your Fik'r. "Transmission of the mind" training sessions can develop extra-sensorial faculties and open your "inner eye" commonly referred to as the "Third Eye".

***   ***   ***

18-What Is An-Hayya'h? Is It The Original Source Of Life?

The Answer

An-Hayya'h "A-haYA, Aelef-hayat"

- **1-Origin:** Derived from the Anakh A.Ha.YA
- **2-Numerical value:** 1111, also Al-Lef 111.
- **3-Meaning:** As defined in the "Anunnaki Encyclopedia"; "An-Hayya'h" could be the most important word in the whole literature of the Anunnaki Anakh, and Ulema, as well as in the written history of humanity, because it deals with:

1-Origin of man on earth;

2-How humans are connected to the Anunnaki;

3-Importance of water vis-à-vis humans and Anunnaki;

4-The life of humans;

5-Proof that it was the "Woman" who created man, Adam and the human race via her Anunnaki identity;

6-The return of the Anunnaki to earth;

7-Humanity salvation, hopes, and a better future for all of us; a gift from our ancestors and creators, the Anunnaki.

I will try to explain the whole concept as clear as possible, because it is extremely difficult to find the proper and accurate word or words in our terrestrial languages and vocabularies.

The word **"An-Hayya'h"** is composed of:

- o **1-"An" or "A"** (Pronounced Aa), or "Aelef "(Pronounced A'lef). It is the same letter in Anakh**,** Akkadian, Canaanite, Babylonian, Assyrian, Ugaritic, Phoenician, Moabite, Siloam, Samaritan, Lachish, Hebrew, Aramaic, Nabataean Aramaic, Syriac, and Arabic. All these languages are derived from the Anakh. (Note: The early Greeks adopted the Phoenician Alphabet, and the Latin and Cyrillic came from the Greek. The Hebrew, Aramaic and Greek scripts all came from the Phoenician. Arabic and most of Indian scriptures came from the Aramaic.

- o The entire Western world received its languages from the Phoenicians, the descendants of the Anunnaki). "An" in Anakh (Anunnaki language), means one of the following: 1-Beginning; 2-The very first; 3-The ultimate; 4-The origin; 5-Water.

- o On earth, this word became "Alef" in Phoenician, Aramaic, Hebrew, Syriac and Arabic. Alef is the beginning of the alphabet in these languages. In Latin, it's "A" and in Greek is "Alpha". In Hebrew, the "Aleph" consists of two yuds (Pronounced Yood); one yud is situated to the upper right and the other yud to the lower left. Both yuds are joined by a diagonal *vav*. They represent the higher water and the lower water, and between them the heaven. This mystic-kabalistic interpretation was given to us by Rabbi Isaac Louria. Water is extremely important in all the sacred scriptures, as well as in the vast literature and scripts of extraterrestrials and Anunnaki.

- o Water links humans to the Anunnaki. In the Babylonian account of the Creation, Tablet 1 illustrates Apsu (male), representing the primeval fresh water, and Tiamat (female), the primeval salt water.

These were the parents of the gods. Apsu and Tiamat begat Lahmu (Lakhmu) and Lahamu (Lakhamu) deities. In the Torah, the word "water" was mentioned in the first day of the creation of the world: "And the spirit of God hovered over the surface of the water." In the Chassidut, the higher water is "wet" and "warm", and represents the closeness to Yahweh (God), and it brings happiness to man. The lower water is "cold", and brings unhappiness because it separates us from Yahweh (God), and man feels lonely and abandoned. The Ten Commandments commences with the letter "Alef": "Anochi (I) am God your God who has taken you out of the land of Egypt, out of the house of bondage."

The letter "Alef" holds the secret of man, its creation and the whole universe (Midrash). In Hebrew, the numeric value of "Aleph" is 1. And the meaning is: a-First; b-Adonai; 3-Leader; 4-Strength; 5-Ox; 6-Bull, 7-Thousand; 8-Teach.

According to Jewish teaching, each Hebrew letter is a spiritual force and power by itself, and comes directly from Yahweh (God). This force contains the raw material for the creation of the world and man. The Word of God ranges from the Aleph (the very first letter) to the Tav (the last letter) in Hebrew. In Revelation 1:8, Jesus said: "I am Alpha and Omega, the beginning and the ending."

In John 1:1-3, as the Word becomes Jesus, the Lord Jesus is also the Aleph and the Tav, as well as the Alpha and the Omega. In Him exists all the forces, and spiritual powers of the creation. Jesus is also connected to water, an essential substance for the purification of the body and the soul, this is why Christians got to be baptized in water.

In Islam, water is primordial and considered as the major force of the creation of the universe.

The Prophet Mohammad said (From the Quran): "Wa Khalaknah Lakoum min al Ma'i, koula chay en hay", meaning: And WE (Allah) have created for you from water everything alive." The Islamic numeric value of Aleph and God is 1.

To the Anunnaki and many extraterrestrial civilizations, the "An" or "Alef" represents number 1, also Nibiru, the constellation Orion, the star Aldebaran, and above all the female aspect of the creation symbolized in an Anunnaki woman "Gb'r" (Angel Gabriel to us) have the humeric value of 1.

- **2-Hayya'h** (Also A-haYA, Aelef-hayat) means: a-Life; b-Creation; c-Humans; d-Earth, where the first human (female human was the first created human on earth) was created. In Arabic, Hebrew, Aramaic, Turkish, Syriac, and so many Eastern languages, the Anunnaki words "Hayya'h" and "Hayat" mean the same thing: Life. Quite astonishing! But the most striking part of our story is that the original name of Eve is not Eve, but "Hawwa" derived directly from Hayya. How do we know this?

  o Very simple: Eve's name in the Bible is "Hawwa", also "Chevvah". In the Quran is also "Hawwa", and in every single Semitic and Akkadian script, Eve is called Hawwa or Hayat, meaning the giver of life; the source of the creation.

  o Now, if we combine the 2 words: An +Hayya'h or Hayat, we get this: Beginning; The very first; The ultimate; The origin; Water + Life; Creation; Humans; Earth, where the first was created; Woman. And the whole meaning becomes: The origin of the creation and first thing or person who created the life of humans was a woman (Eve; Hawwa) or water.

  o Amazingly enough, in Anakh, woman and water mean the same thing, because woman represents water according to the Babylonian, Sumerians and Anunnaki tablets, as clearly written in the Babylonian-Sumerian account of the Creation, Tablet 1. And I have more surprises to share with you: The Anunnaki who created us genetically some 65,000 B.C. lived on earth with us, in Iraq (Sumer, Mesopotamia, Babylon) and Lebanon (Loubnan, Pheonicia, Phinikia).

They taught our ancestors how to write, how to speak, how to play music, how to build temples, how to navigate, as well as geometry, algebra, metallurgy, irrigation, astronomy, you name it. But the human races disappointed them, for the early human beings were cruel, violent, greedy and ungrateful. So, the Anunnaki gave up on us and left earth. The few remaining Anunnaki living in Iraq and Lebanon were killed by savage military legions from Greece, Turkey and other nations of the region. The Anunnaki left earth for good. Other extraterrestrial races came to earth, but these celestial visitors were not friendly and considerate like our ancestors the Anunnaki. The new extraterrestrials had a different plan for humanity, and their agenda included abduction of women and children, animal mutilation, genetic experiments on human beings, creating a new hybrid race, etc…

The Anunnaki did not totally forget us. After all, many of their women were married to humans, and many of our women were married to Anunnaki. Ancient history, the Bible, Sumerian Texts, Babylonian scriptures, Phoenician tablets, and historical accounts from around the globe recorded these events.
You can find them, almost intact, in archeological sites in Iraq and Lebanon, as well as in museums, particularly the British Museum, the Iraqi Museum and the Lebanese Museum. So, before leaving us, the Anunnaki activated in our cells the infinitesimally invisible multi-multi--microscopic gene of An-Hayya'h. It was implanted in our organism and became a vital composition of our DNA.

Humans are not yet aware of this, as we were not aware of the existence of our DNA for thousands of years.
As our medicine, science and technology advance, we will be able one day to discover that miniscule, invisible, undetectable An-Hayya'h, exactly as we have discovered our DNA. An-Hayya'h cannot be detected yet in our laboratories. It is way beyond our reach and our comprehension. It is extremely powerful, because it is the very source of our existence.

- o Through An-Hayya'h, the Anunnaki remained in touch with us, even though we are not aware of it. It is linked directly to a "Conduit" and to a "Miraya" (Monitor, or mirror) on Nibiru. Every single human being on the face of the earth is linked to the outer-world of the Anunnaki through An-Hayya'h. And it is faster than the speed of light.
- o It reaches the Anunnaki through "Babs" (Star gates).
- o For now, we will call it "molecule" or "bubble". This molecule travels the universe and reaches the "Miraya" of the Anunnaki through a "Conduit" integrated in our genes and our brain cells by the Anunnaki some 65,000 years ago. But what is a "Conduit"? I will explain below. Does every human possess a "conduit"? The answer is yes.
- o All humans have a "Conduit" just like the Anunnaki, because it is part of our DNA.

It is impossible to explain how a "Conduit" works inside the human brain, and/or how it works for a human being. I will explain it in the Anunnaki's context. The creation of the "Conduit" is the most important procedure done for each Anunnaki student on the first day of his or her entrance into the Academy. A new identity is created for each Anunnaki student by the development of a new pathway in his or her mind, connecting the student to the rest of the Anunnaki's psyche.

- Simultaneously, the cells check with the "other copy" of the mind and body of the Anunnaki student, to make sure that the "Double" and "Other Copy" of the Mind and body of the student are totally clean. During this phase, the Anunnaki student temporarily loses his or her memory, for a very short time. This is how the telepathic faculty is developed, or enhanced in everyone. It is necessary, since to serve the total community of the Anunnaki, the individual program inside each Anunnaki student is immediately shared with everybody. The Anunnaki have collective intelligence and individual intelligence. And this is directly connected to two things: the first is the access to the "Community Depot of Knowledge" that any Anunnaki can tap in and update and acquire additional knowledge.
- The second is an "individual Prevention Shield," also referred to as "Personal Privacy." This means that an Anunnaki can switch on and off his/her direct link, or perhaps better defined as a channel, to other Anunnaki. By establishing the "Screen" or "Filter" an Anunnaki can block others from either communication with him or her, or simply prevent others from reading any personal thought.
- "Filter" "Screen" and "Shield" are interchangeably used to describe the privacy protection.
- In addition, an Anunnaki can program telepathy and set it up on chosen channels, exactly as we turn on our radio set and select the station we wish to listen to. Telepathy has several frequency, channels and stations. When the establishment of the Conduit is complete, the student leaves the conic cell, where the procedure has taken place, and heads to the classroom. Now, the second question is: How does an Anunnaki receive the content of a "Conduit" to allow him/her to watch over us? Through the "Miraya" (Please see Miraya in "Anunnaki Encyclopedia" to learn how it works).

The Anunnaki created the "Conduit", the "Miraya" and the "An-Hayya'h" to watch over us, even though we do not deserve it.
The Anunnaki have been watching us, monitoring our activities, listening to our voices, witnessing our wars, brutality, greed and indifference toward each others for centuries. But they did not interfere. But now, they will, because they fear two things that could destroy earth and annihilate the human race:

1-The domination of earth and the human race by the Greys;

2-The destruction of human life and planet Earth on the hands of humans.

The whole earth could blow up. Should this happen, the whole solar system could be destroyed. For we know, should anything happen to the Moon, the earth will cease to exist. This is an absolute truth and a fact accepted by all scientists. "An-Hayya'h" is our umbilical cord, our birth cord that attaches us to the Anunnaki.

No matter how silly and crazy this concept might look to many of us, one day, we will accept and possibly we might understand its mind-boggling mysteries, when our science, technology and mind explore wider dimensions, and reach a higher level of cosmic awareness and intelligence.

But this is not the whole story about An-Hayya'h; the most delightful and comforting aspect of it, is the hope, peace, a brighter future, and a better life we can accomplish and reach when we discover how to use it without abusing it.

Every one of us can do that. If in your lifespan, you remain unable to attain these results, your An-Hayya'h will always be there for you to use before you depart this earth.

It will never go away, because it is part of you. Without it you couldn't exist. Just before you die, your brain out of the blue wills active it for you. Seconds before you leave earth (Not your body, not your soul) your mind will project the reenactment of all the events and acts (bad and good) in your life, past, present and future, and "zoom" you right toward your next nonphysical destination, where and when you judge yourself, your deeds, your existence and decide whether you wish to elevate yourself to a higher dimension, or stay in the state of nothingness and loneliness. No, you will not return to earth, nor your soul will migrate to another soul or another body, because the Anunnaki do not believe in reincarnation or a return to earth.

Earth is the lowest sphere of existence for humans. Thus, you are always connected to the Anunnaki in this life and the next one.

- **4-Code/Use according to mythology and esoterism:** Because it is the source of life, An-Hayya'h as a word entered the sacred language of the "Intellect" and communication medium of the enlightened teachers. It was pronounced 7 times at the beginning of each "Ij-Ti.Mah" (Reunion) of the elders. Some believe that the first letter of this word "Heh", not An, had supernatural healing powers. Talismans were created to hold the "Heh". The Templars of the Island of Malta honored it and engraved on their swords. The Phoenician-Jewish-Aramaic-

Arabic "Heh" if illustrated as two letters, it creates the shape of an esoteric rose. And the rose was the early secret and esoteric symbol of many secret learned societies, and Crusaders who were searching for the Philosophical Stone in Palestine.

- **5-Benefits:** No pragmatic visible application. However, it could facilitate negotiations between sympathizers of the occult and practitioners of "Al Sihr". The legendary alchemist Nicholas Flamel used it in many of his metal transmutations formulas. Allegedly, the letter "Heh" was found on a measuring tape retrieved at the UFO crash site in Roswell. If you join the two ends of the letter, you get the sign of infinity. You can do that just by drawing a straight line between the top and bottom of the letter. Many historians believed for centuries, that the infinity sign was a Greek symbol. The truth is, the infinity sign is a numerical form for 2 parallel words. The Ulema used it as a mental stimulus for extraterrestrial entities plasmic apparitions. According to the Book of Rama-Dosh, the converted "Heh" letter…in the possession of an honorable person creates wealth, and opportunities for prosperity. In tarot, the magician begins to work under the sign of infinity.

Using the infinity sign, the magician of the Tarot make financial difficulties disappear. If you draw the "HEH" twice side by side on a candle, you will increase your chances of financial success. It appears a ridiculous story for the rational person, and I totally agree. Ironically, 3 out 4 "scientific" persons I knew and who ridiculed the whole idea, tried it at least once.

*** *** ***

19-What Is Ar. Hal?
Is It Going Back In Time?

The Answer

Anunnaki branching out and changing individuality in multiple universes

- **1-Origin:** Derived from the Anakh Aa. R'Hal.Ra
- **2-Numerical value:** 888
- **3-Meaning:** According to the "Anunnaki Encyclopedia", this is a very difficult phenomenon to comprehend.
  - To understand the concept, the closest metaphor in human terms would be that if you wish you could do something differently, change the past, change a life decision, like perhaps, going back in time to a point before you have made a bad decision.
  - Or, if you think that you could do some good if you could change an entire event. In the Anunnaki's case, they have the solutions for these dilemmas. An Anunnaki can split himself/herself in two, or more if necessary, and move on to a universe that is very much like the one they live on (Nibiru).
  - There are so many universes, and some of them do not resemble Nibiru at all.
  - If an Anunnaki wishes to branch out and move on, he/she must study the matter very carefully and make the right selection. And the branching, or splitting, results in exact copies of the person of the Anunnaki, both physically and mentally. At the moment of separation, each separate individual copy of an Anunnaki grows, mentally, in a different direction, follows his or her own free will and decisions, and eventually the two are not exactly alike. So what do they do, first of all?
  - The old one stays where he/she is and follows his/her old patterns as he/she wishes.
  - The new one might land one minute, or a month, or a year, before the decision he/she wants to change or avoid. Let's take this scenario for instance; Some 30,000 years ago in his life-span; an Anunnaki male was living a nice life with his wife and family. But he felt that he did not accomplish much, and suddenly he wanted to be more active in the development of the universe; a change caused by witnessing a horrendous event such as a certain group of beings in his galaxy

destroying an entire civilization, and killing millions of the inhabitants, in order to take over their planet for various purposes. It happened while an Anunnaki was on a trip, and he actually saw the destruction and actions of war while he was traveling. It was quite traumatic, and he thought, at that moment, that he must be active in preventing such events from occurring again, ever. So, he went back in time to be in a spot to prevent these fateful events from happening again. There, in that new dimension, the Anunnaki leaves his former self (A copy of himself) as a guardian and a protector. The other copy (Perhaps one of the original ones) is still on Nibiru.

- **4-Code/Use according to mythology and esoterism:** There is no connection to mythology and esoterim. The "Branching Out" phenomenon occurred in one of the designated locals of the Anunnaki Hall of Records, also called in terrestrial term "Akashic Records."
- **5-Benefits:** The possibility of visiting other worlds, dimensions and civilizations.
- **6-Geometrical presentation/Symbol:** Not applicable

*** *** ***

20-Year 2012: Is It The Date Of The End Of The World?

2085: Is It The Date Of The Return Of The Anunnaki?

2022: It It The Year When Anunnaki And Mankind Meet Face To Face, And The Destiny Of Humans Will Be decided Upon For Good?

The Answer

2012: Is It The Date Of The End Of The World?
2085: Is It The Date Of The Return Of The Anunnaki?
2022: It It The Year When Anunnaki And Mankind Meet Face To Face, And The Destiny Of Humans Will Be decided Upon For Good?

Possibilities and Scenarios:

- 2012 marks the end of the Mayan calendar. It has no relation whatsoever with the return of the Anunnaki. Any advanced theory pertaining to this date is not backed up by science. Such assumption is pseudoscience. It is my belief that Mr. Burak Eldem was the first writer to suggest that the Anunnaki will return in 2012. Again, this "assigned" date could not be backed by astronomy or any other science. It is evident that people are confusing the Mayan calendar that ends in 2012 with the Anunnaki return or intention to return. Some authors suggested that the Mayas and the Incas have some sort of link to the Anunnaki, because of their extensive knowledge in astronomy and cosmology. The same thing was said about the Sumerians who mapped the heavens. Yet, there is no date for their return to earth in the Sumerian texts.

- According to Dr. Sitchin, the next passage of Nibiru will occur in the year 2085. This means that the Anunnaki will show up in 2085. Any scientific data to substantiate this idea? No. However, Dr. Sitchin must have his own reasons and logic for advancing such a theory. On what foundation did he cement his assumption? I don't know. I respect the man and admire his pioneering work. But, I have no clues how Dr. Sitchin came up with this date.

- How about the 2022 scenario? The only reference made to the date 2022 was found in the Ulema manuscript called "The Book of Rama-Dosh." In essence, this book is a cosmological-metaphysical-philosophical work allegedly based upon science, astronomy and quantum physics. Yet, at the time it was written or compiled, quantum physics theories did not exist. How did they know about quantum physics, and anti-gravity law, remain an unsolved mystery.

*** *** ***

104

The book also described *ad infinitum* the return of the Anunnaki and their plan for humanity. According to the Ulema book, The Anunnaki's return has been already announced to leading figures in several countries, and official terrestrial authorities of various ethnicities. Some suggested that India was chosen as the landing "terminal."

Others believe that the United States government is moe likely to be the Anunnaki's destination. This was based upon the fact (?) that American military scientists and a group of astrophysicists at NASA and top-echelon big names at NSA have learned about the Anunnaki's return (Including the date of the return) from an extraterrestrial race currently living on earth.

Some of these extraterrestrials work at Dulce base, and some other places in Arizona, Nevada, Puerto Rico and Mexico. How accurate are those claims? Nobody knows.

*** *** ***

- On the map of speculation we have 3 proposed dates so far:
- 1-According to Dr. Sitchin, the return of the Anunnaki shall occur sometime in 2085.
- 2-According to independent researchers and "fans" of the Mayan Calendar, the Anunnaki will return in 2012 and this could change humanity's fate and brings the world to a catastrophic end.
- 3-According to the Ulema, the precise date is 2022.

What is my personal opinion? I don't know. However I tend to have confidence in the Ulema's perspective. The 2022 date was mentioned by the Ulema in 690 A.D., long time before the Sumerian texts were translated and brought to the limelight in the Western world. How did the Ulema know about this date?

Was this date given to them verbatim by the Anunnaki?

I put this question to one of the righteous men of the Ulema group. He said that they knew from the Anunnaki Code. So, I asked again: What is the Anunnaki Code?

And he replied: "A sequence of numbers, phrases, symbols and geometrical forms."

It was still unclear to me, so I asked again: "What number, phrases, symbols and forms you are talking about?" And he said (smiling):

The numbers belong to a calendar established by a Phoenician secret society called "The Circle Of The Serpent". And he added: "Nothing to fear at all. The Serpent will not bite you. The Serpent is a metaphor…a symbolic representation of the ultimate knowledge; the knowledge of the origin of man, nature of sin, and secret healing powers.

The Serpent symbol, was highly revered in antiquity and appeared in many writings and works of the brightest men in history, including Socrates, Archimedes, Ibn Sina, Maimonides, Ibn Batouta, St. Augustine, Nicolas Flamel, the scribes of Melkart, Baal and "Shams Al Maaref Al Koubra."

Today in modern science, and particularly in medicine, the serpent is extremely valuable.

Do your homework, and you will find out how many vaccines, anti-poisoning formulas, and cures were extracted and developed from serpents and snakes. I asked him again: "Fine with the serpent story, why don't you tell me more about the numbers…This is what I am interested in."

And he replied: "The numbers can be found in the numeric values of the Phoenician Alphabet and the secret attributes of the Creator of the Universe, the God ordinary folks never knew. Each given number corresponds to another number that summarizes distances between stars and planets in various galaxies, including our Milky Way.

Some of these numbers, if aligned in certain order with Phoenician letters, will reveal celestial maps and the exact locations of planets and "destinations" the Anunnaki will use as "stations" and terminals for their space travel in direction of planet earth.

The value and importance of the Alphabet are not manifested in linguistic assets and effective communication only, but in hidden messages revealed only to those enlightened masters who will never use science and technology to destroy humanity and dominate others.

He continues: Every single word in our language, as well as in many ancient languages of the Near East, contains many secrets.

Ask a Rabbi, and he will tell you all about it. Ask a Gnostic and will explain to you the secret messages hidden in the Bibleverses' numbers.

Without numerology, our physical world will remain an unsolved mathematical theorem!" and he ended his elaborate response with: "At one time in old days, Alchemy was highly respected, until greedy and disillusioned individuals began to use it for personal gain, deceiving the innocent.

Alchemy started with a secret code of numbers.

These numbers as they were assembled in the "Divine Formula" allowed the Templars to prosper...I can't go further...."

PHRASES:

On phrases: I asked him about these phrases and what kind of relation they had with predicting future events and the return of the Anunnaki. He said: "One of the most important gifts given to mankind was teaching early humans how to write and how to read. Without the ability of reading and writing, history of civilization will be forgotten, and no lesson from the past can be remembered and taught to future generations. When the Anunnaki realized that man was ready to understand and assess events, to rationalize and take proper actions, to follow their instructions and use creative and resourceful ways to carry assigned duties, then, and only then, the Anunnaki decided to teach man how to read and how to write. They did not teach the whole population. They chose those who showed compassion toward others, a quiet and serene nature, and commitment to preserve the secret messages of words, nouns, and sacred phrases.

I think Jesus knew a lot about these words and managed to penetrate the veil of secrecy of the most powerful words on earth.

Without certain phrases Jesus used, he could have not performed miracles. Some phrases contain the power to pulverize a person, as well as the power of healing and brining dead people to life.

SYMBOLS AND GEOMETRICAL FORMS:

"And how about the symbols and geometrical forms. Can you tell me something about their practical use and how are they related to the return of the Anunnaki?" I asked. And he replied: "You can interpret symbols as a form of algebra, but at a higher level of a scientific knowledge. Symbols are not drawings. They are the soul of science. Dr. Fermi used them very well...Unfortunately they led to mass destruction and annihilation of hundreds of thousands of people...And geometrical forms belong to "sacred architecture."

No, it is not a fantasy or a myth, magic or illusion.

It is pure science. Those geometrical forms were used in teleportation.

How do you think our ancestors built the Pyramids, Stonehenge, and Baalbeck? He asked me. And he continued...

"Do you thing they used crane, winches, and bulldozers?

They didn't!

Geometrical forms are also used in reading celestial maps, locations and navigation of the stars and planets. In fact, they dictate stars rotations, gravity, and cosmomagnetism. Without them, we will not be able to foresee future events and prevent catastrophes from happening.

They are the language of the future. But you have to understand the concept of future. Future is not what is going to happen in years to come...Future is already written in geometrical forms...they contain dates, places, locations, destinations and transmutation of events...."

*** *** ***

Confusing? Perhaps.

Was I not totally confused, but intrigued and fadscinated? Yes!

Worth exploring? No doubt!

"An open mind is wealth" said Dr. Tayarah, one of the enlightened masters of Ulema.

21-Do Anunnaki Have Social Classes?

The Answer

Yes, Anunnaki, have social classes.

The Anunnaki's society is divided into two classes: The lower class and the higher class. Both are under the control of a "Sinhar" or a "Baalshalimroot-An'kgh." Baalshalimroot-An'kgh means: Greatest Leader.

Sinhar means: Leader or Ruler.

When the word "Sinhar" is attached to "Mardack" or "Marduck", the new meaning becomes: Leader of the Ultimate Energy.

Why "Ultimate Energy" is so important? Because the Anunnaki do not believe in the God we know and worship.

To the Anunnaki, the universe was NOT created by God.

The universe is "What It Is" or "Creation by Itself". It gets more and more complicated when we try to understand the psyche of the Anunnaki, and how this psyche defines the elements of the universe in a very strange and complicated language. Consequently, trying to fully understand their language using our terrestrial vocabulary and perception of life is a fruitless effort.

There is nothing metaphysical to it.

It is simply a scientific lexicon our mind cannot grasp.

History has taught us, that as the level of knowledge reaches a higher standard, and technology advances, language changes and new terminology is automatically added to our lexicon and expressions.

The same principle applies to the language of the Anunnaki which reflects an extremely advanced level of technology.

And this is the reason behind our inability to understand their language, and how they describe the universe. Let's for now, forget about all these semantics and galactic jargon, and return to the Anunnaki's social classes:

1-The lower class of the Anunnaki consists of the Nephilim.

2-The higher class of the Anunnaki consists of the Sinhar-Harib.

3-Baalshalimroot-An'kgh is the Anunnaki's greatest leader. He rules both classes. His name means the following:

A-Baal: God; Creator; the Leading Force of creation;

B-Shalim: Friendly Greetings; Message of the Leader; Peace; Root: The Way; Direction of Victory;

C-An'kgh: Eternity; Wisdom; Eye of Great Knowledge; the Infinite; the Ever-Lasting Energy.

*** *** ***

The second in command is Adoun Rou'h Dar, also Adon-Nefs-Beyth. His name means the following:
A-Adoun or Adon: The Lord; God; The Ultimate One;
B-Rou'h or Nefs: The Spirit; The Original Creative Force; the Soul; the Mind;
C-Dar, Beit or Beyth: Residence; the House of the Lord. Members of the higher class of the Anunnaki are 9 foot tall. Their lifespan averages 350,000-400,000 years.

The Igigi did co-exist with the Anunnaki, and shared some traits with them, but they were totally dissimilar in their physical shape, and had different intentions as far as the human race was concerned.

The Igigi are 245 million years older than the Anunnaki. Scholars like Sitchin and Gardner have equated the Anunnaki with the Nephilim. This is not totally correct. The lower class of the Anunnaki are the Nephilim, although many historians call them sometimes Anakim or Elohim.

The higher class of the Anunnaki is ruled by Baalshalimroot, and his followers or subjects are called the "Shtaroout-Hxall Ain", meaning the inhabitants of the house of knowledge, or "those who see clearly."

Ain: The word "Ain" was later adopted by the early inhabitants of the Arab Peninsula. "Ain" in Arabic means "eye".

In the secret teachings of Sufism, visions of Al Hallaj, and of the greatest poetess of Sufism, Rabiha' Al Adawi Yah, known also as "Ha Chi katou Al Houbb Al Ilahi" (The mistress of the divine love), and in the banned book *Shams Al Maa'Ref Al Kubrah* (Book of the Sun of the Great Knowledge), the word "eye" meant the ultimate knowledge, or wisdom from above.

"Above" clearly indicates the heavens. Later on, it was used to symbolize the justice of God or "God watching over us." And much later in history, several societies and cultures adopted the "eye" as an institutional symbol and caused it to appear on many temples' pillars, bank notes, money bills, and religious texts.

*** *** ***

Freemasons and Illuminati favorite symbol is the Anunnaki's eye. And as everything changes in time and takes on different forms and meanings, the 'eye' became a 'triangle,' a very secretive and powerful symbol.

George Washington carried this triangle with him wherever he went, and wore it during official ceremonies. If you double and reverse the triangle, you get the Star of David.

This very triangle is visible on many extraterrestrial spacecrafts and on uniforms of military personnel in secret American military bases underground, working on alien technology and propulsion systems.

The triangle became the insignia of the New World Order.

On February 17, 1,953, an American millionaire by the name of Paul Warburg who was involved with secret organizations and the Freemasons in Virginia and Washington, DC, shouted before the Senate of the United States of America: "We shall have world government whether or not you like it, by conquest or consent."

The 'Triangle' can be a negative force. When integrated without balance and cosmic harmony.

In other words, used without spatial equilibrium, in architectural design and lined up on territories' maps, the triangle becomes a negative force on the map. If the three sides of the triangle are separated, such separation can cause serious health problems.

The triangle becomes three lines of negative energy. This energy is not easily detected; nevertheless it runs strong and deep underground.

People who live above these lines suffer enormously.

In many instances, this negative power or current can negatively affect the present and future of many human beings.

Similar to some Ufologists who can identify UFOs' hot spots on earth, usually above ground, descendants of the extraterrestrials can identify and locate the negative currents underground. Each country has these negative currents or circuits underground. I do not wish to scare my readers, but I must inform you that some American states are located above these lines. For example, Mississippi, Alabama, the northern part of Washington, DC, and two areas in Brooklyn, New York share this misfortune.

*** *** ***

112

22-Do Anunnaki Believe In "God?

The Answer

Anunnaki's god is not the same "God" we worship on earth.

The grand leader of the Anunnaki (Called the creator of energy), and other Anunnaki kings and commanders of the first three expeditions to earth were worshiped by the early human races as gods. The Anunnaki do not believe in a God in the same way we do, even though they were the ones who created and originated the early forms of all our religions on earth. However, those Anunnaki who brought religion to earth were of a lower class of the Anakh (Anunnaki).

The god (Yah-Weh) they brought to earth and planted in the mind of primitive humans, was a vengeful and terrifying god; a fact the Gnostics and early scholars of the Coptic Church in Egypt were fully aware of. Their doctrines show their disdain for such a god, and consequently, they called him the 'Creator of Evil and Darkness.'
Later on in history, the Gnostics began to spread the word that this earth was not created by the God of the Church, but rather by an evil demi-god.

The more advanced human beings who interacted with the Anunnaki shared similar beliefs.
Today, if humans would learn about all this, the religious aspect of our beliefs would be most difficult to reconcile.
Members of an early Anunnaki expedition to Phoenicia taught the Phoenicians how to develop their language, and revealed to them the secret powerful names and attributes of Baalshalimroot.

They instructed them not to use these words for ill purposes. Particularly, the word 'Baalazamhour-Il' is never to be pronounced or written.
Later on in history, the Habiru (Hebrew) religiously observed this instruction, and thus, pronouncing the name of God became forbidden in Jewish tradition.

However, the Anunnaki did reveal to the Phoenicians and Sumerians seven positive and powerful names/attributes of the Grand Leader (Call him God in terrestrial terms).
If well used, these words can bring prosperity, good health, and salvation in moments of difficulty and despair.

The prophet Mohammad learned these seven words from an early Christian ascetic, a Sahara hermit called Raheb Bouhayra.

Today, Muslims all over the world are aware of these seven words or names. They call them in written Arabic 'Asma' Al Lah Al Sabha' Al Housna,' meaning the seven lovely names of God.

These names do not have numerical value or secret meanings as many scholars claim, simply because they were not originally written in a geometrical form, and did not correspond to a "true god". (Note: None of these words appeared on the alleged hieroglyphic measuring tape that the Americans found at the UFO crash site in Roswell. The symbols and geometrical signs Americans found in Roswell were biochemical symbols.)

Also, early names of the Hebrew God were of an extraterrestrial origin. It is true that the ancient Sumerian texts and records mentioned names of some of the Anunnaki leaders such as Utu, Ningishzida, Ninki, Marduk, Enki, Enlil, Inanna, but the greatest name of all was Baalshalimroot, also referred to as "Baalshalimroot-An'kgh."

He was not depicted by the Anunnaki as a god. Terah, the father of Abraham, mistakenly worshiped Baalshalimroot-An'kgh as "God".

Early Semites made the same mistake when they worshiped the leaders of the Anunnaki as gods, later to be called Bene Ha-Elohim, meaning the children of the gods. The Anunnaki never introduced themselves as gods.

The Jewish words "El Elyon" and "Yahweh" (Jehovah) were taken directly from the Anunnaki's written language. The original word was "Yah'weh-El' Ankh" and El Elyon was "Il Ilayon-imroot."

Some scholars equated the Anunnaki with the Nephilim. This is not totally correct. The lower class of the Anunnaki are the Nephilim, although many historians call them sometimes Ana-KIm or Elohim.

Elohim was interpreted by the early human race including the Hebrew as "GOD" or "My Lord".

Elohim is the plural of Eli. And Eli became "god" in many Semitic languages, including Hebrew and Aramaic.

It has the same meaning in Aramaic, Hebrew, Phoenician, Akkadian and Arabic. And it was frequently used in reference to God. Even Jesus Christ used it. On the cross, Jesus said in Aramaic: "Eli, Eli, Lama Shabaktani", meaning: "My God, my God, why hast thou forsaken me?

The higher class of the Anunnaki (RafaaTH) is ruled by Baalshalimroot, and his followers or subjects are called the

.

'Shtaroout-Hxall Ain,' meaning the inhabitants of the house of knowledge, (Mistakenly, the Aramaic and Hebrew texts refer to as: House of God) or 'those who see clearly. At one point in ancient times, the Anunnaki told the Phoenicians that there is no god (One God) ruling over the entire universe.

However, the high priest of Melkart (Chief god in Tyre, Carthage and many regions in the Near and Middle East) instructed the temple's priests to mislead the people, and spread the word that the Anunnaki were celestial gods visiting earth and were constantly working with the Phoenician gods

---

In the early tales about Kadmos (Kadmus), the Phoenician prince who lived around 2,000 B.C. according to Herodotus of Halicarnassus (482-B.C.-426 B.C.), the concept of one god instead of many gods began to surface.

It was based upon the belief that the Anunnaki followed one supreme leader who created the entire human race. But even then, the term "god" did not mean the "God" we worship today.

Kadmos was the first Phoenician scholar and thinker who knew that "God" did not create mankind, and that the universe was not created by the supreme god or gods of the Phoenicians, the neighboring Near Eastern civilizations or the Anunnaki. Kadmos was and still is one of the brightest minds in the history of humanity; he was recognized by the ancient Greeks (Hellenes) as the creator of the Alphabet.

Kadmos founded the legendary city of Thebes and built the first acropolis in ancient Greece. The Greeks called him Kadmos, and to honor him, they called the city of Thebes "Kademeia" (From Kadmos) after him. Many words and letters from the Phoenician alphabet derived from the Anunnaki language (Ankh).

Kadmos wrote down its final format according to the instructions of the Anunnaki. So, he knew what he was talking about; he knew from the Anunnaki that there is no such thing as one god (Judeo-Christian God) who created Adam, Eve, and all of us, because he was one of their students.

23-Where Did The Anunnaki Create Their First Colonies On Earth?

The Answer

Where Did The Anunnaki Create Their First Colonies On Earth?

449.000 years ago, under the leadership of Enki, the Anunnaki landed on Earth. The Anunnaki established their first colonies on the lands surrounding Phoenicia, Syria and Iraq. But their first cities and housing facilities were erected near Baalbeck, followed by Eridu. The Anunnaki used a sort of laser beams-anti-gravity tools to lift and transport enormous stones exceeding 1,500 tones each to build their first labs, landing and launching pads and to strengthen their gold mines.

- Their operations extended to regions neighboring Iran, Jordan and Israel.
- Years later, they concentrated their mining projects in Sumer, where they built enormous cities. However, during their first expedition, the Anunnaki did not relinquish the colonies they established in Phoenicia (Baalbeck and Tyre).
- The first Anunnaki's expedition included a multitude of scientists, topographers, ecologists, irrigation experts, engineers, architects, metallurgists, mineralogists, and military men.
- The objectives and purposes of this expedition were not exclusively gold mining and the extraction of rich minerals from earth's oceans and seas. However, assessing the natural resources and enormous wealth of earth in minerals and gold, the Anunnaki quickly realized that they needed a larger man-power; something they did not anticipate. Thus, it became necessary to bring more Anunnaki to Earth. Consequently, more landings were en route. And gold mining became the Anunnaki new quest.

*** *** ***

24-Are The Anunnaki Immortal?

The Answer

Are The Anunnaki Immortal?

Immortality is a concept created by the human race. And because it is understood and measured by time and duration, this concept is no longer a reality. For we know that time becomes irrelevant or non-existent beyond our solar system. On aliens' planets, time and space as two separated things or two separate "plans" do not exist. The M theory as well as the parallel universe and multiple universes theories can explain this phenomenon to a certain degree.

- So, if there is no time per se, by itself, the notion or concept of immortality is not applicable.
- The Anunnaki do not think like us. They don't define immortality as we do, because they do not equate immortality with duration or with "Time".
- No, the Anunnaki don't believe in immortality, even though they can live up to 400,000 years. Is there an after-life once those 450,000 years come to an end?
- Yes. The Anunnaki calculate, plan and duplicate everything, All Anunnaki have a double; they reproduce themselves while alive.
- It means, they create copies of themselves and store those copies.
- These copies retain everything including memory. And they can repeat this process for ever. However, there is a limit. And this occurs when the last bio-cell is no longer strong enough to create the energy needed to keep the mind functioning and the body's organs working perfectly.

*** *** ***

25-Do The Anunnaki Speak Or Understand Our Languages?

The Answer

Do The Anunnaki Speak Or Understand Our Languages?

> **Languages on earth:** All our spoken languages derived directly from extraterrestrial languages. And all terrestrial languages derived from the Phoenician Alphabet.
> Many of the Phoenician linguists and early creators of their Alphabet borrowed numerous words and expressions from the higher class of the Anunnaki. Ancient Phoenician texts and poems, recorded on tablets found in Tyre, Sidon, Ugarit, Amrit, and The Island of Arwad included reference to symbols and words taken from the written language of the upper class of the Anunnaki.

The first genetically created race could not speak, and the concept of language was completely unknown to humans. Thousands of years later, the Anunnaki taught the new race of humans how to speak, read, and write. Members of an early Anunnaki expedition to Phoenicia taught the Phoenicians how to create their language, and revealed to them the secret powerful names and attributes of Baalshalimroot.

They instructed them not to use these words for ill purposes. Particularly, the word "Baalazamhour-Il" is never to be said, spelled, or written. Later on in history, the Hebrews religiously observed this instruction, and pronouncing the word of name of God became forbidden.

The language of the Anunnaki was taught to the early Phoenicians who lived in the ancient cities of Tyre, Sidon, Byblos, Afka and Batroun. Phoenicia borrowed her Alphabet from the Anunnaki. The 7 powerful names and attributes of the Anunnaki's grand leader were given to the early Phoenicians in a ritual ceremony in Tyre.

- Yes, Extraterrestrials are capable of speaking and understanding many languages, including our own.
- They assimilate and "compute" words and sentences with mathematical formulas and numerical values.

122

- Some extraterrestrials have limited vocal chords capabilities, but they can very quickly acquire additional vocal faculties by rewinding sounds and vibes.
- Contrary to what many contactees and others said, extraterrestrials from higher dimensions do not talk like computerized machines. They have their own language but also they can absorb and assimilate all the languages on earth in a blink of an eye via the reception and emission of a "spatial memory." At first, the voice of an alien from a higher dimension sounds like an old record that was played at the wrong speed – fast, squeaky, scratching. Then the sound adjusts itself, and the voice becomes a normal human voice. A very pleasant human voice.
- Many of the Anunnaki's letters cannot be pronounced by Westerners because of the limitation of their vocal chords.

*** *** ***

Anunnaki's language used by Americans: The American top military scientists who work in secret military bases and aliens' laboratories on earth have an extraterrestrial lexicon, and use it constantly.

In that lexicon, or dictionary, you will find variations of Phoenician and Sumerian symbols.

Some letters represent maritime and celestial symbols and measurements.

The fact that the Americans are still using this extraterrestrial language should be enough to convince you that the US deals with extraterrestrials, and Zeta Reticuli descendants, live among us, otherwise why would anyone learn a language that cannot be used to communicate with people who speak it and write it?

On some of the manifestos of military parts used in anti-gravity secret laboratories underground in the United States, several letters were borrowed from the "Enuma Elish" of Sumeria and regularly appeared on the top right corner of each document. In the eighties, those Sumerian numbers were replaced by an Americanized version.

Military personnel at other American military bases in Mexico, Australia and underwater in the Pacific do not use an extraterrestrial lexicon.

The original language of the Anunnaki is still intact and is currently being used by top American scientists and researchers who work in secret American-Aliens military bases in the United States and Mexico.

In 1947, the first attempt was made by American linguists, who previously worked at the OSS (Precursor to the CIA), to decipher it. They tried to compare it with the Sumerian, Hebrew, Armenian and Phoenician Alphabet, languages which are directly derived from the Anunnaki's written language. The problem they faced and could not resolve were the geometrical symbols included in the written Anunnaki's texts. But in 1956, they cracked down the puzzle.

Those mathematical figures hold great secrets regarding an alien advanced technology used for peaceful and constructive purposes.

The American military intelligence and what's left from Dr. Fermi's group at Los Alamos wanted to use this alien technology for military purposes. The Anunnaki have two kinds or styles of languages; one is spoken and the other one is written. The spoken language is the easiest one to learn, and it is used by the Anunnaki's population. The written one is exclusively used in books and consists of twenty-six letters. Seven of these letters represent the planets that surround their planet.

*** *** ***

26-What Is The Anunnaki Liquid Light?

The Answer

What Is The Anunnaki Liquid Light?

- The Liquid-Light is an Anunnaki electro-plasma substance that appears like luminous watery substance, and it is called "Nou-Rah Shams."
- In Anakh (Anunnaki language), Menou-Ra actually means the following: Nou, or Nour, or sometimes Menour, representing light. It has the same meaning in many Semitic languages. Shams means sun. The Ulema in Egypt, Syria, Iraq and Lebanon use the same word in their opening ceremony.
- Sometimes, the word Nour becomes Nar, which means fire. This is intentional, because the Ulema, like the Phoenicians, believed in fire as a symbolic procedure to purify the thoughts. This created the word Min-Nawar, meaning the enlightened or surrounded with light.
- If you know any Hebrew, you might remember that Menorah means a lamp. It's all connected. Later, the Illuminati used it as well.

*** *** ***

27-What Is Mah-RIT?
Is It Anunnaki Steroids?

The Answer

What Is Mahrit? Is It Anunnaki Steroids?

- Mah-RIT is humanity's early form/formula of what we call today steroids; an early genetic product created by the Anunnaki in the ancient Phoenician city of Amrit, in Syria co-built by the remnants of the Anunnaki and early Phoenicians from Tyre and Sidon. Amrit is one of the most puzzling, mysterious and enigmatic cities in recorded history. It was the stage for a cosmic war between many ancient nations; the birth of the "Olympiads"; and the world's first Anunnaki-Phoenician medical center. But recent archeological excavations on the Island of Arwad revealed that this island gave birth to the "Olympiads", and not Amrit as it was suggested by historians.
- Mah-RIT was first used by Inanna when she created the first 7 prototypes of the human race.
- Phoenicians used Mah-Rit quite often. It was supplied by the priests of god Melkart.

*** *** ***

28-What Is The Anunnaki ME.nou-Ra?

The Answer

What Is The Anunnaki ME.nou-Ra?

- MEnour "ME.nou-Ra" is a sort of a light (Plasma laser) used by the Anunnaki to purify the body and thoughts.
- All Anunnaki students entering the classroom in an Anunnaki Academy must purify their bodies and minds.
- The purification exercise occurs inside a small room, entirely made of shimmering white marble.
- In the middle of the room, there is a basin, made of the same material, and filled with a substance called Nou-Rah Shams; an electro-plasma substance that appears like 'liquid-light.' It actually means, in Anakh, The Liquid of Light.
- Nou, or Nour, or sometimes Menour, or Menou-Ra, means light.
- Shams means sun.
- Nour in Arabic means light.
- The Ulema in Egypt, Syria, Iraq and Lebanon use the same word in their opening ceremony.
- Sometimes, the word Nour becomes Nar, which means fire. This is intentional, because the Ulemas, like the Phoenicians, believed in fire as a symbolic procedure to purify the thoughts.

*** *** ***

130

29-Anunnaki Code Predictions And Revelations

The Answer

Code Predictions and Revelations

> The Anunnaki Code is an effective tool to foresee forthcoming events in the immediate and long term future.
>
> The expression or term "foreseeing" is never used in the Anakh language and by extraterrestrials because they don't foresee and predict. They just calculate and formulate. In spatial terms, they don't even measure things and distances, because time and space do not exist as two separate "presences" in their dimensions. However, on Nibiru, Anunnaki are fully aware of all these variations, and the human concept of time and space, and have the capability of separating time and space, and/or combining them into one single dimension, or one single "frame of existence".
>
> Anunnaki understand "time" differently from us. For instance, on Nibiru, there are no clocks and no watches. They are useless.
>
> Then you might ask: "So, how do they measure time? How do they know what time is it… now or after 10 minutes, or in one hour from now?"
>
> The answer is simple: If you don't need time, you don't need to measure it.

However, on Nibiru, Anunnaki experience time and space as we do on earth. And they do measure objects, substances, distances and locations as we do on earth. But they rarely do. The Anunnaki (in addition to the Nordics and Lyrans) are the only known extraterrestrials in the universe to look like humans, and in many instances, they share several similarities with the human race. This physiognomic resemblance explains to a certain degree, the reason for Anunnaki to use "time".

*** *** ***

To "calculate and formulate" information and to acquire data, Anunnaki consult the "Code Screen". Consulting the screen means: Reading "Events Sequences". Every single event in the cosmos in any dimension has a code; call it for now a "number".

Nothing happens in the universe without a reason. The universe has its own logic that the human mind cannot understand. In many instances, the "logic of Numbers" dictates and creates events. And not all created events are understood by the extraterrestrials. This is why they resort to the "Code Screen".

Activation of the "Code Screen"

Activating the Code requires two actions or procedures:

1-Preparing the grid or cadre.

This demands clearing all the previous data stored in the "pockets" of the net.

"Net" resembles space net as usually used by quantum physics scientists. They do in fact compare space to a net. According to their theories, the "net" as the landscape of time and space bends under the weight of a "ball" rotating at a maximum speed. The centrifugal effect produced by the ball alters the shape of the net, and consequently the fabric of space. And by altering space, time changes automatically.

And as time changes, speed and distances change simultaneously.

Same principle applies to stretching and cleaning up the net of the screen containing a multitude of codes of the Anunnaki.

"Pockets" means the exact dimension and a space an object occupies on the universe net or landscape. No more than one object or one substance occupies one single pocket; this is by earth standard and human level of knowledge. In other parallel words, more than one object or one substance can be infused in one single pocket. But this could lead to loss of memory. Yes, objects and substances have memory too, just like human beings; some are called:

a-"space memory",
b-"time memory",
c-"string memory",
d-"astral memory",
e-"metal memory", etc…the list is endless.

Thus, all pockets containing previous data are cleared. And now they are ready to absorb and store new data. How do they clear the data? I have no clues. And no human on the face of the earth knows!

2-Feeding the "Pockets": Retrieving Data.

All sorts and sizes of data are retrieved and stored through the "Conduit".
The "Conduit" is an electroplasmic substance implanted into the cells of the brain. I am not going to repeat the lengthy description of the characteristics and properties of the "Conduit". Please refer to my book "Anunnaki Encyclopedia".

*** *** ***

3-Viewing the Data:

Retrieved data and information are viewed through the "Miraya", also called "Cosmic Mirror". Some refer to it as "Akashic Records". It is not! In-depth description of the "Miraya" is provided in the book "Anunnaki Encyclopedia"

*** *** ***

4-Revisiting The Past:

Can the Anunnaki revisit the past? In other words, can they travel back in time? The answer is yes. This concept might seem absurd to many. But quantum physics professors and theorists have already explained this in papers they have published. And once again, let me remind you that I have explained the phenomenon of going back in time in the "Anunnaki Encyclopedia."

*** *** ***

5-Going Forward in the Future

Can the Anunnaki go forward in time and meet with the future? Yes, they can! One Ulema told me that future events have already happened at some level and in some spheres. It is just a matter of a "waiting period" for the mind to see it.

*** *** ***

134

Yes, they did. But please remember, the Anunnaki do not "predict". They just "see" the future as briefly explained before. The book "Anunnaki Encyclopedia" listed some of their predictions. Here are some excerpts from the book:

2,034 A.D.: The secret code of the Bible will be revealed. Part of the code will be used to predict the future. Humanity will finally know the true identity of Yeshua (Jesus), Moshe (Moses) and Mouhammad (Mohammad). The original voice of Jesus in Aramaic, several Biblical figures and greatest personages in our history will be found and recorded on the "Memory Screen" replacing tapes and CDs.

2,031-2,033 A.D.: Humans will have spatial-galactic-extra-sensorial faculties' implants. And Electro-magnetic telepathy will be developed, thus reducing time and space limitations. Many will be able to revisit the past and foresee the immediate future.

2,029 A.D.: Several American bases will be created on Mars and the moon. The Americans will reverse the anti-gravity laws. Several stargates will fill our skies, and become fully operational and totally controlled by American scientists.
Humans will be able to store their memory on a computer chip. Cinema will become 3 dimensionally animated.
American, Russian and French astrophysicists and scientists will discover and recapture voices and sounds from humanity's past, going back to the dawn of creation.

2,028 A.D.: The Vatican becomes an icon of the past. Life expectancy in the United States (lifespan average) will become 130 years. Americans will conquer many diseases, to name a few: AIDS, cancer, Alzheimer, thanks to new technology and very advanced scientific knowledge gained from extraterrestrials.
Official extraterrestrial embassies and delegations will be established on earth.

2,027-2,026 A.D.: By November 2,026, The United States will resurface as a major key player in world's affairs and regain its universal leadership. The American Dollar will have a face-lift.
Puerto Rico becomes a major spatial base for extraterrestrials. Many extraterrestrial bases will be created on earth, the majority in the United States.
By the end of 2,027, the United States will emerge as the absolute and ultimate power on earth, and will intensify its cooperation with several extraterrestrial civilizations. This will lead to the creation of a new extraterrestrial-terrestrial lexicon on earth.

2,026 A.D.: A new powerful and global religion will be established on earth, created by new scientific development and a direct contact with extraterrestrial civilizations. Many will convert to this new religion except the Muslims. Islam and a form of extraterrestrial-spiritual religion will become the two major religions on earth.

Islamabad will be declared the official capital of Islam on earth. The United Arab Emirates, Qatar, Kuwait, Bahrain, and Saudi Arabia will fall in the hands of the World Islamic Council controlled by Pakistan. India will lose Kashmere.

2,025 A.D.: Afro-Americans become the majority in the United States. Islam will unify all Muslim countries, and several Islamic countries will acquire the atomic bomb. Muslims in Europe will constitute 72% of the French population, 64% of the Scandinavian countries, and 91% of the African Continent.

A major military confrontation between Muslim countries and Israel will decimate many nations on the globe. Tibet will become an independent country.

A military alliance between Pakistan, Malaysia, Indonesia and 29 Muslim countries will shift the world's military, nuclear, commerce and peace balance. England will be totally alienated in Europe.

However by the end of 2,025 England will regain global influence. Lebanon will be fully absorbed by Islam, and a major Christian Lebanese exodus will begin; many will settle in Canada, Brazil and France. Malta will play a major role on the map of world's affairs. The Anunnaki will interfere to put an end to the humans' madness.

2,022 A.D.: Threat to humanity: In the "Anunnaki Encyclopedia", see listing under 2,008: Humanity, *hope for.*

2,022 A.D., September. The Higher Council of the Anunnaki learned that the aliens intend to attack earth on a massive scale by 2,022. A major confrontation with aliens will happen in September 2,022; the consequences are not totally clear, nor predictable. However, extraordinary events will occur, including global ecological changes, extraordinary advance in medicine, a global unified monetary system that will unite the market of 125 countries, but the United States will refuse to take part in it, and this refusal could lead to the collapse of the American financial influence worldwide, and force American banks' branches abroad to go out of business. The American Dollar is no longer a hard currency.

30-What Is The Secret Meaning Of Haf-nah, The Symbol Of Mushrooms?

The Answer

What Is The Secret Meaning Of Haf-nah, The Symbol Of Mushrooms?

Although it might appear insignificant and silly in the context of extraterrestrial civilizations and Anunnaki's literature, the mushroom was a very important symbol in the early Anakh (Anunnaki language) scripts given to the Phoenicians and later on to King Solomon. Mushroom in Anak is "Haf-nah", and it represents many things such as: a-fecundity, b-occult power; 3-heredity; 4-life; 5-genetical reproduction; 6-and even a sexual symbol referring to a woman. Ancient Sumerian, Persians and Phoenicians myths tell us how patriarchs used an extraction from mushroom and mixed it with an Anunnaki female DNA to create a secret race of creatures capable of building huge edifices and temples.

Legend has it that the Templars learned this secret while digging in the basements and underground tunnels of the temple of King Solomon.

The Book of Rama-Dosh elaborated on this mixture and described how "Haf-nah" was used to create an extraordinary quasi-human race capable of performing miracles and teleporting stones of an immense dimension.

In the early Phoenician language, "Haf-na" meant: a-hand; b-grabbing; c-instrument. Ironically and interestingly enough, if you read the Christian Arabic translation of the Bible you will find this phrase: "Haf-nat Tourab".

And this is mind-boggling, because it refers to the creation of Adam, in other words the creation of the human race. In Arabic, "Haf-na" means: a-What a hand can grab; b-A small quantity.

The contemporary meaning of the word "Tourab" in Arabic is: a-sand; b-dirt. Now, if you add Haf-na+Tourab, you get this: The hand grabs dirt. And this is how the Christian Arabic Bible interprets the creation of Adam; God grabbed with his hand dirt from the ground.

So, the mushroom, hand, and dirt are enigmatically connected in the creation's script of the ancients. (Please refer to my Book "Ulema: Code and Language of the World Beyond", coming in June 2008.)

The meaning of the name of the great Perseus, founder of the Perseid Dynasty, and builder of the Citadel of Mycenae is: "The Place of the Mushroom", and various illustrations of the mushroom appear abundantly on churches' columns. Another striking example is the figure of the Biblical Melchizedek that appeared on a façade of the "Cathedral de Chartre" in France, holding a chalice in the shape of a mushroom, symbolizing life, and perhaps the "Holy Grail", as interpreted in the literature of Cathars, Templars, and many enlightened eastern secret societies. It was also interpreted as the "Divine-Human Vessel", meaning the womb of Virgin Mary; the very womb that gave birth to Jesus.

In ancient Phoenician and Akkadian traditions closely related to the Anunnaki, the mushroom as a chalice represents the creative power of the female.

More precisely, the fecundity of a female Anunnaki goddess, giver of life and all living creatures.

This fecundity source came in the form of a mitochondrial DNA.

Also, the secret extracted liquid of the mushroom represented the "Light Liquid" known also as "Elixir of Life". (Book of Rama-dosh).

On many Templars' pillars and Bourj (upper part of a medieval fortress or a castle) in Syria, Malta and Lebanon, the mushroom is carefully illustrated as a "Flower of Life" known to the Phoenicians, Habiru (Hebrew), early Arabs, Sumerians and Anunnaki as: a-Wardah; b-Ward; c-Vardeh (Almost the same word in all these languages), symbolizing the "blooming of life".

At one point in history, the mushroom's figure was used by the Templars of St. John of Malta as the symbol of the Holy Grail.

And in other passages, the mushroom represented a head; the head of a leader. Some historians thought that the leader was Baphomet, while others believed that is was "Noah", and another group believed it was the Prophet Mohammed, and finally, there is a group of learned masters who claimed that is was the "Khalek of Markabah".

Familiar? Khalek is "God", and "Markabah" is a spaceship (UFO).

The Anunnaki's mushroom symbol gave birth to the "Cult of Head". There is nothing in the world more stimulating and captivating than deciphering buried ancient linguistic-religious symbols and languages.

31-Who Is Nafar JinMarkah?
Was He The Early Human On Three Legs?

The Answer

Who Is Nafar JinMarkah? Was He The Early Human On Three Legs?

- Nafar Jinmarkah, is the name of humans on three legs: The Anunnaki were geneticists and engineers with a strong appreciation for aesthetics. Per contra, the Igigi created a very primitive form of living beings on earth, exactly as humans created unappealing early forms and shapes of robots, and related mechanical devices, at the dawn of robotics. These robots were functional but not pretty to look at, and the Igigi considered the early quasi-humans to be not much more than machines with limited mental faculties.
- The early forms of humans were created by the Igigi, and looked like apes.
- The earth was extremely cold at that time, and the Igigi had to cover the human bodies with lots of hair to protect them from the elements. It took the quasi-human race thousands of years to evolve into an early human form, and even then not totally human, still looking like apes.
- Some of them had bizarre skulls and facial bones.
- The Igigi actually experimented a bit with the early human-forms. First, they created the "Nafar Jinmarkah" meaning 'individual on three legs.' They consisted of a very strong physical body but lacked agility. Those bodies were created to carry heavy weight. The three legs' purpose was to support heavy loads they could lift and carry.
- Later on, the Igigi worked on a new human form that consisted of a body with two legs, to bring speed and better agility. Yet, early humans remained terrifying, nothing like the Biblical descriptions.
- The Igigi tried four times. They experimented in four different ways. Each time, they faced a problem in designing the human skull. Early Igigi creators did not want to put brains in the skull so human-forms-bodies would not think. These early human-forms were the world's first robots.
- The Anunnaki were the ones who created the brains for the humans. These early brains contained two million cells. But the Anunnaki too worked several times on the prototypes of humans. In their final genetic experiments, the Anunnaki programmed humans with the thirteen original faculties.

*** *** ***

142

32-Do Anunnaki Have Extra-Senses And Particular Powers?

The Answer

Do Anunnaki Have Extra-Senses And Particular Powers?

- The Anunnaki have an astonishing range of extra-senses and incomprehensible powers.
- Almost all extraterrestrials possess multiple physical-mental faculties that can be called extra-senses.
- The Anunnaki and the Artyrians have 13 different kinds of extra-senses, ranging from physio-biological to mental-sensorial. They are NOT neurological.
- The Naryans have 17 senses. Some of the most fascinating senses are:
- **A-**The ability of freeing themselves from the limitation of time and space and sensing the "ultra dimension"; in other words, they are able to feel and sense the infinitesimal frequencies that constitute the dividing waves or walls between each dimension and/or multiple universes.
- Those dividing lines are waves and they expand and react spatially like rubber bands. There are no other words or expressions in the human vocabularies we can use to describe these "existences".
- **B**-They can totally eliminate and sense the effect of heat and cold and mentally regulate the temperature degrees of the environment. Also they can adjust others' bodies' temperature for health and therapeutic reasons, because they can sense the body's weaknesses and strengths. In terrestrial terms, they can see the aura. But it goes beyond aura, because aura is produced bio-organically and can be detected either visually or through scientific apparatus.
- The Anunnaki can easily jam any communication and transmission device on earth, and disable any military and scientific apparatus and equipment instantaneously.
- Extraterrestrials and particularly the Anunnaki and the Grays know very well all missiles installations and locations on earth, whether on the surface, underwater or underground. They can disable their delivery systems in a fraction of a second.
- The Anunnaki have conquered the laws of anti-gravity.
- The Anunnaki can bend time and space.

- The Anunnaki can navigate the universe and reach unimaginable destinations and travel mind boggling distances in a very short time using "Babs", stargates and wormholes.
- An Anunnaki can transpose and transport himself/herself to several places simultaneously, and appear in the same time in multiple locations, always conserving his/her properties and physical-mental capacities. This can be done through various techniques such as using a "Double", another "Copy" of himself/herself, de-fragmenting the molecules of his/her physical body and recreating identical molecules in another dimension. Anunnaki are physical, mental, vibrational and multi-dimensional.
- Anunnaki can transmute metals into any other metal, including gold.
- Anunnaki can alter the properties of any liquid, soft and hard substances.
- Anunnaki can live up to 400,000 years.
- Through their "Miraya" (Cosmic Monitor), the Anunnaki can watch and follow any event happening on many other planets.
- Anunnaki can travel into the future and the past. They can alter the events they have created in the past, and influence occurrences to happen in the future.

*** *** ***

33-Are The United States Air Force And NASA Currently Using Extraterrestrial Technology?

The Answer

Are The United States Air Force and NASA Currently Using Extraterrestrial Technology?

Anthropologist and psychologist, Dr. Boylan, shed a strong light on the issue. He stated that:

- The B-2 Stealth bomber is manufactured by Northrop-Grumman. The Air Force describes it as a low-observable, strategic, long-range heavy bomber capable of penetrating sophisticated and dense air-defense shields. Retired Air Force Colonel Donald Ware passed on Dr. Boylan information from a three-star general he knows, who revealed to him in that the B-2 (Stealth bombers) have electro-gravitic systems on board; and that this explains why our *21 Northrop B-2s cost* about a billion dollars each.

- The Aurora SR-33A is a moderate-sized spacefaring vehicle. The late National Security Council scientist Dr. Michael Wolf of MJ-12, has stated that the Aurora can operate on both conventional fuel and antigravity field propulsion systems. He further stated that the Aurora can travel to the Moon. Wolf had also disclosed to Dr. Boylan that the U.S. has a small station on the Moon, and a tiny observation post on Mars. Dr. Boylan doubts that Dr. Wolf would characterize the Aurora thus, unless it was a vessel already used in making such trips. He disclosed additionally that the Aurora operates out of Area 51 (Groom Dry Lake Air Force Station), at the northeast corner of the Nellis AFB Range, north of Las Vegas, Nevada.

- The Lockheed-Martin X-33A military spaceplane is a prototype of Lockheed's other spaceplane, the single-stage-to-orbit re-useable aerospace vehicle, the National SpacePlane. Lockheed-Martin does not say too much about its winged, delta-shape X-33 VentureStar, except to say that we are building it. To be at that stage of development for its public-program SpacePlane, clearly Lockheed-Martin has already long since built prototypes, as well as an unacknowledged military version, which Dr. Boylan dubbed the X-33A. The 'A' suffix stands for antigravity. Colonel Donald Ware, USAF (ret.) told Dr. Boylan that he had recently learned from a three-star General that the VentureStar X-33 has an electrogravitics (antigravity) system on board.

- This virtually assures that the unacknowledged military antigravity version, the X-33 A, must surely also have electrogravitics on board. It is possible that what Dr. Boylan called the X-33A is the Aurora craft which Dr. Wolf described. The Lockheed X-22A is a two-man antigravity disc fighter. The late Colonel Steve Wilson, USAF (ret.), stated that military astronauts trained at a secret aerospace academy separate from the regular Air Force Academy at Colorado Springs, CO. These military astronauts then operate out of Beale and Vandenberg Air Force Bases, Northern California from those bases, these military astronauts regularly fly trans-atmospherically and out into space. One of the aerospace craft they use, Colonel Wilson reported, is the X-22A. Another informant, 'Z', aka '*Jesse*', who formerly worked at the NSA, told Dr. Boylan that the Lockheed X-22A antigravity fighter disc fleet is equipped with Neutral Particle Beam directed-energy weapons, that it is capable of effecting optical as well as radar invisibility, and that it is deployable for worldwide military operations from the new U.S. Space Warfare Headquarters, located in hardened underground facilities beneath 13,528' King's Peak in the Wasatch Mountains' High Uintas Primitive (Wilderness) Area, 80 miles east of Salt Lake City. Dr. Boylan publicly stated that he heard from an Army engineer, formerly TDY'ed to NASA, who shall remain unnamed at his request. He also confirmed that Lockheed had made the X-22A, the two-man antigravity fighter disc which Dr. Boylan had seen test-flown in a canyon adjacent to the main Area 51 operations zone. He explained why he had seen the X-22A so nervously flown during that test flight. He said that the original X-22A had had a standard altimeter hard-wired into it, but that such an instrument would give faulty readings in the craft's antigravity field, which bends space-time. He had recommended that they instead use a gradiometer, which would function better. Apparently his suggestion was finally taken up, "since in more recent years I have seen the X-22As flying more smoothly and confidently at high altitudes over and near Area 51" said Dr. Boylan. Another informant who wishes his identity kept private related operational details about military deployment of antigravity disc craft which sound like the X-22A. He reports: 'During operation Desert Storm a close relative of mine was in charge of a Marine Division right on the front. In the first days film footage and especially video-cams which a large number of G.I.s had were impounded, so they wouldn't capture any sensitive material. Iraq was pumped up and Gung-Ho, since they had well over 50,000 troops ready to charge us, and since we only had about 3500 they knew of, and they knew [that], because of the close proximity of troops we couldn't nuke them, so, they were assuming piece of cake. Wrong! 'Two pictures my relative confiscated from one of his officers showed:

1-A large disc-shaped craft slightly in front of our men with a high intensity beam of light emitting out of it; then,

2.Where men, equipment, etc. was [had stood], there only remained dark charcoal-like spots on the desert floor. We have had this technology for quite a while.'

The described disc was clearly an antigravity, levitating, aerial-weapons platform in the U.S. arsenal. Quite possibly it was the Lockheed X-22A two-man discoid craft, the real DarkStar, of which the unmanned drone X-22 DarkStar is but an aircraft 'cover' program to disguise the existence of this manned antigravity fighter disc, the X-22A. Further, as 'Z' noted, the real manned discs come equipped with the latest Neutral Particle Beam weapons, which take apart the target at the molecular level. Star Visitor craft do not incinerate humans. Only human military fighters are so deployed. So the above report does not deal with any extraterrestrial event.

- The Nautilus is another space-faring craft, a secret military spacecraft which operates by magnetic pulsing. It operates out of the unacknowledged new headquarters of the U.S. Space Command, deep under a mountain in Utah. It makes twice-a-week trips up to the secret military-intelligence space station, which has been in deep space for the past thirty years, and manned by U.S. and USSR (now CIS) military astronauts. The Nautilus also is used for superfast surveillance operations, utilizing its ability to penetrate target country airspace from above from deep space, a direction not usually expected. It is manufactured jointly by *Boeing's Phantom Works* near Seattle and *EU's Airbus Industries Anglo-French consortium.* Dr. Boylan stated: "During travel to Washington State several years ago, I had a conversation with a former Boeing executive who worked in their Phantom Works, Boeing's black projects division, (roughly the equivalent of Lockheed's Skunk Works). The executive confirmed what I had earlier learned from an intelligence insider: that *Boeing* had teamed up with Europe's *Airbus Industrie* to manufacture the Nautilus."

- The TR3-A 'Pumpkinseed' is a super-fast air vehicle. The 'Pumpkinseed' nickname is a reference to its thin oval airframe, whose contours resemble that seed. It may be the craft identified as using pulse detonation technology for propulsion in a sub-hypersonic regime, and also uses antigravity technology for either mass-reduction or complementary field propulsion at higher speed levels. As air breathers, these Pulse Detonation Wave Engines (PDWEs) could theoretically propel a hypersonic aircraft towards Mach 10 at an altitude in excess of 180,000 feet. Used to power an trans-atmospheric vehicle, the same PDWEs might be capable of lifting the craft to the edge of space when switched to rocket mode.

- The TR3-B 'Astra", is a large triangular anti-gravity craft within the U.S. fleet. Black projects defense industry insider Edgar Rothschild Fouche wrote about the existence of the TR3-B in his book, "Alien Rapture." Dr. Boylan's ex-NSA informant, 'Z', also confirmed that the TR3-B is operational. 'Z' had this to say about the TR3-B triangular antigravity craft. TR3-B. This is the code name for what everyone on Earth has seen. It is a very large triangular-shaped re-entry vehicle with anti-gravity. It is what the November, 2000 issue of *Popular Mechanics* identified as the Lenticular Reentry Vehicle, a nuclear-powered flying saucer, the first version of which went operational in 1962, [the version which Popular Mechanics illustrated.] It was used in Gulf War's early hours with electromagnetic-pulse/laser cannons. It literally sat mid-air, firing long-, medium-, short-range to take out antennas, towers, communications, air traffic control towers, TV dishes and centers, etc. For three hours, these three triangles (TR3-Bs) just sat there blowing up everything in sight. Then the *Stealth fighters* had fun for the rest of the day into the early evening next night. Then followed carpet bombings from high altitude B-52 Strato-Fortresses. They dumped all the old, aged Vietnam-era crap (munitions); a third blew up and the rest [were] duds. Anyways, the TR3B has been in testing since the '60s. But it has only been perfected for the last 8 years since 1992. It is a good remake of what President Truman first saw, (The Roswell semi-circular craft). It is compartmentalized, built by *the Skunk Works* (Lockheed-Martin's classified plant at Palmdale, CA) and Boeing [Phantom Works, Seattle]. It is housed in Utah. 'Z' was reminding of his earlier revelation that the U.S. Space Command has located its prime headquarters and antigravity space-launch fleet facility beneath King Mountain, the tallest mountain in the Wasatch Range east of Salt Lake City, Utah.
- Northrop Aircraft Corporation has manufactured its Northrop antigravity disc, (designation unknown), which Dr. Boylan dubbed the 'Great Pumpkin', from its brilliant ruddy golden-orangish glow. Dr. Boylan said: "I first saw these craft operationally test-flown in 1992 above the Groom Range ridge line at Area 51, Nevada. Later I saw the same intensely burning-bright orange-gold craft that I had seen above Area 51 being test-flown sixty miles north of Los Angeles, in the Tehachapi Mountains east of Edwards Air Force Base. There the Northrop has its secret saucer manufacturing works buried deep within the mountains. I saw the same intensely burning-bright orange-gold craft test-flown above Northrop's mountaintop test bed there as I had seen above Areas 51/S-4." When energized these discs emit their characteristic intense glow. It is reasonable to assume that this is due to strong ionization, and that electrogravitics is the methodology of their field propulsion.

- The XH-75D or XH Shark antigravity helicopter, is manufactured by *Teledyne Ryan Aeronautical Corporation* of San Diego. USAF Colonel Steve Wilson reported that many of these XH-75Ds were assigned to the *Delta/National Reconnaissance Organization Division* which retrieves downed UFOs. That Division is also implicated in mutilating cattle as a psychological warfare program on the American public, to try to get citizens to fear and hate extraterrestrials through assuming that aliens are the ones cutting up the cattle. Colonel Wilson also leaked a drawing of the XH-75D Shark.

- The TAW-50 is a hypersonic, antigravity space fighter-bomber. Dr. Boylan stated: "A defense contractor with whom I have been in communication leaked to me details of this U.S. Advanced TAW-50 warcraft. Developed during the early 1990s, the capabilities of this war-bird are jaw-dropping. And the technology shows that the Defense Department did not fail to utilize what it learned combing through the wreckage of various UFO crashes." The TAW-50 was jointly developed by the *Lockheed-Martin Skunk Works* (Palmdale-Helendale, CA) and *Northrop* (undoubtedly at their undeclared Anthill facility within the Tehachapi Mountains, northwest of Lancaster, CA.) Both companies have a history of development of secret anti-gravity craft at these Mojave Desert facilities. The TAW-50 has speed capabilities well in excess of Mach 50, a number the contractor calls 'a very conservative estimate'. Its actual speed is classified. Since Mach-1 is 1,225 kilometers per hour, (approximately 748 mph), this means that the TAW-50 is capable of moving considerably faster than 38,000 mph. In comparison, the velocity required to escape Earth's gravity is 25,000 mph. Therefore the TAW-50 is capable of going into space, and does. The TAW-50 has a SCRAM (supersonic ramjet) propulsion system for passing through the outer atmosphere. The TAW-50 utilizes electrogravitics to maintain its own artificial gravity while in weightless space, as well as to nullify the vehicle's mass during operations. The TAW-50's power supply is provided by a small nuclear power generator that the contractor said is Normal-Inert. The contractor said that the space plane uses electromagnetoferrometric power generation by the immersion of pellets in heavy water (deuterium) and specially-designed coil superconductive magnets, which yield enormous amounts of free electrons when placed in an immersion which has been triggered into an oscillating field-state flux. The TAW-50 has a crew of four. Nevertheless, the TAW-50 flies so fast that it requires computers to fly it. These were developed by American Computer Company, who derived them from its *Valkyrie XB/9000 AI* [artificial intelligence] Guidance series. They utilize a RISC Milspec Superchip. There are 180 of them in the flight control system, and 64 more in the weapons guidance system, the contractor reported.

It can carry a combined payload of glide bombs and a package of MIRV (Multiple Independently-targeted Reentry Vehicles, mil-speak for a group of intercontinental ballistic missiles), each of which can seek out and strike a different target. The MIRV pack also contains reentry-capable balloon countermeasures to make it very difficult for laser and other defensive weapons to track down where the real MIRVs are and intercept them. The TAW-50 is armed with its own Kill Laser system, which can track and immolate SAM (Surface-to-Air missiles), STTA (Surface-To-Trans-Atmosphere missiles), ATA (Air-To- Air missiles), and ATTA (Air-To-Trans-Atmospheric missiles). The TAW-50's killer lasers can also knock down high-performance fighter interceptors. The TAW's Kill Laser is much smaller than the earlier 1980s-era SDI (Star Wars program) models, and has a miniaturized cooling core and 500 times the wattage.

The contractor said it uses a spontaneous nucleonic burst to trigger the lasing (laser) effect. In addition, the TAW-50 is armed with micro-superexplosive HyperDart missiles. These are just a little larger than ordinary aircraft cannon ammunition, but travel at hypersonic speed for up to three minutes, and have enormous explosive capability. One HyperDart can blow apart a MiG fighter anywhere within 20 feet of the HyperDart. The TAW-50 carries several hundred HyperDarts. Because the TAW-50 is designed to operate in space, it has on board a two-day air supply. This air supply can be extended by using its scoop system and traveling into the upper atmosphere to harvest more oxygen. The contractor did not reveal the size of the space fighter-bomber except to say, 'It's a pretty big thing.'

The performance of the TAW-50 makes it virtually impossible to defend against. A-It can hide in orbit many hundreds of miles into space, orbiting at times at 22,000 mph. B-Then, without warning, it can dive straight down through the atmosphere at over 38,000 miles per hour on an 80-degree attack vector, reverse direction within 150 feet of the ground with very little loss of motion and without a glide turn, and almost instantly go vertically straight up at over 38,000 mph until long after it leaves the atmosphere and resumes orbiting in space.

The contractor told Dr. Boylan: "Those electrogravitics allow it to change its mass to almost nothing in a moment, and reverse direction in a second, increase its acceleration to so many times G (Earth's gravity) it's not funny, yet they are able to nearly nullify the G-force on the pilots.

153

They (the electrogravitics) are fourth-generation, with the ability to bring it to a complete standstill in under 2 milliseconds, if need be, without crushing the pilots, and keep it there for quite some time."

The contractor added, "It's far too fast for tracking radars…what military aims its radars straight up?' The TAW-50 can be refueled and rearmed in orbit by docking with the secret undeclared Military Space Station that is in orbit. The entire refueling and rearming procedure takes under 10 minutes. Who mans the gas pumps? Military astronauts trained at the Secret Air Force Academy, located in the hills immediately west of the official Air Force Academy at Colorado Springs, CO. These military astronauts rotate duty by traveling to and from Vandenberg Air Force Base on other military antigravity vehicles."

The Cape Canaveral Space Shuttles have carried the arming platforms ('classified *Defense Department payloads*') up to the secret Military Space Station. The contractor reported that with a few extra tanks of LOX (liquid oxygen), the TAW-50 could fly to the Moon and back. As of 2002, the U.S. has 20 TAW-50s in its arsenal. But, as the contractor commented, 'You could take out an entire nation in under 10 days with only 10 of these, doing three attacks a day. One can wipe out an entire city the size of suburban Cleveland in a single attack without having to use any nukes at all.' A-The electrogravitics for the TAW-50 was produced by GE Radionics. B-Pratt & Whitney designed the SCRAM atmospheric penetrator technology. C-American Computer Company created the artificial-intelligence supercomputers. The contractor said he could not tell me anything else. And it was clear he did not want his name used. So, this is what is known.

- The Northrop Quantum Teleportation Disc? Are the above the current state-of-the-art in advanced aerospace craft? No. There have been advances beyond "mere" antigravity field propulsion. Quantum particulate physics is now being used to update a variety of aerospace craft and their weapons systems. On a recent (09/16/05) field trip to the boundary of Area 51, during a middle-of-the-night observation, Dr. Boylan saw first one, then another, and finally six brightly-lit objects suddenly appear at approximately 1000' (305 meters) height above the desert floor. The intensely-glowing, ruddy, golden-orangish ionization field surrounding these craft appeared identical to the field around the Northrop antigravity disc. Dr. Boylan said: "But in the 13 years since I had last observed the Northrop discs above Area 51, and at their Tehachapi Mountains manufacturing site, considerable progress has been made." In 1992, the Northrop disc slowly rose vertically from its flight pad and gradually reached flight altitude. But in 2005 these craft are able to depart from their flight pad and suddenly appear at flight altitude without any visible ascent.

154

> And it is not a matter of their ionization field having been turned off during ascent for stealth purposes. The ionization field comes with electrogravitic field propulsion. If the ionization were turned off, the craft would have fallen from the sky. Rather what appears to be going on is that the Northrop engineers have incorporated quantum physics principles into the propulsion. Simply stated, Northrop appears to have harnessed quantum entanglement to achieve quantum teleportation. To the observer the craft simply ceases to exist on the flight pad and instantly begins to exist at, (in this case), 1000 feet altitude.

If the interpretation of this observation is correct, then there exists an 11th entry in the U.S. antigravity arsenal, the Northrop Quantum Teleportation Disc. If the black-budget scientists keep advancing along these lines, we could foresee the day when a fleet of Air Force craft suddenly "cease to exist" on the air base runway and instantly appear at 35,000 feet altitude over a target city halfway around the globe. (Source: Dr. R. Boylan)

*** *** ***

34-Are There Animals On Nibiru?

The Answer

Are There Animals On Nibiru?

Answer: YES! And they are well-treated!

- The Anunnaki believe that the early animals on earth were created by evil spirits (Mental- non dimensional entities.) Anunnaki did not want to create animals. While working in their genetic laboratories on creating new life forms, outside the human or quasi human border line, and by trial and error, one formula produced cats. The cat in the Anunnaki's language is called Bessa.
- In Coptic and Arabic and other Semitic language, the cat is called Bess or Bessa; strange similarity for two separate civilizations that are apart by million light years. The Anunnaki, upon noticing that the female cats responded joyfully to the sound of music and water falls, they added to their genetic formula an extra sensorial faculty to enhance their hearing.
- There is something unusual in the Anunnaki's genetic creation of cats, because their cats don't have gender. Only female cats live on their planet, and they reproduce constantly without mating obviously; their reproduction process occurs in genetic laboratories.
- One of the gifts that the Anunnaki gave the early friendly monarchs of the earth was a set of cats. You can see this gift illustrated in the history and mythology of Egypt. This is another connection or relation between the lineage of the early pharaohs and the Anunnaki.
- Also the cats of the Anunnaki have psychic powers. Although they don't sense fear and danger like earth's cats, they predict weather and atmospheric anomalies. And another unique characteristic – they can talk. They talk to the Anunnaki via vocal expressions. It's not a fully cohesive language that uses nouns, adjectives, verbs, or sentences; it is a series of uttered words and conversational expressions.

- Only one kind of cat exists. And this breed looks a bit like Siamese but with white fur and rainbow of blue and gray around the neck. They are double the size of our cats. The color of their eyes is very light blue.
- Birds: There is infinity of types and colors. All genetically created by the Anunnaki, and they all sing. And yes, they give eggs.
- On Ashtari (Nibiru) and Zeta Reticuli, you will not find insects, only butterflies, because they blend well with the beauty of the landscape and they were also created by genetic formulas. Interestingly enough, the genetic formulas were not created by highly advanced scientists, as on earth. The Anunnaki's children created those life forms, and genetic engineering is part of their schools' curricula.

*** *** ***

35-What Kind Of Relation Eve And Her Children Had With God And The Anunnaki?

The Answer

What Kind Of Relation Eve And Her Children Had With God And The Anunnaki?

There is a vast literature about Eve, and lots of contradictory accounts about her true nature, her origin, her DNA, and above all, her relation with the Anunnaki, the "Gods" and the Judeo-Christian-Muslim God. Eve appeared in the Sumerian texts, in Phoenicians epics, in the Bible, in the Quran, in the Gnostics books, and in the Ulema's manuscripts. Eve story in the Bible is the less credible one.

Excerpts from the Gnostic Books:

"And the first ruler saw the female virgin standing with Adam, and saw that the living, luminous afterthought had been shown forth within her. And Aldabaoth became filled with lack of acquaintance. Now, the forethought of the entirety learned of this, and sent certain beings, who caught life (Zoë) out of Eve. And the first ruler defiled her, and begot on her two sons—the first and the second, Elohim and Iaue. Eloim has the face of a bear; Iaue, the face of a cat. One is just, the other is unjust: Iaue is just, Elohim is unjust. It established Iaue in charge of fire and wind, and established Elohim in charge of water and earth. And it called them by the names Cain and Abel, with trickery in mind. And to the present day sexual intercourse, which originated from the first ruler, has remained. And in the female who belonged to Adam it sowed a seed of desire; and by sexual intercourse it raised up birth in the image of the bodies. And it supplied them some of its counterfeit spirit. And it established the two rulers in charge of realms, so that they ruled over the cave."

In other words, Eve had a direct relationship with the ruler. The nature and identity of the rulers are not clear. But an alert mind can assume that the ruler was the God of the earth, the creator of the human race.

*** *** ***

162

- The Sumerian texts convey almost a similar message. In many passages of the Anunnaki-Sumerian scriptures, the Anunnaki Creators of the human race were physically intimate with their creations.
- Enki was the most visible one. In the Gnostics books, the "Ruler" is a divinity and a creator. In The Sumerian texts, EN.Ki is a king, a god and a creator.
- Both created the same woman. However, according to the Sumerian texts and Anunnaki Mythology, it is not absolutely clear whether EN.KI was the original and sole creator of Eve, because many other Sumerian deities participated in the creation of mankind, such as Angel Gabriel known as Gb'r, Inanna, to name a few.

Quite often, humans who were genetically created by the Anunnaki were "produced" from and by a mixture of the DNA of an Anunnaki, usually a god or a goddess, and an earthy element. This element was described as either clay or specie of a primitive human being. The intervention of an Anunnaki god was a prerequisite. Thousands of years later, the Bible told us that Eve too received a divine help in the creation of her first two sons; they were fathered by the "Lord" not by Adam.

This could and would astonish the Christians. Eve conceived Cain and Abel with the help of God. Only her third son Seth was the result of her union with Adam. And Seth came to life in Adam's likeness.

So how did Cain and Abel look like?

The Bible does not provide an answer. From Genesis: 4:1 "…and she bore Cain saying. "I have gotten a man with the help of the Lord. And again, she bore his brother Abel…" Genesis 5: 3 "When Adam had lived a hundred and thirty years, he became the father of a son in his own likeness, after his image, and named him Seth."

The Gnostics books shed a bright light on this situation; Cain was created by the Anunnaki god EN.KI and a woman called KaVa, (Also Havvah and Hawwa) which is the original name of Eve in the ancient texts written thousands of years before the Bible was written and assembled. This is the official version of the Gnostics.

This means that Cain is not 100% human. Cain's blood is ¾ or ½ Anunnaki. The other two sons of Eve, Abel called "Hevel", and Seth called "Sata-Na-il" were less than ½ genetically Anunnaki, because they were the offspring of KaVa (Eve) and Ata.Bba (Original name of Adam).

*** *** ***

- Cain was superior to his brother Abel at so many levels, because he was the offspring of an Anunnaki.
- Abel was inferior to Cain, because he was the offspring of an earthy element. The superiority of Cain was documented in the Bible, because the Bible (Old and New Testaments) clearly stated that Cain "rose far above Abel"!

What can we conclude from this hypothesis?

We can conclude that

1-Eve and Adam were not from the same race. Genetically, they were different.

2-Consequently, the offspring people (first human race) of Eve were the result of a breeding by Gods.

3-The children of Abel and Cain were genetically modified to fit the scenario of the Anunnaki.

4-The creation of the human race happened earlier, much earlier than the date suggested by Jewish, Christian and Muslim scriptures.

5-All human races came from the primordial female element: EVE.

*** *** ***

36-What Is The Nature Of The Ulema

The Answer

What are the Ulema? Are they gods, angels, and spirits?

*** *** ***

The Ulema are not gods, angels or spirits.
The Ulema are divided into two categories, called "Dara-Ja".
1-Category One: "The Enlightened Teachers". They are humans living on earth. And they are called "Mou.NA Wa.Rin"
2-Category Two: The super beings, called "Guardians". They live in various higher physical and non-physical dimensions.

1-Category One: The Enlightened Teachers "Mou.NA Wa.Rin"

They are a group of thinkers, philosophers and scientists. They are the custodians of important books and ancient manuscripts about the origin of mankind, the creation of the universe and human races, and a multitude of subjects pertaining to vital aspects of humanity, "intelligent beings" and other dimensions that are closely connected to humans.

The Ulema group was also called the "Society of the Book of Rama-Dosh". The Ulema do not discuss religions. Although, many of them belong to various religious beliefs and faiths.

Three of the most important manuscripts (very ancient texts) they keep in utmost secrecy and with an enormous reverence are:

1-**The Book of Rama-Dosh,** also called the Book of Radosh.

Main topic: The origin of mankind, and how various extraterrestrial races genetically created the human race.

2-**Shams El Maaref Al Koubra** (The Sun of the Great Knowledge).

Main topic: The study of superior beings who live in higher physical and non physical dimensions, and who are watching over us.

3-**Al Hak** (Justice and Truth).

166

Main topic: Laws that allow mankind to live righteously on earth and allow human beings to prepare themselves for the next life. Guidance for the next journey is provided in metaphors and parables.

The Ulema group was created during the time of Hiram, the Phoenician King of Tyre. It included illustrious astronomers, astrologers, physicians, mathematicians, scientists, philosophers and metaphysicists from Sumer, Phoenicia, Syria, Palestine, Egypt and Greece. Later on, leading figures of the Knights of St John of Malta, The Templars, The Wise Men of Arwad, and Hiram-Grand Orient Masonic Rites' members joined the Ulema group.

Mou.NA Wa.Rin means: Those who have received the light of the great knowledge.

*** *** ***

2-Category Two: The super beings, called "Guardians"

The "Guardians" are not human beings. And they are not spirits either.

Humans were taught to believe that the world (seen and unseen) consists of a physical life on earth, and a spiritual life after death.

The Ulema's views are different.

According to The Book of Sun of the Great Knowledge, the world or universe usually referred to as *existence* "Wu-Jud" contains more than a physical life and a spiritual life.

Wu Jud consists of 11 dimensions. Humans are aware of three dimensions on earth. The fourth is the one that exists in the next life.

That is the limit of their understanding and interpretation of the world; the physical and spiritual.

To the Ulema, existence, including human existence goes beyond the fourth dimension. The "Guardians" live in the fourth, fifth, six, and seventh dimensions. In the eight dimension, live the "Ultimate Ones". And so on…

Thus, the "Guardians" who live in the fourth, fifth, six and seventh dimensions are noble entities who regularly communicate with chosen human beings and enlightened teachers for various reasons and purposes.

The "Guardians" are not physical beings, however, they can manifest to us in any shape or form using a "Plasmic" organism or substance that the human mind cannot comprehend.

The Ulema receive knowledge and guidance from the "Guardians".

What is the relationship between humans and Ulema?

*** *** ***

1-The Physical Ulema:

The "physical" Ulema who live on earth are not very much different from the rest of us, as physical humans. But on other levels, they are very different from human beings. For instance (to name a few)

- 1-They do not age as rapidly as we do. A seventy year old Ulema look like a forty five year old man.
- 2-Ulema live longer than ordinary human beings. Their lifespan on earth is approximately 135 years.
- 3-They are vegetarians. Yes, they do drink, but with moderation. Some smoke, but not cigarettes. Their tobacco is made out of aromatic dried fruits.
- 4-They have an enormous compassion toward animals. In fact, they communicate so well with animals, the majority of them except crocodiles, snakes, insects carrying bacteria and diseases, and four reptiles' species. Animals sense their presence and welcome them. Ulema have developed a sign language to facilitate their communication with animals. And usually, animals respond in the same manner.
- 5-Ulema are well-versed in many languages. And they are fond of languages of ancient civilizations, including those of vanished cultures. Ulema learn foreign languages very easily and rapidly. Usually, an Ulema learns a foreign language in less than a week.
- 6-Ulema can read a voluminous book and memorize it in its entirety in less than three hours.
- 7-Ulema can foresee the future and predict events to happen in several dimensions, including our own.
- 8-Ulema are in constant contact with the "Guardians".
- 9-Ulema knowledge in arts, science, history and religions is limitless. Etc…

These qualities and gifts allow them to fully understand the human psyche, read our minds, and sympathize with our tastes, needs and aspirations. They are socially active, however, they do not reveal themselves to the rest of us, nor get involved in groups' activities.

They dislike organized religions, politics, fanaticism, prejudices, stock markets, financial interests, publicity, egoism, and excessive authority.

It is not so easy to gain membership in their groups and societies. Membership is by invitation only. And the membership procedures and initiation process, formalities, and rituals are rigorous. Many applicants have failed because of the tests they had to go through.

2-The Non-Physical Ulema:

The non-physical Ulema do not reveal themselves to us. They communicate with the physical Ulema on an exclusive basis through:

- 1-Secret codes and a visual language.
- 2-Ectoplasmic apparitions.
- 3-Transmission of mind.
- 4-Visitations through "Ba'abs".
- 5-Telepathy triggered by a "Conduit" implanted and activated in the brain' cells.

Ordinary human beings are not trained nor prepared to communicate with them. They can't see them, and they can't sense their presence, even though sometimes they are very close to them.

*** *** ***

37-What Are The Plans Of The Anunnaki For Their Return In 2022?

The Answer

What are the plans of the Anunnaki for their return in 2022?

The Anunnaki are coming back to clean the earth. As was mentioned in a previous question, they created the earth, started developing the life forms, fostered the evolutionary process, and managed to accumulate an enormous amount of useful knowledge, all of which they telepathically transferred to Nibiru, where it was much appreciated. Unfortunately, the knowledge leaked to the Grays at Zeta Reticuli, and they decided to use the humans, and sometimes the cattle, in their doomed experiments that were geared to save their own miserable race. While doing this, they sadly contaminated the pure genetic material the Anunnaki so painstakingly created, and the humans that resulted were no longer suitable for the study. That was the reason why the Anunnaki deserted their research on earth.

Now, after receiving pertinent information over the last forty years, the Anunnaki had decided to come back and clean up their creations. Whether they are doing it out of benevolence, or because they wish to pursue their laboratory work, we do not as yet know. But one thing is clear – **any human being heavily tainted by the Grays' DNA will be destroyed.** Some, who are lightly contaminated, will be evaluated further, but in another dimension, so as not to endanger the cleaned up earth. Those who are not contaminated will remain on earth, which will be immeasurably improved by the removal of the contaminated humans. The Anunnaki know who is contaminated, and what is the contamination level, by using the Conduit, so to them it is extremely easy to make the selection. This process of selection will be extremely fast, a matter of minutes.

Since most humans do not have a functional Conduit, only a latent one, we must use other ways to find out what is our chances for survival so we can take steps to improve the odds; this will be done individually, each person must examine his or her level. **You will not be helped by joining a religious group, or going to therapy, or any other form of relying on someone else.** You will have to do your own work, but it is not difficult to find out. Figuring it out requires thought and introspection only.

*** *** ***

The Grays' DNA have created greed, violence, and unbelievable cruelty within our nature. Such characteristics were not part of the original DNA material used to create humans, since the original DNA was given by the Anunnaki themselves, who had intended to create humans **in their image**.

Therefore, each person must examine his or her life carefully. The list of offences is extremely long, but here are some examples of people who are contaminated by the Grays' DNA. They are divided into three groups. If any of these traits exist in you, if you have committed any of these atrocities, try to remove them as soon as possible from your life – if you wish to survive after 2022. But even with all your hard work, **there is no guarantee.**

People who exhibit heavy Grays' DNA contamination

- Those who torture or support torture by others, **for any purpose whatsoever**
- Murderers (unless in self defense, which sometimes occurs in situations such as domestic abuse by a contaminated spouse)
- Rapists
- Child molesters
- Child abusers
- Senior abusers
- Spouse abusers
- Those who commit violent robberies
- Illicit drug manufacturers, distributors and pushers
- Those who engage in enslaving women, girls and young boys in prostitution rings
- Criminals who use their form of religion as an excuse for their heinous crimes; this include all religious fanatics, such as suicide bombers
- Those who destroy lives by depriving them of ways to support themselves, for their own greed. This include the top echelon of corporate executives, who have lost any sense of humanity in their treatment of thousands of people and feel that this is "strictly business"
- Elected officials who have sold out for power and greed, and who are willing to destroy their own countries to aggrandize themselves
- Elected officials who are willingly participating in destroying the ecology of the planet because of their close association with the oil and other forms of commercial energies producing countries and their corrupt rulers.

- Any politician, military personnel, or anyone else who is engaging in trade with the Grays, allowing them to continue the atrocities in exchange for technical and military knowledge
- Lawyers and judges who play games at the legal system for their own gain, sending free, child molesters, murderers, and other violent offenders in the name of "reasonable doubt"
- Those who destroy lives and reputations by "identity theft"
- Those who torment animals. These include not only people who hurt and mutilate animals for their own sick pleasure, but also those who support dog fights, cockfights and bullfights, those who beat their horses, donkeys, or dogs, those who "legally" mutilate cats by removing their claws or hurting their vocal cords, owners of puppy mills who force female dogs to reproduce by "animal rape," and those who abandon their animals, or chain them indefinitely, sometimes allowing them to die by such neglect.

*** *** ***

People who exhibit medium Grays' DNA contamination:

- People who believe that discipline requires physical punishment (in children or adults)
- Middle echelon executives who "only take orders" from their superiors as their corporations are destroying the economy of their own countries to save their own skin
- Those, who in the name of fashion and beauty, have hurt countless young girls who have succumbed to eating disorders, some of whom have actually died, while the owners and designers made a fortune for themselves
- Irresponsible parents who allow their children to grow up with Grays' values rather than human and Anunnaki values
- Hunters of animals who believe they are doing it only for food but do not feel a joy in killing
- Owners of "factory farms" whose animals are not tormented, but live a miserable life
- People who eat any form of meat (the Anunnaki believe in strict vegetarian diet, supplemented by milk and eggs from animals that are treated humanely and allowed to live out their life comfortably and die naturally)

*** *** ***

174

People who exhibit light Grays' DNA contamination

- People who are willing to advertise products that may be harmful, for gain
- People who are willing to import products that may be harmful, for gain
- People who object to social reform that may help the greater number of others, such as health care or better equalization of income, for gain
- People who are engaged in the fur trade
- People who are willing to influence others through brain wash advertising, such as the cosmetic industry, for gain
- Racists, sexists, and ageists, who are willing to allow their prejudices to influence their behaviour to others
- People who are willing to spend millions of dollars on frivolous pursuits (diamond studded collars for dogs, who really don't care about anything but love and food? $200,000 wedding cakes?) while millions around them are starving
- People actively engaged in aggressive take-overs, thus destroying the livelihood of many
- Anyone deliberately sending a computer virus for "fun"

This is only a partial listing. Examine your heart, there may be other reasons to assume you are contaminated. There are only fourteen more year to the final date.

*** *** ***

38-What Will Happen In 2022, When The Anunnaki Return?

The Answer

What Will Happen In 2022, When The Anunnaki Return?

Many things at so many levels: Physical, spiritual, mental, multidimensional, vibrational, intellectual, and religious. We will try to explore some of the possibilities, scenarios and theories.

***   ***   ***

As mentioned in a previous question, the Anunnaki are returning in 2022 to clean the earth. This will happen through a cataclysmic event, the like of which can hardly even be imagined by us, but is child play to the Anunnaki, who have done it all before on other planets, many times. The procedure will take a very short time, a few minutes only, but is, as always, elaborately and securely planned by the Anunnaki.

The Anunnaki will bring a bubble of a special substance, resembling anti-matter but not destructive, and cause it to touch the earth's atmosphere. It will be exactly the size of earth. As soon as the two globes touch, all the humans that have been lucky enough not to be contaminated by Grays' DNA, and all the animals, plants, and those inanimate material which the Anunnaki wish to preserve (such as beautiful and historic monuments, art-filled museums, and great libraries, in addition to the homes of those saved) will be stripped from earth and absorbed into the bubble.

The fish, and other animals who need water, will be taken to a created ocean within the bubble. The birds will have plenty of places to perch on. Nothing will be hurt or damaged – the humans and animals will feel nothing – they will be secure within the bubble. It is unlikely that they will even retain a clear memory of the event, because the Anunnaki would not wish them to be traumatized.

Then, the earth will be cleaned of all our pollution. For lack of better description, try to imagine a huge vacuum cleaner removing all the landfills, eliminating all the plastics, all the dirt, all the smog from the air, and all the filth from the ocean. In a few short minutes, the earth will be sparkling clean, a pristine planet, the way it was when the Anunnaki had first created it. How they dispose of the garbage is not clear to us – it involves a very high technology which we simply do not as yet understand.

The beautiful clean planet is now ready to be repopulated, and in an instant, the humans, animals, plants, and inanimate objects would be returned to earth. Anunnaki guides will be there for the humans, who would naturally need quite a bit of help to adjust to the new life.

In the meantime, the issue of the rest of humanity is resolved as well. As mentioned in a previous question, there are three groups of humans the Anunnaki will attend to. Those who are not contaminated have already been taken back to the cleaned planet.

Those who are heavily contaminated, and who are engaging in cruelty, greed, and violence for their own gain, have no chance at all. They will simply be destroyed, and there is no need to even think about them any further.

What is left are those who are the medium-level of contamination, and the lighter level.

These groups had received a warning to mend their lives, fourteen years before the event of 2022. Some of the people of light level contamination would have completely cleaned themselves through their efforts, and therefore would have been transferred, as clean beings, into the bubble.

Others had remained lightly contaminated.

Those of medium level contamination, who obviously require more work, would be divided into those who had succeeded in the cleaning, and had brought themselves into a light level contamination.

Those who remain medium level, who did not do the work of cleaning properly, will be destroyed with the heavily contaminated ones.

All that remains now is the group of light contamination level, and if they wish to save themselves, they must go through the Ba'abs, or Star Gates, into other dimensions, so that they could be evaluated by the Anunnaki. If they can be cleaned, they go back to earth. If not, they will live out their lives in another dimension, where conditions are much like our own earth before the cleaning.

They will lead a normal life, but will not be able to reproduce, so eventually they will die out.

As for those who go through the Ba'abs, the procedure is extremely difficult. Ba'abs exist everywhere.

There are huge, magnificent Ba'abs that are used regularly by the Anunnaki to cross from one dimension to another. But there are also small ones, located in the street, in a tree, in an apartment building, in your own home, you name it.

They will become visible when the bubble clashes with the earth, and those who were not taken into the bubble, or were not destroyed, must find their way into a Ba'ab. All Ba'abs look the same – they are a circle of shifting light of rainbow colors, very clearly defined. People wishing to enter a Ba'ab must hurl themselves against it, and it will open and absorb any number of travelers.

As soon as you enter the Ba'ab, you are already in another dimension.

It is extremely frightening, a deep blackness illuminated by explosions, thunderbolts, and streaking comets.

There is a very high level of a stormy, whoosh-like sound – the noise can be deafening – and the traveler is swept with violent speed forward, unable to resist or help the move, and constantly twirled and twisted in one direction, and then the other. The traveler will feel dizzy, disoriented, and scared, and this lasts for an indefinite amount of time. When this part is over, the traveler is thrown by a huge gust of wind into a tunnel, which is so brightly lit by orange, yellow, and white light, it is impossible to keep one's eyes open for more than a few seconds at a time. The traveler hears horrible shrieks, screams, and howling of wind, and when the eyes are open, he or she sees bizarre faces, weird creatures, and unknown vehicles which always seem almost on the verge of colliding with the traveler, but somehow never do. After a while, the traveler is thrown out of the tunnel into solid ground, which may be quite painful but not permanently harmful. The light becomes normal and the sounds stop.

At that point, the travelers have reached their destination. It looks much like earth, but it is empty of people or animals, and plants and houses look very dim, as if the traveler found himself in virtual reality. Then, the traveler begins to see people materialize against the cardboard like background. This takes time, the images of people float as if from thin air, but then, all of a sudden, reality shifts and the travelers find themselves in a real world.

The animals, incidentally, will never materialize.

All of them have been returned to earth, to their proper places, as mentioned before.

They are not needed here, since no animal labor or the eating of animals is permitted by the Anunnaki, who abhor such practices. In this dimension, the travelers will meet a few Anunnaki, who will direct them to their evaluation and possible cleaning. We do not know how this procedure works, and in truth, it does not matter very much, since only those who made it would be returned to earth.

Those who cannot be cleaned will be sent, through a Ba'ab, to the dimension we have mentioned before, where they will live out their lives, but will not be able to reproduce. The Anunnaki do not wish to kill them, since they are not inherently evil like the heavily contaminated ones. But they cannot let them reproduce the bad DNA; the Anunnaki do not indulge in sentimental pity, and are fully aware that any form of evil should not be allowed to exist.

39-What is going to happen to organized religions?

The Answer

- The very first thing the Anunnaki will do when they land on earth will be the reorganization of the human race, readjusting the structure and substructure of our societies.
- The Anunnaki believe that without a new social order, humanity will remain in chaotic state and violent conditions.
- The first change they will bring to earth consist in totally eliminating organized religions, for instance, the Vatican will be reduced to a historic icon. Churches, temples, synagogues, ashrams and particularly beautiful cathedrals will become public libraries and centers for the fine arts.
- The Anunnaki will explain to the human race that the God we worshipped on earth was an invention of the primitive minds of the early human race.
- Anunnaki will explain to the human race that the idea of one god, master of the universe, originated from the belief in many gods in the early days of the history of humanity but for several reasons, the number of deities shrunk to one.
- The early prophets, and some of the founders of great religions, saw the Anunnaki as gods. For example, Enki became Yahweh. And before Yahweh, he was all sort of things, such as Adon, Adonis, Melkart, Zeus, Brahma, you name it. So the foundation of religion was a fragment of imagination of primitive and uninformed and confused minds of the human race. However, something good came out of it, such as the Christian charity, the Jewish Tzedakah, the Buddhist non-violence philosophy, the Islamic protection of the orphans and forgiveness. All these virtues, although they are no longer in use today, were a positive aspect of the invention of religion.
- There will be no more churches, synagogues, or any other centers of worship. All that will be replaced by the concept of God as All-That-Is.
- All the famous "Stars" of religion, such as televangelists, fanatic extremists, those who advocate phantasmagorical ideologies such as the Rapture, etc., will have been eliminated.

40-How Will The Earth Be Protected From Further Contamination From The Grays?

The Answer

- The Anunnaki will create an electro-plasma-laser shield around the orbit of the earth, preventing any hostile extraterrestrial civilization from conquering earth.

- The shield will be an invisible "plasmic belt" surrounding the whole planet earth.

- The "plasmic belt" will look like like a zone of extremely extensive heat that will melt anything that might try to go through it.

- On the inside, the mind of the human beings will be constantly monitored by Anunnaki societies on earth, which report directly to the High Council on Nibiru.

- A new "Conduit" will be implanted in the brain cells of each human, so a new "form" of a "global truth" governing the whole earth, and based totally on scientific facts will shape up social code and ethics, thus eliminating erroneous personal interpretations of law and order. It is no longer special interest groups, influential lobbying organizations, and powerful lawmakers will dictate laws and influence jurisdictions.

- The Anunnaki believe that a negative and a malicious mind is as dangerous as an atomic weapon. Therefore, he Anunnaki will eliminate all forms of governmental institutions, installations and places, such as NATO, European military posts, strategic ballistic (missiles and nukes) launching pads and bases, The White House, City Halls, European Fund, The Internal Revenue Service, the KGB, the CIA, International Money Fund, the United Nations, World Bank, mansions for governors, so called palaces of justice, and military high command centers, and all establishments that reflect authority over people and create fear in the hearts and minds of populations. They will disappear. And since they will no longer exist, a greater sense of security and feeling of personal autonomy, freedom, and new sense of individual security will come to life.

- The Anunnaki will eliminate all the dangerous secret organizations controlled by entities such as the New World Order, and the Grays who are currently working with official authorities and military scientists in many centers in the U.S., on the surface, underwater, and underground, all potential dangers and risks of war, as well as threat to humanity peace and happiness, such as global military confrontations, invading other countries, tortures, executing officials and heads of states of foreign countries, dominating world markets, greedy monetary systems, atomic annihilation, thus elevating the human race to a higher standard of spirituality, cosmic awareness, and global peace on earth.

- Nations will no longer be judged by their super military power and military might, but by the creative accomplishment of the mind, collective consciousness of their people, and their contribution to the human race as "one race" on earth.

- People will no longer be judged, assessed and rated by the color of their skin, physical looks, wealth, assets, eminence and the importance of positions and status they enjoy and monopolize.

*** *** ***

41-How Will The Human Mind Benefit From The Anunnaki Connection?

The Answer

- What the Anunnaki will do will not impose on you new beliefs that bring chaos to your mind, and/or confuse you in your daily transactions.
- The Anunnaki will delete those beliefs that were created by institutions that deprived you physically, mentally, and spiritually from evolving, such as the belief or concept that without confessing your sins to your priest you will not be absolved from your sins and you will not enter the kingdom of God, or such as if you don't convert to Islam, and follow the message of the Prophet Muhammad, you will not enter Heaven.
- Those are the concepts that have controlled the mind of humans for centuries. By demonstrating scientifically and physically what really works, what really is the "honest truth for humanity", the human mind will be given the opportunity to see the whole truth.
- All be based on scientific explanation, and since the mind will evolve, by conquering new scientific frontiers, the spectrum of the human intelligence will increase infinitely.
- Therefore, the human mind will have an extremely developed center of knowledge, and will tap into the depot of collective intelligence, and consequently voluntarily selects what fits and meets the physical, spiritual, mental and intellectual needs of the person.

*** *** ***

188

42-Is It A Mind Control Situation?

The Answer

In a previous answer, you say: "A new Conduit will be implanted in the brain cells of each human, so one kind of truth based totally on scientific truth will shape up social code and ethics, thus eliminating erroneous personal interpretation of law and peace."That sounds like a new form of mind control and like an incredible invasion of each person's privacy. How do you explain that?

*** *** ***

- In a way, yes, we will be controlled for a limited amount of time.
- Each individual will have a different time of such control, which will only last until the more advanced faculties will be developed.
- This involves hard work on the part of each human, but the rewards, as mentioned in a previous answer, will be vastly greater than the effort.
- One must remember that having the "Conduit" allows one to connect with the Akashic Records, the greatest depot of knowledge imaginable.
- Some of us will develop faster than others, but since only those who have no Grays' contamination will survive anyway, they will be more than ready to understand the need for such temporary control, that will greatly improve the human race.
- The Anunnaki themselves have a telepathic connection to each other, the same as will be imposed on us, and they know how to use it with discretion and ethical behaviour.

*** *** ***

190

43-How Will The "Conduit" Be Installed?

Does it require surgical operation? Is this a kind of implanting a third eye in our brain as some Hindu and Buddhist talked about?

The Answer

- Installing the "Conduit" in the brain cells does not require a surgical operation.
- In terrestrial terms, it's like activating your cellular phone without going to the telephone company.
- It's like transferring money from your account to another account, without going physically to a bank, carrying money bills and notes, and physically giving this amount to a bank clerk to deposit it in another account. It is transferred automatically via wire, a non physical operation.
- But with the Anunnaki, it will be a higher level of a more advanced technology, that the human mind will understand in due time.

***   ***   ***

192

44-What Will Happen To The Teachings Of Jesus, Moses, Mohammed, And Buddha, If The Anunnaki Demolish All Religions And Our Religious Beliefs Systems?

The Answer

- The Anunnaki will abolish all forms of organized religions, but not the code of ethics, fairness, and justice.
- For instance, the mind will be fertilized with a device that will enable the human being to tap into a higher sphere of knowledge.
- One example would be the possibility of mankind to go back in time and listen exactly to what the founders of religion have said. Not what their followers have created as doctrines and dogma for their own benefits and personal interests.
- Religious systems based upon organized establishments will be eliminated.
- The human mind will be able through the implanted "Conduit" and the "Miraya" to go back to the time of Jesus and listen to his sermons and teachings. Humans will go back in time, and will see Jesus walking in the streets of Nazareth, Bethlehem, and Jerusalem, and they will be able to listen to him at Mount Olive, and by doing so, they will be able to retrieve the true message. They will compare the teachings of Jesus, automatically, with what the Church, its doctors, its bishops, and its governments, invented and fabricated. They will have the two versions, the original one, and the new one invented by organized religions.
- In summary, the Anunnaki are not abolishing religions because they will be taking us straight to the original message of religions, to the very source. Instead, they will eliminate the bureaucratic, governmental, financial, and business aspect created by those who became the custodians of religions, and unfortunately, erroneously, influenced our mind, ethics and way of life.

*** *** ***

45-You Said That The Anunnaki Will Impose On Humans a Vegetarian Diet.

So what will replace meat? Will the Anunnaki give us new directions about feeding the world with soy, wheat, etc.?

The Answer

You Said That The Anunnaki Will Impose On Humans a Vegetarian Diet. So what will replace meat? Will the Anunnaki give us new directions about feeding the world with soy, wheat, etc.?...

- Although many anthropologists, scientists and doctors of nutrition made it clear that the human body needs meat for physical and mental development, because they found out that back in history when our early ancestors started to eat meat, their brain size increased, and their mental faculties developed rapidly, and while this is true, humans who kill animals and eat their flesh will be forever isolated from cosmic civilizations which are more developed, richer, and more rewarding.

- In the eyes of the Anunnaki, only savage creatures kill other living creatures (Referring to animals) to feed themselves.

- Anunnaki do not advocate eating meat, because it deprives living creatures from living. And by their standard it is a crime.

- However, taking into consideration the physical development needs of the human body, the Anunnaki will substitute meat with a new sort of sea food that will grow in the sea and which will have the taste of fish, and also all the necessary nutrients.

- Also, they will develop certain DNA in trees, capable of producing milk-like substance and fruit that will taste exactly like meat, and it would be much more nutritious, and beneficial to the physical and mental needs of humans.

*** *** ***

46-What Will Happen To The Vast Numbers Of Animals That Used To Live In Farms For Consumption Purposes, And Are No Longer Consumed, Since Everyone Is Vegetarian?

The Answer

- They will have a very peaceful life, like many of the animals that currently live on Nibiru such as cats, butterflies, and a wide variety of birds and aquatic creatures in the seas.

- Anunnaki, when they created humans, they installed minds instead of feelings.

- The Anunnaki did not find animals to be communicative and intelligent in general, and they based their judgement on those monstrous beasts that roamed the earth at its dawn, such as dinosaurs and crocodiles, which incidentally, were not created by the Anunnaki. So when many of us will no longer exist on earth, nor in other dimensions, the animals will be left in peace to live out their lives, but will not reproduce any further.

- Animals will become self-sufficient because the Anunnaki will allow them to regain part of their lost animal kingdom.

*** *** ***

47-What Will Happen To All The Homeless Pets, Whose Infected Owners Were Destroyed?

The Answer

> **What Will Happen To All The Homeless Pets, Whose Infected Owners Were Destroyed?**

- The animals have a sort of animal conduit that intuitively will link them to animal communities.
- They will join the newly established animal kingdoms in areas where humans will not have access to.
- The animals will be relocated to places in zones where they will not be exposed to dangers from other, bigger animals that could devour them.
- Because the Anunnaki consciously will alter the DNA of humans to a degree where the human race will lose taste and interest in meat, the same thing will happen with animals, big and small.
- It will be an earthy-cosmic cleansing in taste and physical priorities.
- The animal will live on natural resources on earth.

*** *** ***

48-What Will Happen On Earth During The Final Clash With The Anunnaki?

The Answer

- As we have explained in a previous answer, the Anunnaki will start the cataclysmic event of 2022 by removing all the clean, uncontaminated humans, all the animals, the plants, and the inanimate objects they wish to preserve, by taking them into the bubble they have brought to clash with the earth.

- This bubble is made of non-destructive, anti-matter like substance, and it will protect everything placed in it from harm, until the cleansing of the earth will be completed.

- We have also explained what would happen to those humans who are only lightly contaminated. They will go through the Ba'abs, or Stargates, to face a journey into the unknown, with the hope of being cleaned and saved. They have no guarantee, but going through the Ba'abs and risking their lives is the only chance they have.

- The question remaining now is, what is going to happen to those who have remained on earth – those who are contaminated with evil to the extent that they cannot be saved?

- First, one must remember that in an instant, the houses these people lived in, any animal that they have had, all the plants of the earth, and many other buildings, will disappear in a blink of an eye.

- For a short time, these people will find themselves in an environment that is already totally alien and frightening.

- Some may remember the warnings of the Anunnaki, started fourteen years before the event and constantly repeated but ignored by many.

- Others may have never even noticed the warnings, and so they have no clue as to what is happening.
- None of that matters, since one must also remember that these people are evil to the core, that nothing can reclaim them because they have nothing which is good in their minds, and that the Anunnaki have absolutely no mercy and no sentimentality about evil and its redemption.
- The Anunnaki firmly believe that all evil should be destroyed, if at all possible.
- At this point, the sun and the moon, depending on the time zones, would seem to be eclipsed.
- This will not happen naturally, but rather, the whole sky, over the entire world, will be covered with spaceships and mother spaceships.
- A massive ceiling of metal shapes of machinery, gadgets, wheels, and shifting lights will be created.
- They will be ominously silent, as if waiting. Looking at this from below will be so frightening that many people will lose their heads.
- Some will try to hide, some will run around in circles, not knowing where to go. In crowded, urban areas, they will create stampedes, killing each other in the process.
- Others will run into their churches, trying to pray, and the churches will ring their bells.
- Some of the religious leaders were saved or gone through the Ba'abs, and so have disappeared already.
- Those who are false and contaminated will still try to call their congregations, feeling that perhaps that would be a way to salvation.
- In various cities, people will try to reach their governments, without much success.
- The only officials that have stayed on their posts will issue orders to avoid any interference with the extraterrestrials, since it will make everything even more dangerous and no one on earth has the technology to match.
- The officials' orders will be ignored, particularly by those in rural areas, who are used to self sufficiency.
- These people will confront the Anunnaki, start shooting at them with their guns.
- As in other areas, which of course have had many good people living in them, only the violent ones have remained, since the others have already escaped.
- Acting stupidly, they will annoy the Anunnaki with their inept shooting until the Anunnaki decide to paralyze them with special beams of light, for a limited time. When the beams' effects wear off, some will resume their doomed attempts to fight, and at this point the Anunnaki will go into the final stage.

- From the bottom of the spaceships, they will diffuse a special substance that will land in huge, swirling streams.
- It is a black liquid, mixed with light and electricity, and some strange sparkling particles, which are a form of energy or radiation.
- It smells like fire and brimstone, but strangely, it is cold to the touch. Yet, it burns everything that touches it.
- This is a tool of annihilation, a tool that no one can fight.
- The substance will slither inexorably over the ground, the buildings, and the stranded cars like icy cold lava waves.
- It will sweep away many people, killing them instantly. Once it covers a large area, it will begin to coagulate, and as it does so, will expand and rise up, foot by foot, until it reaches the height of eight storied buildings.
- Slowly, it will harden, solidifying itself into steel-like state.
- Huge stacks of smoke will rise up into the sky, cars will melt, buildings will collapse, and fires will start everywhere, not only by the touch of the substance, but spontaneously, when the wind carries the particles of energy into flammable materials.
- The fire and brimstone smell will now mix with that of burning flesh and of melting metal, plastic and rubber.
- Then, all of a sudden, the substance will stop growing, and assume the appearance of craggy mountains, with sharp edges and canyons.
- The very few who have escaped, who have now nowhere to go to, will try to climb on the substance, since the earth itself will be buried in it.
- This will be futile, since the substance will be too slippery for the climb.
- They will start to fall and slip, and be instantly killed.
- These conditions will continue all over the entire world for two days; no one will be left alive on the scorched earth.
- On the third day, all the spaceships will leave, and in twenty-four hours, the substance and all it consumed will turn to dust.
- The earth will be ready for the vast cleaning. For that purpose, other spaceships will appear, of completely different appearance.
- The new ones will not be circular like the others, but crescent shaped, and of pleasant colors, nothing frightening about them.
- They will activate the vacuum system that we have mentioned in a previous answer, to ready the earth for a new life.

*** *** ***

49-The End Of The World According To Science And Sociology

The Answer

How will it all end? Some say we are likely to go with a bang, others predict a slow lingering end, while the optimists suggest we will overcome our difficulties by evolving into a different species.

According to Sir Martin Rees, author of Our Final Century, astronomer royal and professor of cosmology and astrophysics at the University of Cambridge, humans only have a 50-50 chance of making it through the 21st century without serious setback. "Some natural threats, such as earthquakes and meteorite impacts, remain the same throughout time, while others are aggravated by our modern-interconnected world. But now we also need to consider threats that are human induced."

So what are the greatest threats to humans and can we do anything about them?

Below, 10 scientists talk about their greatest fears and explain how society could be affected. Afterwards we estimate each threat in two ways: first, the chance of it occurring in our lifetime (the next 70 years); and, second, the danger that it would pose to the human race if it did happen (10 = making humans extinct, to one = barely having an impact on our lives).

1-Climate Change:

Nick Brooks is a senior research associate at the Tyndall Centre for Climate Change Research at the University of East Anglia: "By the end of this century it is likely that greenhouse gases will have doubled and the average global temperature will have risen by at least 2C. This is hotter than anything the Earth has experienced in the last one and a half million years. In the worst case scenario it could completely alter the climate in many regions of the world. This could lead to global food insecurity and the widespread collapse of existing social systems, causing mass migration and conflict over resources as some parts of the world become much less habitable. I don't think that climate change will sound the death knell for humans, but it certainly has the potential to devastate."

206

Chance of temperatures rising more than 2C (the level considered to be dangerous by the European Union) in the next 70 years: High.
Danger score: 6.

*** *** ***

2-Telomere Erosion:

Reinhard Stindl, a medical doctor at the University of Vienna, says every species contains an "evolutionary clock", ticking through the generations and counting down towards an inevitable extinction date: "On the end of every animal's chromosomes are protective caps called telomeres. Without them our chromosomes would become unstable. Each time a cell divides it never quite copies its telomere completely and throughout our lifetime the telomeres become shorter and shorter as the cells multiply. Eventually, when they become critically short, we start to see age-related diseases, such as cancer, Alzheimer's, heart attacks and strokes. However, it is not just through our lifetime that telomeres get shorter. My theory is that there is a tiny loss of telomere length from one generation to the next, mirroring the process of ageing in individuals. Over thousands of generations the telomere gets eroded down to its critical level. Once at the critical level we would expect to see outbreaks of age-related diseases occurring earlier in life and finally a population crash. Telomere erosion could explain the disappearance of a seemingly successful species, such as Neanderthal man, with no need for external factors such as climate change."
Chances of a human population crash due to telomere erosion during the next 70 years: Low.
Danger score: 8.

*** *** ***

3-Viral Pandemic:

Professor Maria Zambon is a virologist and head of the Health Protection Agency's Influenza Laboratory: "Within the last century we have had four major flu epidemics, along with HIV and Sars. Major pandemics sweep the world every century, and it is inevitable that at least one will occur in the future. At the moment the most serious concern is H5 avian influenza in chickens in south-east Asia.

If this virus learns to transmit from human to human then it could sweep rapidly around the world. The 1918 influenza outbreak caused 20m deaths in just one year: more than all the people killed in the first world war. A similar outbreak now could have a perhaps more devastating impact. It is not in the interests of a virus to kill all of its hosts, so a virus is unlikely to wipe out the human race, but it could cause a serious setback for a number of years. We can never be completely prepared for what nature will do: nature is the ultimate bioterrorist."

Chance of a viral pandemic in the next 70 years: Very high.

Danger score: 3.

*** *** ***

4-Terrorism:

Professor Paul Wilkinson is chairman of the advisory board for the Centre for the Study of Terrorism and Political Violence at the University of St Andrews: "Today's society is more vulnerable to terrorism because it is easier for a malevolent group to get hold of the necessary materials, technology and expertise to make weapons of mass destruction. The most likely cause of large scale, mass-casualty terrorism right now is from a chemical or biological weapon. The large-scale release of something like anthrax, the smallpox virus, or the plague, would have a huge effect, and modern communications would quickly make it become a trans-national problem. In an open society, where we value freedoms of movement, we can't guarantee stopping an attack, and there is a very high probability that a major attack will occur somewhere in the world, within our lifetimes."

Chances of a major terrorist attack in the next 70 years: Very high.

Danger score: 2.

*** *** ***

5: Nuclear War:

U.K. Air Marshal Lord Garden is Liberal Democrat defense spokesman and author of Can Deterrence Last?: "In theory, a nuclear war could destroy the human civilization but in practice I think the time of that danger has probably passed. There are three potential nuclear flashpoints today: the Middle East, India-Pakistan and North Korea. Of these, North Korea is the most worrying, with a hair-trigger, conventional army that might start a war by accident. But I like to believe the barriers against using a nuclear weapon remain high because of the way we have developed an international system to restrain

nuclear use. The probability of nuclear war on a global scale is low, even if there remains the possibility of nuclear use by a rogue state or fanatical extremists."
Chance of a global nuclear war in the next 70 years: Low.
Danger score: 8.

*** *** ***

6-Meteorite Impact:

Donald Yeomans is manager of Nasa's Near Earth Object Program Office at the Jet Propulsion Laboratory in California: "Over very long timescales, the risk of you dying as a result of a near-Earth object impact is roughly equivalent to the risk of dying in an aeroplane accident. To cause a serious setback to our civilisation, the impactor would have to be around 1.5km wide or larger. We expect an event of this type every million years on average. The dangers associated with such a large impactor include an enormous amount of dust in the atmosphere, which would substantially shut down sunlight for weeks, thus affecting plant life and crops that sustain life. There would be global firestorms as a result of re-entering hot ejecta and severe acid rain. All of these effects are relatively short-term, so the most adaptable species (cockroaches and humans, for example) would be likely to survive."
Chance of the Earth being hit by a large asteroid in the next 70 years: Medium.
Danger score: 5.

*** *** ***

7-Robots Taking Over:

Hans Moravec is a research professor at Carnegie Mellon University's Robotics Institute in Pittsburgh: "Robot controllers double in complexity (processing power) every year or two. They are now barely at the lower range of vertebrate complexity, but should catch up with us within a half-century. By 2050 I predict that there will be robots with humanlike mental power, with the ability to abstract and generalise. These intelligent machines will grow from us, learn our skills, share our goals and values, and can be viewed as children of our minds. Not only will these robots look after us in the home, but they will also carry out complex tasks that currently require human input, such as diagnosing illness and recommending a therapy or cure. They will be our heirs and will offer us the best chance we'll ever get for immortality by uploading ourselves into advanced robots."
Chance of super-intelligent robots in the next 70 years: High.

Danger score: 8.

*** *** ***

8-Cosmic Ray Blast From Exploding Star

Nir Shaviv is a senior lecturer in physics at the Hebrew University in Jerusalem, Israel: "Once every few decades a massive star from our galaxy, the Milky Way, runs out of fuel and explodes, in what is known as a supernova. Cosmic rays (high-energy particles like gamma rays) spew out in all directions and if the Earth happens to be in the way, they can trigger an ice age. If the Earth already has a cold climate then an extra burst of cosmic rays could make things really icy and perhaps cause a number of species to become extinct. The Earth is at greatest risk when it passes through a spiral arm of the Milky Way, where most of the supernova occur. This happens approximately every 150m years. Paleoclimate indicators show that there has been a corresponding cold period on Earth, with more ice at the poles and many ice ages during these times. We are nearly out of the Sagittarius-Carina arm of the Milky Way now and Earth should have a warmer climate in a few million years. But, in around 60m years we will enter the Perseus arm and ice-house conditions are likely to dominate again."
Chance of encountering a supernova in the next 70 years: Low.
Danger score: 4.

*** *** ***

9-Super-Volcanos:

Professor Bill McGuire is director of the Benfield Hazard Research Centre at University College London and a member of Tony Blair's Natural Hazards working group: "Approximately every 50,000 years the Earth experiences a super-volcano. More than 1,000 sq km of land can be obliterated by pyroclastic ash flows, the surrounding continent is coated in ash and sulphur gases are injected into the atmosphere, making a thin veil of sulphuric acid all around the globe and reflecting back sunlight for years to come. Daytime becomes no brighter than a moonlit night. The global damage from a super-volcano depends on where it is and how long the gas stays in the atmosphere. Taupo in New Zealand was the most recent super-volcano, around 26,500 years ago. However, the most damaging super-volcano in human history was Toba, on Sumatra, Indonesia, 74,000 years ago.

Because it was fairly close to the equator it injected gas quickly into both hemispheres. Ice core data shows that temperatures were dramatically reduced for five to six years afterwards, with freezing conditions right down to the tropics. A super-volcano is 12 times more likely than a large meteorite impact. There is a 0.15% probability that one will happen in your lifetime. Places to watch now are those that have erupted in the past, such as Yellowstone in the US and Toba. But, even more worryingly, a super-volcano could also burst out from somewhere that has never erupted before, such as under the Amazon rainforest."

Chance of a super-volcano in the next 70 years: Very high.
Danger score: 7.

*** *** ***

10-Earth Swallowed By A Black Hole:

Richard Wilson is Mallinckrodt Research Professor of Physics at Harvard University in the US: "Around seven years ago, when the Relativistic Heavy Ion Collider was being built at the Brookhaven National Laboratory in New York, there was a worry that a state of dense matter could be formed that had never been created before. At the time this was the largest particle accelerator to have been built, making gold ions crash head on with immense force. The risk was that this might form a stage that was sufficiently dense to be like a black hole, gathering matter from the outside. Would the Brookhaven labs (and perhaps the entire Earth) end up being swallowed by a black hole created by the new accelerator? Using the information we already know from black holes in outer space, we did some calculations to find out if the Brookhaven particle accelerator was capable of forming such a black hole. We are now pretty certain this state of matter won't form at Brookhaven and that the Earth won't be swallowed when these particles collide."

Chance of Earth being gobbled up by a black hole in the next 70 years: Exceedingly low.
Danger score: 10.

*** *** ***

Note: The general public can participate in related debates at: Naked Science: Clash of Crises at www.danacentre.org.uk for full details. Interested people can also take part in the Dana Centre's survey, investigating the nation's biggest fears for the future at www.sciencemuseum.org.uk (Sources: Guardian)

50-Are The Anunnaki Going To Change Our Way Of Life?

Are the Anunnaki going to change the way we do business, what we do to make a living, and are they going to create or abolish some professional institutions?

The Answer

Are The Anunnaki Going To Change Our Way Of Life?
Are the Anunnaki going to change the way we do business, what we do to make a living, and are they going to create or abolish some professional institutions?

- This will be one of the most significant changes that humanity will see, because the Anunnaki will not support any of our greed-infested systems.
- The most profound change will be the abolition of money and every system that is attached to money.
- People will work in their chosen professions (or a new profession that they will adopt, more on that later in this answer) and produce or serve as usual.
- They will not be paid, but they will have everything that they need. Everyone will have a comfortable home, designed to his or her taste.
- Good food for us and for our pets, beautiful clothes, nice jewelry, cosmetics, diapers for the babies, toys, hobby supplies, etc. will always be available in huge cooperatives that will look like excellent supermarkets, open day and night so that no one will ever lack.
- What we consider luxury items will also be available – the Anunnaki have no desire to have us live in austerity.
- We can always have books, TV, radio, home films, etc. We can go to the theater, the ballet, the symphony orchestra, chamber music performances, movies – always for free.
- The only thing the Anunnaki will deprives us off is *excess*.
- There will be no need for hoarding, since everything will always be available, but you will not be able to be richer than your neighbor. Equality will be established, and appreciated by those of us who are not contaminated by the greed and meanness of the Grays.
- Since money will no longer signify, obviously there will not be a need to have places like Fort Knox.
- It is going to be destroyed, and the gold used for ornamental purposes. That is the only reason people will value gold now – its beauty.

- A good artist can create some pretty good pieces from such lovely substance, which will be so widely available after the great change. The same will happen, incidentally, with diamonds, and other gems. Their intrinsic value will disappear, so jewelry will only be appreciated for its intricate and elegant design, not for how many carats a stone weighs.
- Because of that, there will be no need for the IRS, the Social Security system, and other such organizations. The elimination of the money system will cause many professions to disappear, such as:

- Accountants
- Bankers
- Tax preparers
- Security guards
- IRS employees

But money will not be the only "victim." In a society that consists of good people, people who have no need or desire to commit any crime whatsoever, there will be no need for the legal system. All organizations pertaining to the law will disappear, including the Supreme Court. And of course, no prisons. This will eliminate many professions:

- Lawyers
- Judges
- Court clerks
- Prison officials and guards

All governments will be abolished. No elected officials, no presidents, no kings. People who are good do not need anyone telling them how to live, they do it instinctively. This will eliminate thousands of positions:

- Presidents
- Kings
- Governors
- Mayors
- All government employees
- Social workers
- Child agencies

Since the Anunnaki technology is going to keep us healthy, there will be no need for hospitals or clinics, other than those devoted to childbirth, and much of the work there will be done without the need for people. In addition, there will not be any incidents of mental health. This will eliminate the positions of most doctors and nurses, and of additional employees such as:

- Hospital administration
- Hospital billing
- Psychiatrists
- Psychologists
- Hospital janitors

For transportation, we will no longer have the need for cars and airplanes. There will be advanced technology that will allow us a much more efficient forms of transportation and the use of clean and efficient energy, but in the process, we will eliminate the need for any fossil fuels. This will eliminate many professions, such as:

- Gas stations
- Agencies supplying us with electricity and gas
- Car manufacturers
- Airplane manufacturers
- Highway builders

In addition, there will be some miscellaneous professions that will not remain, since they will no longer be appreciated or needed. For example, the fashion industry, with its cruel attempts to make women into slaves of someone else's ideas of beauty, will entirely disappear. Beautiful clothing will be created by individual designers or by any one who likes to indulge in it as a creative hobby. Advertising, of course, will vanish as well. These miscellaneous jobs that will be eliminated include:

- Runway models
- Beauty contest organizers
- Manicurists

- Cosmetologists
- Advertising commercials actors and voice over artists

*** *** ***

This situation should not cause alarm. Those who will lose their professions will be trained for another profession, always entirely of their choice, that will give them pleasure and pride to pursue. Even those who have not lost their profession, but who feel the need for a change, will be encouraged to pursue a career change. As a matter of fact, since the life expectancy of each and every person will be greatly increased, it is expected that many people will have numerous career changes as time goes by. Life long study is always encouraged by the Anunnaki, who consider the acquisition of knowledge the most enjoyable thing a person can do.

> Many professions will change in the way they are perceived. For example, the teaching profession, for both children and adults, will become the most highly respected profession in the world. Librarians will be very highly regarded. Gardeners will be of great importance. Historians and writers will be greatly valued. But of course, in a world that judges a person by what he or she is, not by how much money is accumulated, every profession will be appreciated for its usefulness to the entire community.

*** *** ***

51-What Other Ufologists Think About Nibiru, Anunnaki And Their Return?

The Answer

Different strokes for different folks! We do not have a shortage of ideas and theories. Some highly respected ufologists believe that the Anunnaki's return is imminent. Others are fully convinced that the Anunnaki are gone for good. A group of mainstream Ufology researchers is so quick to assert that Anunnaki are a cruel race, manipulator of humanity's fate, and the cause for chaos on earth, because they have corrupted our governments. Good-spirited readers and authors, admirers of the Anunnaki strongly believe that our creators are our protectors, and will return to earth to elevate us to a higher level of awareness and spirituality.

Is there any physical evidence to any of these theories? Not much! So, why they keep on debating the issue? Well, without debate and further exploration of the subject, we will plunge ourselves in the darkness of ignorance and shut off all possibilities of getting closer to the truth. But what is truth? Any person who claims to know what is the absolute truth is a fool. Not Even Jesus Christ could answer this question when asked by Pontus Pilatus "What is the Truth?" Remember? Probably, that is the only question Jesus Christ never answered during his ministry on earth!

I wish I had more space in this book to include all the theories on the subject. Unfortunately, I don't. So I will select some of the most colorful and informative ones…and coming from authoritative sources.

*** *** ***

Anunnaki And Nibiru:
The Return

A PUFOIN Commentary/Position, by John Jaeger

> An ongoing interest and debate has been Planet X. This allusive planet has been linked to the myths of the Sumerian Tablets, which speak of the returning of Nibiru (a mythical planet said to visit our solar system once very 3600 years due to its elliptical orbit). Nibiru is said to be the home of our forefathers; the original creators of the Human race; the gods of the Old Testament. Is Nibiru real? The writings of the Sumerian Tablets as translated by Zachariah Sitchin and pre-date any known written history, seem to suggest that it is.

Many current day "seers" and "self-proclaimed emissaries of Alien Beings" preach about the coming events, which will include major Earth changes. I'm sure that even without a degree in Rocket Science, any of us can understand just how the arrival of a planetary sized object would impact the forces being applied against this planet, would have a major impact. Of late, we're seeing our weather patterns change; major earthquakes reaching 9.0; storm of the century - every other week (or so it would seem) and let's not forget the sudden increase in activity of volcano's.

The question of Alien existence is still merely a question. Through out the ages, proof has existed to support Alien interaction in our development and progress.

Cave drawings; ancient Hieroglyphics; mid-evil paintings - all show what we've come to identify as the stereotypical saucer or cigar shaped UFO's. We can't deny that these exist and seem to represent something extraordinary.

A study of the myths in the Bible also reveal many interesting discoveries.

The issue can certainly be debated until we're all long gone but it would appear that the stories of the Bible, written around 200 BCE, are actually a re-telling of stories from much earlier on - thousands of years earlier!

The Sumerian's documented the stories of the Bible in the third millennium BCE! Their stories offer some of the best accounts of our creation and the events of early Mesopotamia.

Yet, our Religion-based society continues to propagate the rewriting of our history for its own means.

There is no secret that the canonized version of the Bible from Constantine's' day has left out many relative books.

The Gnostics; Book of Thomas; etc., were not represented because they were either not available at the time or they contradicted the message Constantine wished to deliver to solidify his rule as Emperor.

If you compare the various Christian religions you'll find that different versions of the Bible are used. Some have incorporated the "found books" while others continue to ignore their existence and suggest that they are not legitimate.

Now, consider this. What "if" the events of the Bible are more-or-less true. What "if" the events in the Old and New Testaments really did happen pretty much along the lines we're told they did but... much earlier! There is significant proof to date the Pyramids to around 11,000 BCE for their construction.

Certainly, with our technology of today we could build such monuments to the precision of these great structures - but... what about back in 11,000 BCE?

The Humans of the Bible were farmers and Shepard's. The technology didn't exist to create such structures. Now, look at the Maya and their Calendar.

Their understanding of astronomy and astrology far exceeded their ability to understand the stars yet they provided us with a calendar, which has been exacting.

The examples of technology exist through out our history yet scholars often refuse to consider this when putting together their thesis or journals.

It isn't mainstream science, thus it would bring way too much attention and critique and essentially ruin their career.

But why?

Anyone with a computer can research these facts on their own and come to their own conclusions.

Anyone with common sense can objectively examine the facts and determine that "we're not in Kansas anymore".

By exploring these facts, we change everything we've ever believed in. We start to question our faith. We have to because what we've been taught isn't what really happened. Most lies are based in truth at some point. Often, good intentions turn sour.

Now, add thousands of years into the mix and you'll find an alarming trend of using Religion to control. Fearing God (yet God is good, right? He cares about us and our well-being, right?) and tossing around the Devil has kept Religious leaders in power and often carved the way for Kings to reach a status of divinity among his subjects.

The fact is, if you research you'll find that the events of the Bible just don't add up with the time these events are said to have occurred.

Next, one must consider that the stories of Jesus are a retelling of Pagan myth.

Osiris was also a man-god who was born of a virgin and carried out miracles (which by the way closely parallel those of Jesus nearly word-for-word). If you consider that the Pagan's worshipped many gods and that this belief system dates back long before the Biblical times, the stories of the Sumerian Tablets start to take on a whole new meaning.

In the Sumerian Tablets, the story of Creation and the Garden of Eden are shared. The Great Flood is also a favorite written in the tablets.

These stories aren't changed all that much when represented in the Bible - however, they are manipulated.

The Sumerian Tablets tell of the Anunnaki; a race of beings from Nibiru who created Humans by taking the indigenous beings on Earth and splicing their own DNA with that of the Aliens.

The Anunnaki were greatly advanced beings and created the great monuments found on the Earth; Moon; Mars and other solid planets/moons within our corner of the Universe.

The purpose for creating Humans is also written in the Tablets. Humans were created to be servants of the gods. Many would have called the early humans, slaves. We were used to mine precious minerals such as gold. Still to this day, gold is considered a highly sought after mineral. Researching the Sumerian tablets will also tell you reasons for this unique status of gold.

So, what about the Bible and the stories in the Bible?

Are they fake?

The answer to that will unfold over time, however it is most likely that these events were real at their core. Even the stories of Jesus, were real.

They just didn't occur when we think they did. If you consider the speculative orbit of Nibiru and the suggested 3600 year cycle, we can begin to establish a time-line for these events. First we must be careful not to deviate from what has already been written in our earliest documents (the Sumerian Tablets).

We can extrapolate based on this information but we must stay relatively true to the core or else our own references will be just as flawed as the Bible.

We know that the Pyramids were built around 11,000 BCE.

That means the Anunnaki must have been already here around that time.

Considering that the cycle of Nibiru is this 3600 year cycle, we must conclude that anyone left here was stuck here until the next cycle.

We are told that the gods had long lives but it doesn't seem imaginable that their lives would last the full cycle of Nibiru.

So, we must then factor in the length of time that Nibiru would be accessible from Earth during its orbit.

It has been suggested that the planet would only be visible for a few months but the length of time that it would be accessible might be years if not hundreds of years.

Any advanced culture capable of creating hybrids would be seen as gods to their creations.

We have that technology today. We mix-breed animals to create animals with special traits; colors or behaviors.

We mix-breed plants.

We're on the edge of cloning.

So, the idea isn't so crazy when you consider these things today vs. even 100 years or less, ago.

We must also then consider that there are other beings than just the Anunnaki roaming the Universe.

Now, taking in the orbit of Nibiru and the fact that there were and still may be, alien outposts on Mars and the Moon, we can begin to paint a picture of the events as described in the Bible.

Many have questioned the "virgin birth".

Why is this so difficult a concept to accept?

We have the technology to impregnate a female who has never experienced intercourse. So, right away, the idea of a virgin birth has to be considered plausible based on our own level of technology, today.

If this birth were between an advanced being and a Human, the offspring might have some advanced abilities.

Even if the offspring didn't, the ability of the "father" who IS an advanced being could give that impression should he intervene on behalf of the son. Actually, all of the events spoken of about Osiris/Jesus persona could actually be factual.

To the people of the time, simple things we take for granted today would seem like miracles.

The true problem rests with our version of the Bible. We singularize the gods. One must consider though that the "god" of the Old Testament isn't the same god of the New Testament. A simple review of the Bible will help to identify this. One god ruled with an iron fist.

The other, with mercy and compassion.

There is no doubt that a power struggle would occur between the gods.

If we are indeed offspring of these beings, then we are the best evidence of this.

Thus, it would make sense that there would be "groups" of gods who would have told their servants to honor no other god but himself. It makes sense that this would be the cause for suddenly making the Pagan plurality of gods into the Jewish and Christian singularity of God.

The study of the Pagan beliefs is truly fascinating.

It must be studied with an open-mind because the idea of these deities is so foreign to the common belief system it becomes difficult to absorb.

Next we must consider the myths, which speak of the return of Jesus.

Now, if you take into context the alien equation, the idea of a returning god is not so far-fetched. If the gods are truly on this 3600 year cycle, it would make sense that they've left and will return.

It is also plausible that during this time we've had interaction with other alien beings who do not support the Anunnaki.

The question of whether the Anunnaki are friend or foe can be debated.

If we were created to be subjects of the gods, it would make sense that we wouldn't wish to be their slaves when they return.

The idea of other aliens interacting within our society may be to provide us with advancements so that our awareness level would be high enough to understand the threat and our technology would be advanced enough to provide us with a means of defense.

The question of time-travel must also be called into the equation because of the suggestion of future events. Interestingly, the Bible is an excellent source of what is to come. Unfortunately, we don't often understand this until the events have come to pass.

Could the Anunnaki have the ability to travel through time? Well, while they "could" it seems unlikely because if that were the case, they'd be able to know about our advancements. It seems much more likely that other alien beings are more advanced than the Anunnaki and shared these future events.

These aliens were the "angels" who came to Daniel and John.

They planted the seed of warning in an effort to help guide us along a path, which would allow us to advance in our understanding; our awareness of our place in the Universe and in our technology.

We advance quickly when we use cooperation. The Bible prophecies speak of this oneness within our nature and the need for us to get along and work together.

Obviously, these prophets knew that the only way for us to advance in the time allotted was to get us to "play nicely" with one another. How better to do this than to write a code of ethics (of sorts) for us to live by.

So, what if all of this speculation is true?

What if we were created to be slaves?

What if we are waiting for the return of the gods?

What next?

When?

Well, many of the Native American prophecies tend to point to the year 2012.

The Mayan calendar ends in 2012.

The Hopi Prophecy Rock points to a certain path we must travel, etc.

The Inca prophecies also point to around 2012.

They speak of the coming of the next density of existence.

We've been able to extrapolate that this will be a time of ascension.

This ascension isn't too dissimilar to the "catching up" or the "rapture" as spoken of in the Bible.

Those who've become spiritually awakened (aware of their place in the Universe) will ascend into the next plain of existence.

Those who are still bound by the ways of the creators and the materialistic world will be left to see the return of the Anunnaki (the end of their 3600 year cycle). These people will see great changes in the Earth because of the influence of Nibiru.

They will also see great battles between the Anunnaki and the Humans of Earth. The prediction of 1000 years of peace may only come about at the hands of the benevolent alien beings currently helping us to advance our level of technology.

It would make sense that we will see huge advancements over the next few years as we approach this 2012 deadline. It would also make sense to consider that anytime from now through 2012 that the Anunnaki may be close enough to actually travel in ships to Earth in limited numbers. It would make sense for them to assume that not much has changed since their previous visit. To those who come in advance of their planet, their discoveries may be quite unique. It may even be an Anunnaki who is the "anti-Christ".

It would make sense that the Anunnaki would choose the region of former Mesopotamia (modern Iraq) for their return.

The predictions speak of the anti-Christ coming from this region and gaining power in the European Union.

It speaks of nations coming against Israel.

On a side note, it adds a new light to why the United States and its allies chose to attack Iraq at this time in our history. Are they perhaps preparing for the return of the Anunnaki?

Our nations are working on space based initiatives for planetary defense.

Ronald Reagan spoke of threats from outside of this world in one of his speeches.

He was the first to suggest a space based missile system (Star Wars).

It would seem that our Government's are already interacting with Aliens.

Look at the advancement in our technology over the past 100 years. Are we being prepped for Armageddon?

There will be many view points on similar topics. There will be many who agree and many who disagree. In the end, only the reader can choose to explore for his/herself or continue to stand true to his/her faith and trust in the authority of their Church.

It would be sad for people to not explore the role of Religion in controlling the population.

It would be sad for people to not explore the way the various Churches have changed their doctrine to stay modern with the times.

The RC Church said that the Earth was the center of the Universe and threatened early scientists who offered proof of the contrary.

The RC Church now admits that Evolution is more than just a theory and accepts it as a more plausible means than Intelligent Design - yet, in the scenario explained above, the Intelligent Design is actually a fact!!

How can anyone stand true to Religion when it continues to change its doctrine?

If Religion were unyielding and thus supported by the science, that fortitude to stay true to Religion would be understandable. Unfortunately, science and Religion do not stand together and the only thing bending is Religion.

As spiritual people, we need to have a faith system. We rely upon our faith to help us through tough times.

We pray to God to help us. What if the being that is helping us isn't the God we're praying to but rather, a galactic consciousness intervening on our behalf?

What if it is simply coincidence?

Again, the theories can abound but the facts can not so easily be dismissed by those who are enlightened and want to know more.

Are we in the end-times?

That is merely a matter of personal perception.

The Earth isn't going to end in 2012 and neither is life.

If the Anunnaki are an advanced race and if they return in 2012 en masse, civilization as we know it may change forever.

Look at the events of the past and the cycle of these events. It is pretty likely that the fall of the advanced civilizations will in most cases correlate with the cycle of the Anunnaki.

Look at Egypt; Atlantis and other great early cultures. What happened to them?

Where did they go?

Were they becoming too advanced and a threat to the Anunnaki?

Did those with an understanding of their place in the universe ascend leaving only the materialistic individuals to service the gods?

Have we advanced far enough in this phase of existence to be enough of a challenge to the Anunnaki?

The debate whether there is a "real" planet named Nibiru or Planet X will continue until that equation can be satisfactorily resolved through the finding of such a planet.

226

It stands within reason that at some point in our history there was such a planet.

The discovery of the Sumerian Tablets and other Sumerian artifacts support this finding.

The remains of the ancient Egyptian settlements and kingdom's also support this theory. Therefore, if we are to assume that Nibiru does exist, we can then entertain certain consequences brought about based on this reality.

One of the first questions, which is often presented during discussion is, *"wouldn't the Anunnaki be so far advanced beyond us that our own advancements would mean little?"*

This is an excellent question and one that can also be explained away with relative ease.

In short, the answer is *no*. Their technology doesn't have to be so superior to our current level of advancement.

Without a doubt it is advanced but not necessarily far ahead. The easiest analogy would be that of a person taking a vacation from work but staying at home. It should be said in advance that there are always exceptions to the rule but in this case we'll focus on the majority rather than the minority.

It can be said that most individuals who take a vacation from work and stay home for their holiday will put together a plan for their week. They'll have daily goals for achieving some success on certain tasks, which they've put off simply due to a lack of time. Their intentions are most sincere and the first day of their vacation they wake up late feeling very rested and a bit lazy. They sit in front of the T.V. or some other distraction and get drawn into whatever they are doing. Before they know it, the better part of the first day is gone and their objective for the day hasn't been met. Typically, the vacationer decides they'll accomplish the missed task tomorrow along with the other tasks of the day. The next morning, the vacationer awakens late yet again having stayed up late. Once again, the intention is sincere to accomplish the list of tasks. One thing leads to another and another full day has gone by with the tasks not being completed. This scenario happens for another few days. Finally, it is the last day. The vacationer, realizing that he hasn't gotten any of his tasks done all week has a tough night sleeping and wakes early.

He rushes around trying to fulfill a weeks worth of tasks in one day. Most he accomplishes but some simply get relegated to being completed during his "free time" during his busy work week.

It is probably fair to say that this has happened to everyone at some point in their working career. It is that old "time management" issue. The idea of the "big stone vs. the pebbles" (big stones being high priority items and the pebbles being the less important tasks). We tend to fill our day with attacking the pebbles and often accomplish a lot of the pebble tasks but we still haven't addressed the big stone priority items and thus, haven't made that much of an impact when all is said and done.

This is also what would happen in theory, with a race of beings who lived for a thousand years or more.

What's the rush?

Why would they need to push hard to develop their technology?

What they have, works for them and they get along just fine.

Their planetary cycle doesn't take them close to any other worlds for roughly 3600 years so they have lots of time to prepare for their next assignment.

It is for this reason that it is plausible that the technological advancements of the Anunnaki may not be much further along than the last time they visited our planet. During this time however, humans have advanced. Our life span is at least 1/10th if not 1/20th or greater than their own. We are motivated to the same level as the Anunnaki but we have a short time to achieve our goals thus the perception of advancement would be accelerated to the bystander.

We must consider that the Anunnaki's level of advancement was already more advanced than our own level of modern days, 3600+ years ago. Therefore it would be reasonable to expect that a return of the Anunnaki would mean that they'd still have advanced technology and would still be a "threat" to humans if they so desired.

Since the turn of the 19th/20th century, the advancement of the human technology has been in leaps and bounds over the centuries before. We can certainly look back to Plato and his descriptions of Atlantis or to the Egyptian times and suggest that at some point we had superior technology and we'd be right.

The problem is that this technology was not human - it was someone else's. For the first time in our existence we can say that our advancement is human based, or can we?

We really need to look at where we were at the turn of the 19th century into the 20th century. We had no automobiles. We had no airplanes. We had no indoor plumbing and bathrooms for the most part. In 60 years time, we went from living off the land to going to the moon! What caused that "leap" in our advancement? Sure, we were getting there. Flight was brought about by the Wright Brothers and others back in the early 1900's. But to go from a bicycled powered air craft to rockets in only 50 years seems a bit tilted to the left.

The idea of UFO's has continued to be a part of the mainstream. We can look at paintings from long ago, which depict disk-shaped objects.

We can look to hieroglyphics and see wing-shaped objects; the chariots of the gods. The idea of visitation has been in our face forever. We are just lead to disbelieve what is obvious and natural. The idea of an alien influence within our level of technology has to be given serious merit. It would certainly explain the rapid advancement we've been experiencing. It is plausible to say that based on history and experience that our technological levels are quite a bit more advanced than the public is aware of.

I touched upon the idea of our missing space probes and the sudden trouble our other probes have at very crucial celestial events. Certainly it could be considered a conspiracy theory and disregarded as such that the Government's don't want us to see something so they claim that their telemetry or technology wasn't working. But think about it. If you were in a position of authority and very few could access what you had and you didn't want certain information to get out, what would be the easiest way to prevent it from getting out? You'd just say it wasn't working. Then you'd continue to retrieve your data and go about your business. Just because we lose contact with a space probe doesn't mean it has stopped collecting data. That is something we must remember. Once we've recovered contact, the data would simply be downloaded. Take for example the ESA's probe sent to Titan.

One of the communication channels was turned off so the data wasn't received here but the signals were still sent from the probe so they are trying to see if they can recover this data through other means. That alone has proven my point that the information is still out there - unless the probe itself stops working. We've been told that story too many times. So, conspiracy theory or not, it makes perfect sense to believe that information is being withheld under the guise of National Security. And, for all we know, it may be exactly that.

The idea of alien intervention in our society continues to be apparent.

A previous PUFOIN perspective suggested that benevolent alien beings were working with us to produce technology which will help prepare us for defending ourselves against a return of the Anunnaki (our creators).

Obviously this assessment suggests that the Anunnaki are planning on coming back "as" our gods and again wish to have rule over us as their subjects. Our history is the best evidence of such a scenario and certainly something we must consider.

The Bible is without a doubt a re-documenting of history written about on the Sumerian tablets. The Old Testament clearly shares its roots with the people of Sumer.

The Pagan beliefs also share a history with the people of Sumer and help define the role of the Anunnaki as our gods. The Bible tells of the Nephilim (Nefilim). It is often mistranslated as "fallen angels" but actually means "coming down from above".

The term Anunnaki also has a similar meaning (from Heaven to Earth, etc.) These are referring to the very same beings. Those who interpret the Bible today desire that Nefilim refer to the devil and the other angels who were cast out of Heaven. Even if we accept this reference, it has a very negative tone to it. The idea of these Nefilim returning should be a concern to the humans of Earth because they are either the spiritual beings of evil looking to steal our souls or they are the creators of man looking to re-establish their rule.

The story of the great flood (Noah and the Ark) is explained in the Sumerian tablets as being the result of polar ice cap melting.

The Anunnaki scientists predicted the outcome and knew that the land would be covered with water. The leader of the Earth-based Anunnaki (Enlil) wanted to remove humans from the planet and thus the tablets tell us he told his people to relocate to the tops of the mountains.

This would explain why we've discovered settlements up high in the mountains of the Middle East. One of the scientists who'd created man had mated with a human woman and they had a child together.

He didn't want his child to die and so the tablets tell us that he shared the scientific information with his son. He was told not to speak directly to his son, so he spoke to his tent and within was his son.

He told him to build a boat and gave him the specifications. He told him what to put on the boat, etc. We all know the story of Noah and other than the twist being that it was the son of a god, the story is relatively the same. Approximately 100 years passed and the Ark was finished and the rising waters lifted it off the land. For a year, the boat drifted on the water until it came to rest on land allowing Noah and his family to again begin their life. Enlil wanted to see the removal of humans from the planet. His intention was never to have beings with self-awareness and knowledge. He simply wanted workers who'd take the place of the Anunnaki miners. With knowledge comes awareness of conditions and treatment and thus rebellion. The Earth once again became crowded with humans. The Nefilim were being hunted and killed and the decision to leave was made. The Anunnaki had already taught many humans of the ways of war because of the infighting of the gods. Humans were once again a serious threat due to their numbers. The Anunnaki left Earth and returned to Nibiru. Some remained behind and continued to have children who were bigger and stronger than the average human. Those Anunnaki still desired to rule over the humans and were thus killed over time.

We can extrapolate from this Biblical history that the Anunnaki, for whatever reason, didn't have the technology available to eliminate humans from the Earth.

They had to rely upon natural events and when no natural events could be predicted, they were forced off the planet. It would also make sense that when they are within range to return, they aren't going to be too pleased. If the Anunnaki live thousands of years, it would be possible that the very same who escaped Earth might still live today. It also wouldn't be too far fetched to consider that they'd be a little bit upset with humans for having forced them off Earth.

The fact that Nibiru will be close enough for the Anunnaki to transfer over to their outposts via ships, it can be extrapolated that they will also have at their disposal the means to mass a large assault on our planet to retake their mineral rich world and again begin enslaving humans to mine their minerals.

They look at us no differently than we do an animal who was used to plow the fields.

Thus, it is conceivable that other aliens, benevolent in nature are helping to advance our level of military technology in order to present a formidable defense. It is rare that anyone does something for nothing so it would also make sense that we've entered into some form of agreement with these aliens in exchange for the technology.

Could this explain the human abductions and mutilations?

Perhaps, without our realizing we are being manipulated into fighting a war for aliens who are pretending to be benevolent but who themselves have ulterior motives for our planet?

Again, this all wages in the realm of science fiction but what we do know is that we were created by an alien race in their likeness.

We will meet our gods again and when we do it has been foretold that there will be a great battle for our very existence (Book of Revelations). Whether it'll be the Anunnaki who are our saviors or our doom, only time will tell.

This is presented as food for thought...

230

52-The Return Of The Anunnaki A La Sitchin

The Answer

The Return Of The Anunnaki A La Sitchin

Nibiruans live on the planet Nibiru, which revolves around our sun every 3,600 years. Nibiru is the 12th planet (counting the Sun and Moon) in our local solar system, and is due to cross the orbits of Earth and Mars in the very near future. These astounding statements are made possible by the Sumerian cuneiform deciphering skills of Zecharia Sitchin, a linguist in command of many ancient languages who has set the scientific world on its ear with his astounding interpretations of ancient writings. In 1976, Sitchin's first book, *The Twelfth Planet*, began an odyssey that has literally transformed the field of ancient history; in 1993 came the sixth book in his Earth Chronicle series, *When Time Began*. Among other mind-boggling assertions, this book links the complex calendar of Stonehenge and the puzzling ruins of Tiahuanacu in Peru to the ancient culture of the Sumerians, and by extension, to the Nibiruans, who are also called the Anunnaki.

These are the folks Sitchin insists not only created the Sumerian culture, but who also genetically created human beings as we know them. And yes, they live on this mysterious 12th planet, Nibiru. Without stretching the English language too much, it is safe to say that the information Sitchin presents is as profound as the realism portrayed in the film *Planet of the Apes*. To date, Sitchin has deciphered more then 2,000 clay cylinders from that ancient land on the Persian Gulf that existed some 6,000 years ago. Some of these fragments, which date to 4,000 B.C., are in museums around the world. One fragment in particular, presently in Germany, indicates that Earth is the seventh planet, counting in from Pluto. The time frame here is four millennia before modern astronomy confirmed the existence of Pluto as an actual planet in our solar system. So how did an ancient race of people know this fact? Sitchin says it is because these ancient people did not come from Earth, but from Nibiru. Profound family squabbles eventually caused the Nibiruans to abandon planet Earth, leaving human beings to fend for themselves. These early humans would never possess the ability to travel among the stars like their creators, nor would they possess the immortality of their creators. Eons later, however, we humans finally have sent an intelligently designed satellite probe beyond the confines of our solar system. Are we repeating our past?

This is but one of the perplexing questions Sitchin investigates in the Earth Chronicles. Not only an eminent archeologist, Sitchin is also a formidable analyst of ancient cultures, in fact, perhaps the best ever.

His explicative comparisons of similar but disparate mythologies provide a fuller understanding of world religions. Among other things, Sitchin's investigations indicate that there may be an outpost in orbit around Mars preventing current humans from getting there (a fact verified by both U.S. and Russian space probe problems in that neighborhood). But the primary focus of this impressive research is ancient Sumer.

The decipherment of that culture's clay tablets, buried for millennia, reveals roots that stretch all the way back to 450,000 B.C. The reason Sitchin was motivated to learn to read cuneiform tablets was his initial curiosity as a boy concerning the meaning of "Nefilim", an enigmatic group mentioned in the Old Testament.

Translated, "Nefilim" means "those who came down." "Came down from where" is the starting point that makes the Earth Chronicles better reading than any Sherlock Holmes mystery.

In order to unlock the mystery, Sitchin takes on a journey all around the world to ancient cities and former civilizations. It would be impossible to do justice to his research in such a brief review as this one; however, there are some very significant findings on the existence of this other race of people. Perhaps the most compelling is the "Face on Mars", the structure in the area called Cydonia on the Red Planet. What is it?

If the relationship of the face on Mars is analyzed for its distance to other pyramidal structures also discovered on Mars, the geometric relationship is found to be identical to the distances of the Egyptian Sphinx and the pyramids in the surrounding areas of Egypt.

Sitchin concluded the placement of these pyramids indicates that they served as landing markers for the Nibiruans after they entered the Earth's atmosphere from outer space. Sitchin also has asserted that the early pyramids were not designed by the Egyptians. NBC-TV aired a program on Nov.10, 1993 entitled "The Mystery of the Sphinx", indicating that the Sphinx is 2,000 years older than previously thought.

This corroborates Sitchin's findings that someone other than the Egyptians designed the pyramids. One astounding assertion after another has made Sitchin the most controversial writer of our time because he challenges everything we thought we knew about human civilization.

It's easy to dismiss Sitchin's research in the same way that other people dismiss UFO's, Eric Von Daniken and countless other researchers who claimed to have found evidence for extraterrestrial visitors to this planet.

But Sitchin is well aware of this devil's advocacy, and vaporizes the arguments of skeptics with solid scholarship, including the most rigorous translations of Sumerian text, Vedic tales and excerpts from the original Greek and Hebrew versions of the Bible.

This ability to translate many languages is no small achievement.

Those of us who will never possess the ability to decipher 6,000-year-old clay tablets must trust that Sitchin has done his job accurately.

But his sources reveal an utter integrity, including the finest, most respected citations and references imaginable. The two most recent individuals to pay attention to Sitchin were Colin Powell and Norman Schwarzkopf, the American Generals who were key figures in the recent Gulf War. The landing place of the Nibiruans was in an area once called Eridu, now called Southern Iraq.

The main reason Saddam Hussein was not captured was because he was holding out in an ancient step pyramid constructed by one of those early civilizations mentioned by Sitchin, and which the Americans were loathe to bomb, because of their inestimable historical value.

Once the gloss of the media is removed from concensus reality, an entirely new picture emerges as to who knows what concerning what Sitchin has uncovered. This writer may never know who knows what, but the circumstantial evidence in the Earth Chronicles concerning the Nibiruans is absolutely compelling. Where does one look for their arrival?

Answer: In the Southern skies.

The fact becomes incontrovertible once you study Sitchin. He points out that NASA has located a massive black object in the Southern skies, and the recent reactivation of the telescopes in Argentina and Chile seems to indicate a renewed interest in that portion of the heavens.

Assimilating all the findings is really beyond the ability of any single person; however, a dedicated team could assemble all the relevant information. Though the information would necessarily be classified top secret, Sitchin has in fact laid out all the secrets in the Earth Chronicles. It is now up to us to revamp our own understanding of who we are as a species called humans so we can, as Sitchin says, "be more prepared when the Anunnaki arrive." Many of us will never travel all over the world to visit the ancient observatories. However, Sitchin has, and what he has found concerning the placement of these observatories on the surface of the Earth also is startling. All the observatories are inclined to the Southern hemisphere. They also are on the same Earth latitude. In his latest book, we learn that many of these observatories measure exact lunar and solar risings and settings with an accuracy unmatched by any modern measuring equipment.

The field of astronomy and astrology are made completely understandable by Sitchin, who shows that the concept of "Divine Time" was something these ancient astronomer priests created to predict the arrival of their creators.

Farfetched, to be sure, but when logic and patience are afforded to Sitchin's conclusions, one comes away with the realization that humanity has been misled in regards to our actual origins.

The biochemical research is especially haunting.

Our entire DNA structure is like a Contact time-release capsule.

When we were originally programmed, our basic DNA structure was limited to a double-helix strand.

The triggering mechanism that enables us to function as we do is affected by stellar radiation.

We are now at a place in the orbit around our central galaxy where the radio frequencies of the center of the galaxy, as well as many other star systems, are communicating new information to us. The release of this information, according to Sitchin, coincides with the next arrival of the 12th planet. The arrival of the year 2013, a la Jose Arguelles, synchronizes nicely with the arrival of the 12th planet. The government's attempt to construct a Freedom Space Lab will be aimed to ascertain the whereabouts of Nibiru.

The big question, of course, is what will these beings whom we have confused with gods think of us now? In the past we were not granted the same powers they had, but as a result of thousands of years of genetic selection, we have in some ways become like gods. Most all of the ancient languages have now been deciphered, and the 22 Hebrew letters have been found to contain information based on light-generating systems. Our understanding of torodial force fields, fibonacci series, fractals and open topological vector spaces have been expressed in the language of mathematics. Star fields begin to look more like computer-generated printouts than random points of light in the night sky.

If there is one thing Sitchin has definitely accomplished, it has been to expand the human imagination.

The legendary cultures of Atlantis and Lemuria no longer apear fantastic, but as efforts of other races to survive on planet Earth.

The SETI project, the government's official Search for Extraterrestrial Intelligence has been canceled, and then reactivated by a private consortium of companies. The most recent Mars probe completely disappeared.

The answer given to these enigmas is unsatisfactory, when weighted against the evidence that another race of people is about to visit our planet, as they apparently have many times in the past.

Remember, it takes Earth one year to orbit the sun.

It takes Nibiru 3,600 years, according to Sitchin.

Therefore, one year for the Nibiruans is equal to 3,600 Earth years. In addition to being a top-of-the-line linguist, and maybe the greatest historian of all time, Sitchin also admits to being a Sumerian. He has completed all this research, he says, to prepare us, the human race, for the return of our creators.

The work of Zecharia Sitchin is without question the most mind-stretching cosmology available to date.

Furthermore, it appears unchallengeable academically. Source: Willard Van De Bogart.

53-The Return Of The Anunnaki As The Giants Nephilim

An Encounter with the Anunnaki

The Answer

The Return Of The Anunnaki As The Giants Nephilim
An Encounter with the Anunnaki

What you are about to read in the second part of this article, might appear as a fairy tale, a fabricated lunatic story, or even imbecility at its best, on the surface that is. But there is a warm touch to it, and certain "un je ne sais quoi" veracity. It could be worth something. The story is told by David Wolfiert who had an encounter with the Anunnaki. Mr. Wolfiert appears to be a knowledgeable reader of the Bible, and this encouraged me to include his story in the book. Mr. Wolfiert said...The prophet Isaiah prophesied that the Nephilim/Anunnaki would someday return to earth and even "the Lord" with them. The prophetic utterance was and is, of great importance to mankind in general and of specific importance to various "interested" parties.

According to Dr. Carl Jung, there is no accident or coincidence. If it is no accident or coincidence that the Nephilim/Anunnaki have been demonized, then why? Why has organized Christian religion purposely lied about the giants of Genesis 6:4? My suggestion is that it very well could have been and is, to cover up the truth concerning their lies concerning the Creation story that they have trumped up for all us fishes to swallow, hook, line, and sinker.

The records of Sumer indicate, according to Laurence Gardner, in his book "Genesis of the Grail Kings", that the Anunnaki, and particularly Enki, along with his wife Nin-Khursag, created Adam and Eve. This must be covered up by organized Christian religion, at all costs, in order for their mythical existence to be perpetuated, along with the sin of Eve in the mythical garden. It is part and parcel of their overall scam on mankind.

Isaiah says in his prophecy in his 13th chapter that "Even the Lord, and the weapons of His indignation, to destroy the whole earth..."

This is strong speech. Nothing to be taken lightly. In other words the return of the Nephilim/Anunnaki are coming back to the genesis of the creation of Adam and Eve, to where it all started.

For what reason is it said "and the weapons of His indignation". Notice that the pronoun there is capitalized! This refers to Deity of some sort.

And this Deity is angered, and His indignation is upon the whole earth. What could have ignited "His indignation"? Could it have been the planned and attempted "Extermination" by an alien race, of the race they first created?

Part 2: David Wolfier's story in his own words: "My life experiences with aliens, spacecraft, and the like started fairly early in life, witnessing my first UFO in 1965 out in the large ranch country of New Mexico between Roswell and Ft. Sumner.

Likely place, some might say. It was basically a craft of some sort that came and made contact with "someone" on the ground, put them aboard the craft and flew away, quite rapidly, I might add.

I have never seen or met anyone such is explained like the term "grays", or any kind of alien similar to that.

The only beings that I have had any dealings with are the Nephilim-Anunnaki, that I know of.

It might be a good place to give forth what information that I have, as to what I have observed through my experiences as to what the Nephilim-Anunnaki's appearance are, at least in my experiences.

I have not seen any particular one of them that could be described as a giant.

I am 6 ft. tall and weigh about 200 lbs, athletic build (used to jump out of perfectly good airplanes and run 2 to 5 miles per day.) I have not seen any one of them that was small, but not giants.

Some might have been over 6 ft. but so what?

The most unusual thing about them is their eyes. The physical formation of them is about the same if not the same as ours.

There is something special about their eyes.

I could best describe it as something ethereal about the eyes. It is very difficult to describe, maybe spiritual could be used as a description. Otherwise, they are just as we are, that is, their children and the descendants of Adam and kindred peoples, does it not say that we are made in their image.

The first contact that I can remember was in the 1970's.

There was a bright light, never have seen such a bright light. I had to close my eyes, both my wife and I, and hold our hands over our closed eyes, and we could not hardly stand it, even then. A voice spoke from the light. We were forced to leave organized Christian religion because of what was said to us. But you can't prove that was the Anunnaki, one might say. Yes we can, because of what was said to us, which we must hold as private and can not be shared. In the last half of the 1990's we first became aware of being what some might call, "watched". We had several eye contacts with not only UFO's at very close range, but also very unusual lights at a distance of about 40 to 50 yards. We became aware that we were not alone in our everyday lives. We have in our possession a very close up picture of a hovering or standing on pods UFO at about 100 yards in plain daylight.

239

Along about this time, I had an Out of Body Experience that really solidifies my understanding of the Nephilim-Anunnaki, as regards the demonization of them as "the bad guys" by organized Christian religion. To make a long story short and leave out what I can not relate, I was in a small conference room.

There were rows of chairs with Anunnaki seated facing the chairman in the front of the room. I could not see anything but males, there were females there but I could not see them, as they were sort of hazed out from me. I know why but that is personal...I approached the chairman at the front of the room. I was observing some of the men there. There were absolutely some mighty ones there in that room.

The chairman said to me the following question/statement: "You stay pretty close to the Nephilim?" I replied, "I guess so, I did not know they existed until recently." A respectful, but unified chuckle went across the room. And I grinned and chuckled with them. It was not disrespectful but humorous to them, and I also, for they have been around for a very long time. That was the end of the conference at that point, and the only thing I remember about it. I am sure that there is more to remember but that is not for now. What I have meditated upon from that encounter with the Nephilim-Anunnaki is that they were presenting themselves as beneficial, at least to me, and not wicked giants with fire coming out of their mouths. The moderator was dark headed, simply setting in a normal chair by a table in front of the conference room. He was not unusually large in stature, but again not small, and he had the same unusual ethereal eyes. My post herein is becoming too long so that I can not finish the most important part of my experiences that I can share with you. I must keep that for one more post. One of the most important experiences that I have had with the Anunnaki is this:

It is not the most spectacular episode in my experiences, and I can not say that it is the most important, but it is a tremendously important experience in regards to the overall theme of their return to mankind.

Does the return of the Anunnaki hinge upon the return of Planet X or Nubiru?

Somehow, within myself, my urge is to answer in the negative, however, again, I do not consciously know for sure. There are parts of the meetings that are still unconscious. There is more than one reason for that, security being one.

In the concept of the return of the Anunnaki, I need to make this point and to try to impress those who will listen that I am not aware on a conscious level, nor am I urged from within that that particular event is not in the realm of what I describe as the concept of escape theology. That concept includes the Christian dogma of the rapture, other similar concepts of escape included.

I do not feel that there is anything of the sort in the future of mankind in general. St. John of the Cross described a process that seems to me to replace the escape theory with what he called "Crossing the Abyss." I am not closed minded against any reality.

At the same time, the ancient freemasons created their 33 degrees because they considered the 33 vertebra between the base chakra and the Pituitary gland to be essential steps to full enlightenment.

I was taught that there was no escape between the base chakra and this side of the Pituitary gland's summit.

My instruction from the Anunnaki was to prepare to personally "go through" the "Time of Jacob's Trouble", and to help others to go through also.

I hope that these posts herein will help you to arrive at the level of awareness to enable you to go with me.

The Command Center:

This was an out of body experience that took me into the command center of the Anunnaki.

As I said, it is not the most dramatic as others but it is very significant as part of the continuing saga of Isaiah 13th Chapter.

I came to consciousness standing in an awesome place. It was a very large room. If you draw a circle and then cut the circle in half, I was standing somewhere on the straight line at the back of the room. In front of me was a curved wall about 15, maybe 20 ft high. On this wall were some sort of screens. These screens were of unusual technical quality, and of various sizes.

There were tables between me and the curved wall with what appeared to be some sort of very advanced computers with monitors.

This room did not belong to any government on this earth. I do not know where it was but I can tell you that the governments of this earth are being monitored by the Anunnaki, totally and completely monitored. The men there were of the same description as I have shared before. What I remember that was said to me is of a personal nature and would not mean anything to anyone generally even if shared.

The place had an awesome vibration to it. One of exactness, power vibration was evident. It was a place literally not of this world. There was a general atmosphere that exhibited all the trappings of a military command center but without the human factor of what could only be described as fear. There was a psychological atmosphere of complete control over what they were there for, what was being monitored. It was NOT the confidence of arrogance that is usual in the affairs of man, but a confidence that defies explanation and description. I have always been treated with respect by the Anunnaki, this encounter was no different. I was not treated as a prisoner nor were they worried about what most mankind of that sort fears, intruders with out a clearance, that sort of thing. They were comfortable with me being there, as was I. It was as if I had seen it before. It has been insinuated that these events or experiences are only imagined by my belief system. That misses the point by a long shot. These experiences that I share with you are true and real, and are meant for the readers benefit.

54-The Reptilian And Shape-Shifters Plan For The Densification Of The Planetary Grid Will Not Happen

The Reptilian And Shape-Shifters Plan For The Densification Of The Planetary Grid Will Not Happen

According to Zuerrnnovahh, the first thing that the reptilians and shape-shifters had to do when they came to Earth was to kill the Anunnaki. The Anunnaki had been ruling the Earth for 400,000 years since their arrival from Nibiru. They are extremely long lived and robust, but by the time of Alexander the Great, 333 BC, the space-gods had been replaced by those who found the density of Earth promising. Most of the negative ones came to Earth about 2500 BC, with the Earth's polar alignment on Alpha Draconis or the star called *Thuban*. During such alignments the whole planet is a stargate. The most recent similar alignment was with Polaris in 1951. The Baby Boom generation from 1945 to 1964 has many who have trans-migrated to Earth through Polaris to help re-establish higher spiritual attunement.

On their own planet the shape-shifters are perfectly adapted to high density planetary existence. They also find the cores of planets welcoming. Earth at 5.5 times the specific gravity of water is the densest planet in our solar system. The cores of Jupiter, Saturn, Uranus and Neptune may contain more matter, but they do not have the metals of Earth. The Earth has a thick magnetic envelope too. This contributes to the density grid of the planet. The shape-shifters want to recreate the conditions of their home world on Earth by compressing the grids. The Anunnaki's home world, Nibiru, is the opposite of the shape-shifter's home world. Nibiru, spending most of its 3600 year orbit in interstellar space and scarce on heavy metals, is less dense than Earth. Although the mass of Nibiru is roughly four times that of Earth and surface gravity likewise higher, the grids were open and refined.

The open grids contributed to the near immortality of the Anunnaki.

Life expectancy of humans was higher hundreds of thousands of years ago as the grids were less dense then.

During historic times life expectancy has varied considerably.

Over the past century, in spite of all the Illuminati attempts to kill people through war, famine and disease, life expectancy has increased. This indicates the grids again are opening.

With the Kali Yuga, the grids are compressed and the Anunnaki would find Earth a difficult place to live on.

Hathor, the mother of humanity, was showing extreme old age when last depicted on Egyptian temple wall murals. The Titans were sent into retirement. With the collapse of the ecology for life on Nibiru about 4,000 years ago, there was no home world for the Anunnaki to which to return. Remnants of the Anunnaki still remain on Nibiru, its moons and other moons and planets. Many were stranded on Earth. They were still the gods controlling humanity and the Earth-and the shape-shifters saw an opportunity.

It is likely that Marduk, the eldest son of Enki, became a temporary host or walk-in for a shape-shifter. Likewise Nebu and Set. Marduk, freeing himself of the walk-in, was then imprisoned in Babylon by shape-shifters and later killed in a seaside cave on the Aegean Sea. Saturn was tortured and killed as he could not be subsumed by a shape-shifter.

The shape-shifter adopted the role of Saturn in his temple city under the new name "Molloch" and instituted ritual sacrifice including the killing of children. Wherever ritual sacrifice was coerced onto people, the Anunnaki had been killed and shape-shifters were dominant. There are many examples in the Americas as well as the old world, including sacrifices in Jerusalem. If the Temple in Jerusalem were rebuilt and the old practices re-instituted, the whole world would be appalled. The most grievous rites were aimed at the Hebrew people in order to stop their own realization of their true spirituality.

The Osiris, Isis and Horus rite demonstrated the domination of shape-shifters in Egypt. This rite was written into the gospels in order that the ceremonial sacrifice of Christ (which never actually happened) would continue up to this day in the churches. The bread and wine mass in nations around the world contributes to the compression of the grids and the shortening of life expectancy and limiting of life experience. It blocks communication to the higher self.

Virtually all brick and mortar religious edifices have been controlled in such a way as to block spiritual progress. Religion is a tool wielded by the shape-shifters.

The religions that work best for the shape-shifters are the ones which take elements from ancient wisdom and then corrupt or block the intent of spiritual understanding. Many priesthoods have had shape-shifters at the top. The truly motivated spiritual seeker never finds the answers to his inner longings in such institutions. The Gnostics called such teachings "dry streams" as the waters of life and spiritual understanding had been dammed or diverted away from the followers. The Roman church was called a "dry stream" in many of the Fourth Century scrolls found at Nag Hammadi Egypt.

Even at the time of Julius Caesar, before the creation of the Roman church, the generals were directed by the wealthy senate to destroy the mystery schools of Britain, Gaul, Germany, Palestine, Egypt and Asia Minor. The shape-shifters were in control of Rome and their plan was to destroy republican government and create an empire more directly ruled by them.

The Roman church, One Universal Church For One Catholic Roman Empire, became the plan after the "Caesar is God" debacle failed miserably. Shape-shifters like Nero and Caligula make terrible gods. No Roman citizen believed their emperors were gods. So they cobbled together Jewish, Greek and Egyptian beliefs into something to "captivate" the minds of men. "Captivate" is the operative word in the minds of empire builders.

The Anunnaki under Janus created the Roman Republic and it took six hundred years for shape-shifters to destroy the republican form of governance even hundreds of years after the last Anunnaki was killed. Janus was created by Enki. He had two faces and an androgynous nature. He was the consummate diplomat. Even before Plato wrote his "Republic", Janus had a working model. Janus' symbol as the two headed eagle.

Janus was not homosexual, but a true spiritual androgyne.

There is more truth in a Pagan under the boughs of an oak tree than in a priest in black robes surrounded by ornate masonry. The beliefs of a Pagan predate the Anunnaki and the people of Nibiru had many of the same understandings. Both Pagan and Anunnaki have the term "serpent" associated with them and this term should not be confused with the "reptilian" agenda.

The reptilian and shape-shifter plan for the densification of the planetary grid will not happen.

The very living being who is the planet Earth will not let this compression to occur. The Earth is going to become a star and the grids need to be open for that to come into being. Gaia is directly intervening in the affairs of men and women and stopping the diabolical conspiracy.

There is a lot of off-world assistance too.

55-The Cosmic Deception

The Hoaxed Alien Invasion Scenario

The Cosmic Deception
The Hoaxed Alien Invasion Scenario

It appears to a great number of researchers believes that the return of aliens and particularly the Anunnaki to earth is nonsense. And more precisely, the alien threat. The editor of the group "educate yourself" said: "The fake alien invasion operation has been mentioned by numerous NWO writers over the years. I first read of it in Bill Cooper's book, *Behold a Pale Horse*. Don Croft mentioned in a few of his "Adventures" Episodes that the not-so-secret inner government had obtained large spacecraft from the B-Sirians for the purpose of staging the phony alien invasion scene. Red Elk cautioned against the idea of allowing yourself to be beamed up into alien spacecraft when things get rough. I'm afraid that a lot of people will think that this is the *Rapture*. In fact, the incessant preaching about the coming Rapture may have been a set up to prepare them for this. I don't know for certain, but according to Red Elk, it's not going to be exactly heaven where those people wind up. Bear in mind the larger game: the inner government. had made a secret deal with negative alien groups in 1947 which was formalized in a written treaty in 1954 under Eisenhower. The agenda has grown more negative and destructive as the years rolled on. The Illuminati wants to reduce the world's population down to 400-500 million. The negative aliens, on the other hand, want to take over this planet completely and use it as a stargate jump off point into other dimensions to extend their empire."

The esteemed writer Steven M. Greer MD, Director, The Disclosure Project, asked us to Imagine this: It is the summer of 2001, and someone presents you with a script for a movie or book that tells how a diabolical terrorist plot unfolds wherein both 110 story World Trade Center towers and part of the Pentagon are destroyed by commercial jets hijacked and flown into those structures.

Of course you would laugh, and if you were a movie mogul or book editor, reject it out of hand as ridiculous and implausible, even for a fictional novel or movie. After all, how could a commercial jet, being tracked on radar after two jets had already hit the World Trade towers, make it through our air defenses, into the most sensitive airspace in the world, and in broad daylight on a crystal clear day, slam into the Pentagon! And this in a country that spends over $ 1 billion a day to defend itself! Absurd, illogical - nobody would swallow it!

Unfortunately, there are some of us who have seen these scripts - and of far worse things to come - and we are not laughing. One of the few silver linings to these recent tragedies is that maybe - just maybe - people will take seriously, however far-fetched it may seem at first, the prospect that a shadowy, para-governmental and transnational entity exists that has kept UFOs secret - and is planning a deception and tragedy that will dwarf the events of 9/11.

The testimony of hundreds of government, military and corporate insiders has established this: That UFOs are real, that some are built by our secret 'black' shadowy government projects and some are from extraterrestrial civilizations, and that a group has kept this secret so that the technology behind the UFO can be withheld - until the right time. This technology can - and eventually will - replace the need for oil, gas, coal, ionizing nuclear power and other centralized and highly destructive energy systems.

This 5 trillion dollar industry - energy and transportation - is currently highly centralized, metered and lucrative. It is the stuff that runs the entire industrialized world. It is the mother of all special interests. It is not about money as you and I think of it, but about geo-political power - the very centralized power on which the current order in the world runs. The world is kept in a state or roiling wars, endless poverty for most of Earth's denizens and global environmental ruin, just to prop up this evil world order.

As immense as that game is, there is a bigger one: Control through fear. As Werner Von Braun related to Dr. Carol Rosin, his spokesperson for the last 4 years of his life, a maniacal machine - the military, industrial, intelligence, laboratory complex - would go from Cold War, to Rogue Nations, to Global Terrorism (the stage we find ourselves at today) to the ultimate trump card: **A hoaxed threat from space**.

To justify eventually spending trillions of dollars on space weapons, the world would be deceived about a threat from outer space, thus uniting the world in fear, in militarism and in war.

Since 1992 I have seen this script unveiled to me by at least a dozen well-placed insiders.

Of course, initially I laughed, thinking this just too absurd and far-fetched. Dr. Rosin gave her testimony to the Disclosure Project before 9/11. And yet others told me explicitly that things that looked like UFOs, but that are built and under the control of deeply secretive 'black' projects, were being used to simulate - hoax - ET-appearing events, including some abductions and cattle mutilations, to sow the early seeds of cultural fear regarding life in outer space. And that at some point after global terrorism, events would unfold that would utilize the now-revealed Alien Reproduction Vehicles (ARVs, or reversed-engineered UFOs made by humans by studying actual ET craft - see the book 'Disclosure' by the same author) to hoax an attack on Earth.

249

Dr. Greer continues…Like the movie Independence Day, an attempt to unite the world through militarism would unfold using ET as the new cosmic scapegoat (think Jews during the Third Reich).

None of this is new to me or other insiders: The Report from Iron Mountain, NY, written in the 1960s, described the need to demonize life in outer space so we could have a new enemy. An enemy off-planet that could unite humans (in fear and war) and that would prove to be the ultimate prop for the trillion dollar military-industrial complex that conservative Republican President and five star general Eisenhower warned us about in 1961 (no one was listening then, either...).

So here is the post-9/11 script - one that will be played out unless enough people are informed and the plan can be foiled because they will be unable to fool a sufficient number of citizens and leaders:

After a period of terrorism - a period during which the detonation of nuclear devices will be threatened and possibly actuated, thus **justifying expanding the weaponization of space** - an effort will ramp up to present the public with information about **a threat from outer space**. Not just asteroids hitting the Earth, but other threats. **An extraterrestrial threat**.

Over the past 40 years, UFOlogy, as it is called, combined with a mighty media machine, has increasingly demonized ETs via fearsome movies like Independence Day, and pseudo-science that presents alien kidnappings and abuse as a fact (in some circles) of modern life. That some humans have had contact with ETs I have no doubt; that the real ET contact has been subsumed in an ocean of hoaxed accounts I am certain.

That is, real ET events are seldom reported out to the public. The Machine ensures that the hoaxed, frightening and intrinsically xenophobic accounts are the ones seen and read by millions.

This mental conditioning to fear ET has been subtly reinforced for decades, in preparation for future deceptions. Deceptions that will make 9/11 look trivial.

I write this now because I have recently been contacted by several highly placed media and intelligence sources that have made it clear to me that hoaxed events and story-lines are imminent that will attempt to further ramp up the fear machine regarding UFOs and ET s. After all, to have an enemy, you must make the people hate and fear a person, a group of people, or in this case an entire category of beings.

To be clear: the maniacal covert programs controlling UFO secrecy, ARVs and related technologies - including those technologies that can simulate ET events, ET abductions and the like - **plan to hijack Disclosure, spin it into the fire of fear, and roll out events that will eventually present ETs as a new enemy**. Do not be deceived.

This hogwash, already the stuff of countless books, videos, movies, documentaries and the like, will attempt to glom onto the facts, evidence and first-hand insider testimony of

250

The Disclosure Project, and on its coattails, deliver to the world the cosmic deception that falsely portrays ETs as a threat from space. Do not be deceived.

By commingling fact with fiction, and by hoaxing UFO events that can look terrifying, the Plan is to eventually create a new, sustainable, off-planet enemy. And who will be the wiser?

*** *** ***

You will. Because now you know that after 60 years, trillions of dollars and the best scientific minds in the world pressed into action, a secretive, shadowy group - a government within the government and at once fully outside the government as we know it - has mastered the technologies, the art of deception and the capability to launch an attack on Earth, and make it look like ET s did it.

Dr. Greer adds…In 1997, I brought a man to Washington to brief members of Congress and others about this plan. Our entire team at the time met this man. He had been present at planning sessions when ARVs - things built by Lockheed, Northrup et al, and housed in secretive locations around the world - would be used to simulate an attack on certain assets, **making leaders and citizens alike believe that there was a threat from space**, when there is none. (Before he could testify, his handlers spirited him away to a secret location in Virginia until the briefing was over...) Sound familiar? **Werner von Braun warned of such a hoax, as a pretext for putting war in space**. And many others have warned of the same."

Space based weapons are already in place - part of a secret parallel space program that has been operating since the 1960s. ARVs are built and ready to go (see the book *'Disclosure'* and the chapter with the testimony of Mark McCandlish et al).

Space holographic deception technologies are in place, tested and ready to fire. And the Big Media is a pawn, now taking dictation from the right hand of the king. I know this all sounds like science fiction. Absurd. Impossible. Just like 9/11 would have sounded before 9/11.

But the unthinkable happened and may happen again, unless we are vigilant. Combine all of this with the current atmosphere of fear and manipulation and there is a real risk of suspending our collective judgment and our constitution. But know this: If there was a threat from outer space, we would have known about it as soon as humans started exploding nuclear weapons and going into space with manned travel.

That we are still breathing the free air of Earth, given the galacticly stupid and reckless actions of an out of control, illegal, secret group, is abundant testimony to the restraint and peaceful intentions of these visitors.

251

The threat is wholly human. And it is we who must address this threat, rein it in and transform the current situation of war, destruction and secret manipulation to one of true Disclosure and an era of sustained peace. War in space, to replace war on Earth, is not evolution, but cosmic madness. A world thus united in fear is worse than one divided by ignorance. It is now time for the great leap into the future, a leap that moves us out of fear and ignorance and into an unbroken era of universal peace.

Know that this is our destiny.

And it will be ours just as soon as we choose it.

56-How Do Anunnaki Explain The Relationship Between Jesus and Mary Magdalene?
Was Jesus An Anunnaki?

The Answer

How Do Anunnaki Explain The Relationship Between Jesus and Mary Magdalene?

The Holy Grail topic occupies a paramount part in the Anunnaki manuscript "The Book of Rama-Dosh", because many early Christian thinkers and Gnostics were members of Ulema groups and their affiliates, such as the Cathars, the Templars, and the Knights of St. John Order of Malta. Logically, the followers of Mary Magdalene who created the first "Christian group" in Alexandria, and later on joined the Ulema became interested in the Anunnaki.

Because the Anunnaki society is matriarchal in essence, Mary Magdalene figures prominently in its literature.

For centuries, in the Near East, Middle East, North Africa, Asia Minor, Anatolia and the early Coptic, Aramaic, Syriac, Nabatean, and Anunnaki circles and learned societies, the New Testament was followed, and understood quite differently from the way contemporary Western believers, devoted Christians and hard-core doctors of the Roman Catholic Church do.

In addition to the Gospel of Mary which contained only a few pages about her life, her ministry and relationship with Jesus, several other manuscripts told the true story of Jesus, Mary Magdalene and Christianity. Many of those early religious manuscripts were written by Ulema.

The Ulema circle which consisted of some of the brightest minds of the era who came from various and different cultural, social and religious backgrounds, told the absolute truth about Jesus and Mary Magdalene. Many Ulema were Muslims, Christians, Hindu, Buddhists, Gnostics and free-spirited thinkers and ethicists. However, they shared many things in common, such as the truthful knowledge and essence of the religions that were originated in the Levant (Orient, Middle and Near East), the origin of mankind, the nature of the Anunnaki, substances that compose parallel dimensions, and the concept of "human salvation."

Their knowledge extended to the Old Testament, the New Testament, extraterrestrial civilizations, and the destined future of mankind. To the Roman Catholic Church, the knowledge and teachings of these enlightened teachers were sacrilege and blasphemy…in other words, a direct and an imminent threat to Rome.

The Ulema who taught the principles and code of ethic as prescribed in the Anunnaki Rama-Dosh" book had an ultimate respect for Jesus and Mary Magdalene. However, the Ulema never considered Jesus of Nazareth as a Messiah or God.

In "Revelation of an Anunnaki's Wife", a biography of Victoria, a hybrid woman, half human and half Anunnaki, I co-authored with Ilil Arbel, Ph.D., we devoted an extensive chapter on the relationship between Jesus and Mary Magdalene. What we wrote about was based upon revelations by Victoria depicting her travel in time, to Marseille, where allegedly she met Mary Magdalene in her own home.

Please refer to the book. But briefly, the Ulema/Anunnaki were fully aware of the relationship that existed between Jesus and Mary Magdalene as a married couple.

This leads me to several questions and inquiries I have received from my readers who asked whether Jesus was God, the Son of God, or an Anunnaki?

The Rama-Dosh book describes Jesus as a Rabbi who preached love, compassion and justice.

But also, the Rama-Dosh book depicted Jesus as a rebel with a revolutionary set of mind, however peaceful and loving…

No, Jesus was not an Anunnaki. And Jesus was not God.

The cliché "Son of God" was frequently used by the Essenes in their teachings, and was used to refer to the "righteous ones."

The teachings of the Anunnaki-Ulema did not diminish the importance of Christianity, nor tarnish the image of Jesus. Simply, they shed the light of truth on the origin of Christianity, the nature of Jesus and the important role, Mary Magdalene played in launching this great religion in Alexandria, and her paramount impact on Jesus.

The Roman Catholic Church felt threatened, and feared that its authority over the simple minded and illiterate believers will dissipate.

Christianity as we know it today in the West, is a scenario well-crafted by Emperor Constantine and the mighty Vatican. It is absolutely misinterpreted, fabricated and intentionally re-created by the Roman Catholic Church.

Christianity was never created by Jesus. Christianity is the product and the results of the propaganda of Paul.

The Anunnaki Book of Rama-Dosh, as well as the Anunnaki Miraya (Sort of Akashic Records, so to speak) tell the true story of Jesus, his life in Palestine, Arwad, Phoenicia, Cyprus and France. Also, it describes in detail the episodes of the life Mary Magdalene and Jesus shared in Palestine and France.

Mary Magdalene; The Wife of Jesus: "The Book of Rama-Dosh" describes Mary Magdalene as a relatively young, attractive, and faithful Jewish woman who stood by her man (Jesus). She was the wife of Jesus and their matrimonial union gave birth to healthy children who grew up in Marseille, France. Long time before any book was written in the West about the Holy Grail and Jesus bloodlines, the remnants and descendants of the Anunnaki in the Middle and Near East already told us that Jesus was married, Mary Magdalene was his wife, and the concept of the Holy Grail was nothing else but the lineage of Jesus. These facts were well known and accepted during the first 3 centuries A.D. in the eastern countries.

The Anunnaki literature is not limited exclusively to space-time travel, the genetic creation of the human race, and the captivating Sumerian mythology.

It has also, deep emotions, a human touch, and captivating philosophical, religious, and metaphysical aspects.

After all, many of the ethical codes and laws of societies of the ancient world were given by the Anunnaki to rulers and kings in the Near East, Middle East, Asia and North Africa, including Mesopotamia's King Hammurabi, India's king Dabshalim, Persia's shah Anu Sherwan Kesra, Tyre's King, Hiram, and King Solomon.

However, the Anunnaki did not give the human races laws governing religions and faith, even though some of the lower class of the early Anunnaki who descended on earth brought to the humanity organized religions and fake deities.

They had to do it in order to control and enslave humanity.

The purpose of bringing those religions to earth was to create fear in the minds and hearts of primitive humans.

The early Anunnaki knew that religion is the most effective way and method to control people. And when you religiously control people, you get hold of their lives, way of life, assets, and possessions, present and future. The Roman Catholic Church knew that quite well and practiced these tactics for centuries.

Consequently, any book, any manuscript, any text, any teaching that taught the truth, the factual origin of man, the creation, science, astronomy, studies of the future of humanity, became a direct threat to the power and authority of Rome and its affiliates around the world.

Michael B. a reader asked: "is Jesus Christ the Only Son of God?, or was he a great teacher? An Anunnaki? He alluded several times to his pre-existence. What to me is a simple connecting-of-the-dots gives the conclusion that Ninurta, son of Enlil, incarnated into the son of Joseph and Mary or "possessed" him. The research is very convincing that the Anunnaki leader Enlil was Jehovah-Yahweh…His son Ninurta was designated as his successor…Enki's son Marduk siezed power instead, thus he was termed "The Usurper." This led to "The Pyramid Wars," culminating in nuclear-type weaponry being used…As a way of creating a new covenant with mankind (and breaking the hold of Marduk's, and other, "pagan" cults) the plan was created for Ninurta to form a once-and-for-all religion in which "The Father" would be worshiped, and the rancorous human population would become peaceful and loving.

On at least two occasions, a voice spoke from the clouds, or mists, "This is my son, in whom I am well pleased." So the question becomes, who else could this father-son team be? It seems unlikely that it is Enki referring to his son Marduk because of, among other reasons, all the references to the devil being a serpent, which is the Enki line's trademark. And Jesus gave full "props" to Jehovah-Yahweh and the prophets who spoke for and about him, even saying he was here to fulfill the words of the prophets. Also, "the Father and I are united" and "He who has seen me has seen the Father." None of the books I have on this subject even vaguely hint at this possibility.

As well, I've done several Internet searches, Google and others, and nowhere is this connection made. It seems so obvious to me now that I am amazed that it has not previously been seized upon. (I'm even surprised at myself, but pre-conceived mindsets can be a stubborn obstacle.) If I had to speculate, I would say that the Vatican has this information in its off-limits library, and this is the reason why they, to this day, retain many symbols from the ancient times in their vestments and architecture. I would appreciate any comments…"

*** *** ***

A Brief Note:

1-Jesus is not God.

2-At one time in history in religious sects gatherings (Essenes, Macedonians, etc.), the righteous men were called "Children or Sons of God".

3-Enki is in fact Yahweh.

4-A voice spoke from the clouds, or mists, "This is my son, in whom I am well pleased." This is a fabrication by the scribes and editors of the first copies of the New Testament in Constantinople (Turkey), and Antioch (Syria).

5-" …Conclusion that Ninurta, son of Enlil, incarnated into the son of Joseph and Mary." Another fairy tale created by the Early Christian Church. However, the Gnostics who were true Christians ridiculed the idea!

57-The Unthinkable Thought
What Are The Mysteries of Jesus?

The Answer

"Jesus said, 'It is to those who are worthy of my Mysteries that I tell my Mysteries.'" The Gospel of Thomas

What Are The Mysteries of Jesus?

The Unthinkable Thought

On the site where the Vatican now stands there once stood a Pagan temple. Here Pagan priests observed sacred ceremonies which early Christians found so disturbing that they tried to erase all evidence of them ever having been practiced. What were these shocking Pagan rites? Gruesome sacrifices or obscene orgies perhaps. This is what we have been led to believe. But the truth is far stranger than this fiction.

Where today the gathered faithful revere their Lord Jesus Christ, the ancients worshipped another godman who, like Jesus, had been miraculously born on 25 December before three shepherds. In this ancient sanctuary Pagan congregations once glorified a Pagan redeemer who, like Jesus, was said to have ascended to heaven and to have promised to come again at the end of time to judge the quick and the dead.

On the same spot where the Pope celebrates the Catholic mass, Pagan priests also celebrated a symbolic meal of bread and wine in memory of their savior who, just like Jesus, had declared: "He who will not eat of my body and drink of my blood, so that he will be made one with me and I with him, the same shall not know salvation."

When we began to uncover such extraordinary similarities between the story of Jesus and Pagan myth we were stunned. We had been brought up in a culture which portrays Paganism and Christianity as entirely antagonistic religious perspectives. How could such astonishing resemblances be explained? We were intrigued and began to search further. The more we looked, the more resemblances we found.

To account for the wealth of evidence we were unearthing we felt compelled to completely review our understanding of the relationship between Paganism and Christianity, to question beliefs that we previously regarded as unquestionable and to imagine possibilities which at first seemed impossible.

Some readers will find our conclusions shocking and others heretical, but for us they are merely the simplest and most obvious way of accounting for the evidence we have amassed.

We have become convinced that the story of Jesus is not the biography of an historical Messiah, but a myth based on perennial Pagan stories.

Christianity was not a new and unique revelation but actually a Jewish adaptation of the ancient Pagan Mystery religion. This is what we have called 'the Jesus Mysteries Thesis.' It may sound farfetched at first, just as it did initially to us. There is, after all, a great deal of unsubstantiated nonsense written about the 'real' Jesus, so any revolutionary theory should be approached with a healthy dose of skepticism. But although this book makes extraordinary claims, it is not just entertaining fantasy or sensational speculation. It is firmly based upon the available historical sources and the latest scholarly research. Whilst we hope to have made it accessible to the general reader, we have also included copious notes giving sources, references and greater detail for those who wish to analyze our arguments more thoroughly. Although still radical and challenging today, many of the ideas we explore are actually far from new. As long ago as the Renaissance, mystics and scholars saw the origins of Christianity in the ancient Egyptian religion. Visionary scholars at the turn of the nineteenth century also made com-paxable conjectures to our own.

In recent decades, modern academics have repeatedly pointed towards the possibilities we consider. Yet few have dared to boldly state the obvious conclusions which we have drawn. Why? Because to do so is taboo. For 2,000 years the West has been dominated by the idea that Christianity is sacred and unique, whilst Paganism is primitive and the work of the Devil. To even consider that they could be parts of the same tradition has been simply unthinkable. Therefore, although the true origins of Christianity have been obvious all along, few have been able to see them, because to do so requires a radical break with the conditioning of our culture.

Our contribution has been to dare to think the unthinkable and to present our conclusions in a popular book rather than some dry academic tome. This is certainly not the last word on this complex subject, but we hope it may be a significant call for a complete reappraisal of the origins of Christianity.

THE PAGAN MYSTERIES

In Greek tragedies the chorus reveals the fate of the protagonists before the play begins. Sometimes it is easier to understand the journey if one is already aware of the destination and the terrain to be covered. Before diving deeper into detail, therefore, we would like to retrace our process of discovery and so provide a brief overview of the book. We had shared an obsession with world mysticism all our lives which recently had led us to explore spirituality in the ancient world. Popular understanding inevitably lags a long way behind the cutting edge of scholarly research and, like most people, we initially had an inaccurate and out-dated view of Paganism.

We had been taught to imagine a primitive superstition which indulged in idol worship and bloody sacrifice, and dry philosophers wearing togas stumbling blindly towards what we today call 'science.' We were familiar with various Greek myths which showed the partisan and capricious nature of the Olympian gods and goddesses. All in all, Paganism seemed primitive and fundamentally alien. After many years of study, however, our understanding has been transformed. Pagan spirituality was actually the sophisticated product of a highly developed culture.

The state religions, such as the Greek worship of the Olympian gods, were little more than outer pomp and ceremony. The real spirituality of the people expressed itself through the vibrant and mystical 'Mystery religions.' At first underground and heretical movements, these Mysteries spread and flourished throughout the ancient Mediterranean, inspiring the greatest minds of the Pagan world, who regarded them as the very source of civilization. Each Mystery tradition had exoteric Outer Mysteries, consisting of myths which were common knowledge and rituals which were open to anyone who wanted to participate.

There were also esoteric Inner Mysteries, which were a sacred secret only known to those who had undergone a powerful process of initiation. Initiates of the Inner Mysteries had the mystical meaning of the rituals and myths of the Outer Mysteries revealed to them, a process which brought about personal transformation and spiritual enlightenment. The philosophers of the ancient world were the spiritual masters of the Inner Mysteries.

They were mystics and miracle-workers, more comparable to Hindu gurus than dusty academics.

The great Greek philosopher Pythagoras, for example, is remembered today for his mathematical theorem, but few people picture him as he actually was a flamboyant sage who was believed to be able to miraculously still the winds and raise the dead. At the heart of the Mysteries were myths concerning a dying and resurrecting godman, who was known by many different names. In Egypt he was Osiris, in Greece Dionysus, in Asia Minor Attis, in Syria Adonis, in Italy Bacchus, in Persia Mithras. Fundamentally all these godmen are the same mythical being. As was the practice from as early as the third century BCE, in this book we will use the combined name "Osiris-Dionysus" to denote his universal and composite nature, and his particular names when referring to a specific Mystery tradition. From the fifth century BCE philosophers such as Xenophanes and Empedocles had ridiculed taking the stories of the gods and goddesses literally. They viewed them as allegories of human spiritual experience.

The myths of Osiris-Dionysus should not be understood as just intriguing tales, therefore, but as a symbolic language which encodes the mystical teachings of the Inner Mysteries. Because of this, although the details were developed and adapted over time by different cultures, the myth of Osiris-Dionysus has remained essentially the same.

The various myths of the different godmen of the Mysteries share what the great mythologist Joseph Campbell called 'the same anatomy', just as every human is physically unique yet it is possible to talk of the general anatomy of the human body, so with these different myths it is possible to see both their uniqueness and fundamental sameness. A helpful comparison may be the relationship between Shakespeare's Romeo and Juliet and Bernstein's West Side Story. One is a sixteenth-century English tragedy about wealthy Italian families, whilst the other is a twentieth-century American musical about street gangs. On the face of it they look very different, yet they are essentially the same story.

Similarly, the tales told about the godmen of the Pagan Mysteries are essentially the same, although they take different forms. The more we studied the various versions of the myth of Osiris-Dionysus, the more it became obvious that the story of Jesus had all the characteristics of this perennial tale. Event by event, we found we were able to construct Jesus' supposed biography from mythic motifs previousl3 relating to Osiris-Dionysus:

- Osiris-Dionysus is God made flesh, the savior and 'Son of God'.
- His father is God and his mother is a mortal virgin.
- He is born in a cave or humble cowshed on 25 December before three shepherds.
- He offers his followers the chance to be born again through the rites to baptism.
- He miraculously turns water into wine at a marriage ceremony.
- He rides triumphantly into town on a donkey while people wave palm leaves to honor him.
- He dies at Easter time as a sacrifice for the sins of the world.
- After his death he descends to hell, then on the third day he rises from the dead and ascends to heaven in glory.
- His followers await his return as the judge during the Last Days.
- His death and resurrection are celebrated by a ritual meal of bread and wine which symbolize his body and blood.

These are just some of the motifs shared between the tales of Osiris-Dionysus and the 'biography' of Jesus. Why are these remarkable similarities not common knowledge? Because, as we were to discover later, the early Roman Church did everything in its power to prevent us perceiving them. It systematically destroyed Pagan sacred literature in a brutal program of eradicating the Mysteries -- a task it performed so completely that today Paganism is regarded as a 'dead' religion.

Although surprising to us now, to writers of the first few centuries CE these similarities between the new Christian religion and the ancient Mysteries were extremely obvious. Pagan critics of Christianity, such as the satirist Celsus, complained that this recent religion was nothing more than a pale reflection of their own ancient teachings. Early 'Church fathers,' such as Justin Martyr, Tertullian, and Irenaeus, were understandably disturbed and resorted to the desperate claim that these similarities were the result of 'diabolical mimicry.'

Using one of the most absurd arguments ever advanced, they accused the Devil of 'plagiarism by anticipation,' of deviously copying the true story of Jesus before it had actually happened in an attempt to mislead the gullible! These Church fathers struck us as no less devious than the Devil they hoped to incriminate. Other Christian commentators have claimed that the myths of the Mysteries were like pre-echoes of the literal coming of Jesus, somewhat like premonitions or prophecies. This is a more generous version of the' diabolical mimicry' theory, but seemed no less ridiculous to us. There was nothing other than cultural prejudice to make us see the Jesus story as the literal culmination of its many mythical precursors. Viewed impartially, it appeared to be just another version of the same basic story.

The obvious explanation is that as early Christianity became the dominant power in the previously Pagan world, popular motifs from Pagan mythology became grafted onto the biography of Jesus. This is a possibility that is even put forward by many Christian theologians.

The virgin birth, for example, is often regarded as an extraneous later addition that should not be understood literally. Such motifs were 'borrowed' from Paganism in the same way that Pagan festivals were adopted as Christian saints' days. This theory is common amongst those who go looking for the 'real' Jesus hidden under the weight of accumulated mythological debris. Attractive as it appears at first, to us this explanation seemed inadequate.

We had collated such a comprehensive body of similarities that there remained hardly any significant elements in the biography of Jesus that we did not find prefigured by the Mysteries. On top of this, we discovered that even Jesus' teachings were not original, but had been anticipated by the Pagan sages! If there was a 'real' Jesus somewhere underneath all this, we would have to acknowledge that we could know absolutely nothing about him, for all that remained for us was later Pagan accretions! Such a position seemed absurd. Surely there was a more elegant solution to this conundrum.

THE GNOSTICS

Whilst we were puzzling over these discoveries, we began to question the received picture of the early Church and have a look at the evidence for ourselves.

We discovered that far from being the united congregation of saints and martyrs that traditional! History would have us believe, the early Christian community was actually made up of a whole spectrum of different groups. These can be broadly categorized into two different schools. On the one hand there were those we will call 'Literalists', because what defines them is that they take the Jesus story as a literal account of historical events. It was this school of Christianity that was adopted by the Roman Empire in the fourth century CE, becoming Roman Catholicism and all its subsequent offshoots. On the other hand, however, there were also radically different Christians known as 'Gnostics.'

These forgotten Christians were later persecuted out of existence by the Literalist Roman Church with such thoroughness that until recently we knew little about them except through the writings of their detractors. Only a handful of original Gnostic texts survived, none of which were published before the nineteenth century.

This situation changed dramatically, however, with a remarkable discovery in 1945 when an Arab peasant stumbled upon a whole library of Gnostic gospels hidden in a cave near Nag Hammadi in Egypt. This gave scholars access to many texts which were in wide circulation amongst early Christians, but which were deliberately excluded from the canon of the New Testament -- gospels attributed to Thomas and Philip, texts recording the acts of Peter and the 12 disciples, apocalypses attributed to Paul and James, and so on. It seemed to us extraordinary that a whole library of early Christian documents could be discovered, containing what purport to be the teachings of Christ and his disciples, and yet so few modem followers of Jesus should even know of their existence.

Why hasn't every Christian rushed out to read these newly discovered words of the Master? What keeps them confined to the small number of gospels selected for inclusion in the New Testament?

It seems that even though 2,000 years have passed since the Gnostics were purged, during which time the Roman Church has split into Protestantism and thousands of other alternative groups, the Gnostics are still not regarded as a legitimate voice of Christianity.

Those who do explore the Gnostic gospels discover a form of Christianity quite alien to the religion with which they are familiar. We found ourselves studying strange esoteric tracts with titles such as Hypostasis of the Archons and The Thought of Norea. It felt as if we were in an episode of Star Trek -- and in a way we were.

The Gnostics truly were 'psychonauts' who boldly explored the final frontiers of inner space, searching for the origins and meaning of life.

These people were mystics and creative free-thinkers. It was obvious to us why they were so hated by the bishops of the Literalist Church hierarchy.

To Literalists, the Gnostics were dangerous heretics.

In volumes of anti-Gnostic works -- an unintentional testimony to the power and influence of Gnosticism within early Christianity -- they painted them as Christians who had 'gone native.'

They claimed they had become contaminated by the Paganism that surrounded them and had abandoned the purity of the true faith. The Gnostics, on the other hand, saw themselves as the authentic Christian tradition and the orthodox bishops as an 'imitation church.'

They claimed to know the secret Inner Mysteries of Christianity which the Literalists did not possess. As we explored the beliefs and practices of the Gnostics we became convinced that the Literalists had at least been right about one thing: the Gnostics were little different from Pagans.

Like the philosophers of the Pagan Mysteries, they believed in reincarnation, honored the goddess Sophia, and were immersed in the mystical Greek philosophy of Plato. 'Gnostics' means 'Knowers', a name they acquired because, like the initiates of the Pagan Mysteries, they believed that their secret teachings had the power to impart 'Gnosis' -- direct experiential 'Knowledge of God.' Just as the goal of a Pagan initiate was to become a god, so for the Gnostics the goal of the Christian initiate was to become a Christ. What particularly struck us was that the Gnostics were not concerned with the historical Jesus.

They viewed the Jesus story in the same way that the Pagan philosophers viewed the myths of Osiris-Dionysus -- as an allegory which encoded secret mystical teachings. This insight crystallized for us a remarkable possibility. Perhaps the explanation for the similarities between Pagan myths and the biography of Jesus had been staring us in the face the whole time, but we had been so caught up with traditional ways of thinking that we had been unable to see it.

THE JESUS MYSTERIES THESIS

The traditional version of history bequeathed to us by the authorities of the Roman Church is that Christianity developed from the teachings of a Jewish Messiah and that Gnosticism was a later deviation. What would happen, we wondered if the picture were reversed and Gnosticism viewed as the authentic Christianity, just as the Gnostics themselves claimed? Could it be that orthodox Christianity was a later deviation from Gnosticism and that Gnosticism was a synthesis of Judaism and the Pagan Mystery religion? This was the beginning of the Jesus Mysteries Thesis. Boldly stated, the picture that emerged for us was as follows.

266

We knew that most ancient Mediterranean cultures had adopted the ancient Mysteries, adapting them to their own national tastes and creating their own version of the myth of the dying and resurrecting godman. Perhaps some of the Jews had likewise adopted the Pagan Mysteries and created their own version of the Mysteries which we now know as Gnosticism. Perhaps initiates of the Jewish Mysteries had adapted the potent symbolism of the Osiris-Dionysus myths into a myth of their own, the hero of which was the Jewish dying and ~resurrecting godman Jesus.

If this was so, then the Jesus story was not a biography at all but a consciously crafted vehicle for encoded spiritual teachings created by Jewish Gnostics.

As in the Pagan Mysteries, initiation into the Inner Mysteries would reveal the myth's allegorical meaning. Perhaps those uninitiated into the Inner Mysteries had mistakenly come to regard the Jesus myth as historical fact and in this way Literalist Christianity had been created. Perhaps the Inner Mysteries of Christianity, which the Gnostics taught but which the Literalists denied existed, revealed that the Jesus story was not a factual account of God's one and only visit to planet Earth, but a mystical teaching story designed to help each one of us become a Christ. The Jesus story does have all the hallmarks of a myth, so could it be that that is exactly what it is?

After all, no one has read the newly discovered Gnostic gospels and taken their fantastic stories as literally true; they are readily seen as myths. It is only familiarity and cultural prejudice which prevent us from seeing the New Testament gospels in the same light. If those gospels had also been lost to us and only recently discovered, who would read these tales for the first time and believe they were historical accounts of a man born of a virgin, who had walked on water and returned from the dead?

Why should we consider the stories of Osiris, Dionysus, Adonis, Attis, Mithras and the other Pagan Mystery saviors as fables, yet come across essentially the same story told in a Jewish context and believe it to be the biography of a carpenter from Bethlehem?

We had both been raised as Christians and were surprised to find that, despite years of open-minded spiritual exploration, it still felt somehow dangerous to even dare think such thoughts. Early indoctrination reaches very deep. We were in effect saying that Jesus was a Pagan god and that Christianity was a heretical product of Paganism!

It seemed outrageous.

Yet this theory explained the similarities between the stories of Osiris-Dionysus and Jesus Christ in a simple and elegant way. They are parts of one developing mythos.

The Jesus Mysteries Thesis answered many puzzling questions, yet it also opened up new dilemmas.

Isn't there indisputable historical evidence for the existence of Jesus the man?

And how could Gnosticism be the original Christianity when St Paul, the earliest Christian we know about, is so vociferously anti-Gnostic?

And is it really credible that such an insular and anti-Pagan people as the Jews could have adopted the Pagan Mysteries?

And how could it have happened that a consciously created myth came to be believed as history?

And if Gnosticism represents genuine Christianity, why was it Literalist Christianity that came to dominate the world as the most influential religion of all time? All of these difficult questions would have to be satisfactorily answered before we could wholeheartedly accept such a radical theory as the Jesus Mysteries Thesis.

THE GREAT COVER UP

Our new account of the origins of Christianity only seemed improbable because it contradicted the received view. As we pushed further with our research, the traditional picture began to completely unravel all around us.

We found ourselves embroiled in a world of schism and power straggles, of forged documents and false identities, of letters that had been edited and added to, and of the wholesale destruction of historical evidence.

We focused forensically on the few facts we could be confident of, as if we were detectives on the verge of cracking a sensational 'whodunit', or perhaps more accurately as if we were uncovering an ancient and unacknowledged miscarriage of justice. For, time and again, when we critically examined what genuine evidence remained, we found that the history of Christianity bequeathed to us by the Roman Church was a gross distortion of the truth.

Actually the evidence completely endorsed the Jesus Mysteries Thesis!

It was becoming increasingly obvious that we had been deliberately deceived, that the Gnostics were indeed the original Christians, and that their anarchic mysticism had been hijacked by an authoritarian institution which had created from it a dogmatic religion - and then brutally enforced the greatest cover-up in history.

One of the major players in this cover-up operation was a character called Eusebius, who, at the beginning of the fourth century, compiled from legends, fabrications and his own imagination the only early history of Christianity that still exists today.

All subsequent histories have been forced to base themselves on Eusebins' dubious claims, because there has been little other information to draw on. All those with a different perspective on Christianity were branded as heretics and eradicated. In this way falsehoods compiled in the fourth century have come down to us as established facts.

Eusebius was employed by the Roman Emperor Constantine, who made Christianity the state religion of the Empire and gave Literalist Christianity the power it needed to begin the final eradication of Paganism and Gnosticism. Constantine wanted 'one God, one religion' to consolidate his claim of 'one Empire, one Emperor.'

He oversaw the creation of the Nicene creed -- the article of faith repeated in churches to this day -- and Christians who refused to assent to this creed were banished from the Empire or otherwise silenced.

This 'Christian' Emperor then returned home from Nicaea and had his wife suffocated and his son murdered. He deliberately remained unbaptized until his deathbed so that he could continue his atrocities and still receive forgiveness of sins and a guaranteed place in heaven by being baptized at the last moment. Although he had his 'spin doctor' Eusebius compose a suitably obsequious biography for him, he was actually a monster -- just like many Roman Emperors before him. Is it really at all surprising that a 'history' of the origins of Christianity created by an employee in the service of a Roman tyrant should turn out to be a pack of lies?

Elaine Pagels, one of the foremost academic authorities on early Christianity, writes: "It is the winners who write history -- their way. No wonder, then, that the traditional accounts of the origins of Christianity first defined the terms (naming themselves "orthodox" and their opponents "heretics"); then they proceeded to demonstrate -- at least to their own satisfaction -- that their triumph was historically inevitable, or, in religious terms, "guided by the Holy Spirit." But the discoveries of the Gnostic gospels at Nag Hammadi reopen fundamental questions."

History is indeed written by the victors. The creation of an appropriate history has always been part of the arsenal of political manipulation. The Roman Church created a history of the triumph of Literalist Christianity in much the same partisan way that, two millennia later, Hollywood created tales of 'cowboys and Indians' to relate 'how the West was won' not 'how the West was lost.' History is not simply related, it is created. Ideally, the motivation is to explain historical evidence and come to an accurate understanding of how the present has been created by the past. All too often, however, it is simply to glorify and justify the status quo. Such histories conceal as much as they reveal.

To dare to question a received history is not easy. It is difficult to believe that something which you have been told is true from childhood could actually be a product of falsification and fantasy. It must have been hard for those Russians brought up on tales of kindly 'Uncle Joe' Stalin to accept that he was actually responsible for the deaths of millions. It must have strained credibility when those opposing his regime claimed that he had in fact murdered many of the heroes of the Russian revolution. It must have seemed ridiculous when they asserted that he had even had the images of his rivals removed from photographs and completely fabricated historical events. Yet all these things are true.

It is easy to believe that something must be true because everyone else believes it. But the truth often only comes to light by daring to question the unquestionable, by doubting notions which are so commonly believed that they are taken for granted.

The Jesus Mysteries Thesis is the product of such an openness of mind. When it first occurred to us, it seemed absurd and impossible. Now it seems obvious and ordinary. The Vatican was constructed upon the site of an ancient Pagan sanctuary because the new is always built upon the old. In the same way Christianity itself has as its foundations the Pagan spirituality that preceded it. What is more plausible than to posit the gradual evolution of spiritual ideas, with Christianity emerging from the ancient Pagan Mysteries in a seamless historical continuum? It is only because the conventional history has been so widely believed for so long that this idea could be seen as heretical and shocking.

RECOVERING MYSTICAL CHRISTIANITY

As the final pieces of the puzzle were falling into place, we came across a small picture tucked away in the appendices of an old academic book. It was a drawing of a third-century CE amulet. We have used it as the cover of this book. It shows a crucified figure which most people would immediately recognize as Jesus. Yet the Greek words name the figure 'Orpheus Bacchus,' one of the pseudonyms of Osiris-Dionysus. To the author of the book in which we found the picture, this amulet was an anomaly. Who could it have possibly belonged to? Was it a crucified Pagan deity or some sort of Gnostic synthesis of Paganism and Christianity? Either way it was deeply puzzling. For us, however, this amulet was perfectly understandable.

It was an unexpected confirmation of the Jesus Mysteries Thesis. The image could be that of either Jesus or Osiris-Dionysus. To the initiated, these were both names for essentially the same figure. The 'chance' discovery of this amulet made us feel as though the universe itself was encouraging us to make our findings public. In different ways the Jesus Mysteries Thesis has been proposed by mystics and scholars for centuries, but has always ended up being ignored. It now felt like an idea whose moment had come. We did, however, have misgivings about writing this book.

We knew that it would inevitably upset certain Christians, something which we had no desire to do.

Certainly it has been hard to be constantly surrounded by lies and injustices without experiencing a certain amount of outrage at the negative misrepresentation of the Gnostics, and to have become aware of the great riches of Pagan culture without feeling grief that they were so wantonly destroyed.

Yet we do not have some sort of anti-Christian agenda.

Far from it.

Those who have read our other works will know that our interest is not in further division, but in acknowledging the unity that lies at the heart of all spiritual traditions -- and this present book is no exception.

270

Early Literalist Christians mistakenly believed that the Jesus story was different from other stories of Osiris-Dionysus because Jesus alone had been an historical rather than a mythical figure. This has left Christians feeling that their faith is in opposition to all others -- which it is not. We hope that by understanding its true origins in the ongoing evolution of a universal human spirituality, Christianity may be able to free itself from this self-imposed isolation. Whilst the Jesus Mysteries Thesis clearly rewrites history, we do not see it as undermining the Christian faith, but as suggesting that Christianity is in fact richer than we previously imagined.

The Jesus story is a perennial myth with the power to impart the saving Gnosis which can transform each one of us into a Christ, not merely a history of events that happened to someone else 2,000 years ago. Belief in the Jesus story was originally the first step in Christian spirituality -- the Outer Mysteries. Its significance was to be explained by an enlightened teacher when the seeker was spiritually ripe. These Inner Mysteries imparted a mystical Knowledge of God beyond mere belief in dogmas. Although many inspired Christian mystics throughout history have intuitively seen through to this deeper symbolic level of understanding, as a culture we have inherited only the Outer Mysteries of Christianity.

We have kept the form, but lost the inner meaning. Our hope is that this book can play some small part in reclaiming the true mystical Christian inheritance.

The Pagan Mysteries

"Blest is the happy man
Who knows the Mysteries the gods ordain,
And sanctifies his life,
Joins soul with soul in mystic unity,
And, by due ritual made pure
Enters the ecstasy of mountain solitudes;
Who observes the mystic rites
Made lawful by the Great Mother;
Who crowns his head with ivy,
And shakes his wand in worship of Dionysus." Euripides

*** *** ***

271

Paganism is a 'dead' religion -- or more accurately an 'exterminated' religion· It did not simply fade away into oblivion. It was actively suppressed and annihilated, its temples and shrines desecrated and demolished, and its great sacred books thrown onto bonfires. No living lineage has been left to explain its ancient beliefs. So, the Pagan worldview has to be reconstructed from the archaeological evidence and texts that have survived, like some giant metaphysical jigsaw puzzle. 'Pagan' was originally a derogatory term meaning 'country-dweller,' used by Christians to infer that the spirituality of the ancients was some primitive rural superstition.

But this is not true.

Paganism was the spirituality which inspired the unequalled magnificence of the Giza pyramids, the exquisite architecture of the Parthenon, the legendary sculptures of Phideas, the powerful plays of Euripides and Sophocles, and the sublime philosophy of Socrates and Plato. Pagan civilization built vast libraries to house hundreds of thousands of works of literary and scientific genius. Its natural philosophers speculated that human beings had evolved from animals. Its astronomers knew the Earth was a sphere which, along with the planets, revolves around the sun.

They had even estimated its circumference to within one degree of accuracy?

The ancient Pagan world sustained a population not matched again in Europe until the eighteenth century.

In Greece, Pagan culture gave birth to the concepts of democracy, rational philosophy, public libraries, theatre and the Olympic Games, creating a blueprint for our modern world. What was the spirituality that inspired these momentous cultural achievements?

Most people associate Paganism with either rustic witchcraft or the myths of the gods of Olympus as recorded by Hesiod and Homer. Pagan spirituality did indeed embrace both. The country people practiced their traditional shamanic nature worship to maintain the fertility of the land and the city authorities propped up formal state religions, such as the worship of the Olympian gods, to maintain the power of the status quo. It was, however, a third, more mystical, expression of the Pagan spirit which inspired the great minds of the ancient world.

The thinkers, artists and innovators of antiquity were initiates of various religions known as 'Mysteries.' These remarkable men and women held the Mysteries to be the heart and soul of their culture. The Greek historian Zosimos writes that without the Mysteries "life for the Greeks would be unlivable" for "the sacred Mysteries hold the whole human race together." The eminent Roman statesman Cicero enthuses: "These Mysteries have brought us from rustic savagery to a cultivated and refined civilization.

The rites of the Mysteries are called "initiations" and in truth we have learned from them the first principles of life. We have gained the understanding not only to live happily but also to die with better hope." Unlike the traditional rituals of the official state religions, which were designed to aid social cohesion, the mysteries were an individualistic form of spirituality which offered mystical visions and personal enlightenment. Initiates underwent a secret process of initiation which profoundly trans-r formed their state of consciousness. The poet Pindar reveals that an initiate into the Mysteries "knows the end of life and its God-given beginning."

Lucius Apuleius, a poet-philosopher, writes of his experience of initiation as a spiritual rebirth which he celebrated as his birthday, an experience for which he felt a "debt of gratitude" that he "could never hope to repay."

Plato, the most influential philosopher of all time, relates: "We beheld the beatific visions and were initiated into the Mystery which may be truly called blessed, celebrated by us in a state of innocence. We beheld calm, happy, simple, eternal visions, resplendent in pure light."

The great Pagan philosophers were the enlightened masters of the Mysteries. Although they are often portrayed today as dry 'academic' intellectuals, they were actually enigmatic 'gurus.'

Empedocles, like his master Pythagoras, was a charismatic miracle-worker. Socrates was an eccentric mystic prone to being suddenly overcome by states of rapture during which his friends would discover him staring off into space for hours. Heraclitus was asked by the citizens of Ephesus to become a lawmaker, but turned the offer down so that he could continue playing with the children in the temple. Anaxagoras shocked ordinary citizens by completely abandoning his farm to fully devote his life to "the higher philosophy." Diogenes owned nothing and lived in a jar at the entrance of a temple.

The inspired playwright Euripides wrote his greatest tragedies during solitary retreats in an isolated cave. All of these idiosyncratic sages were steeped in the mysticism of the Mysteries, which they expressed in their philosophy.

Olympiodorus, a follower of Plato, tells us that his master paraphrased the Mysteries everywhere. The works of Heraclites were renowned even in ancient times for being obscure and impenetrable, yet Diogenes explains that they are crystal clear to an initiate of the Mysteries.

Of studying Heraclites he writes: "It is a hard road to follow, filled with darkness and gloom; but if an initiate leads you on the way, it becomes brighter than the radiance of the sun."

At the heart of Pagan philosophy is an understanding that all things are One.

The Mysteries aimed at awakening within the initiate a sublime experience of this Oneness. Sallustius declares:

"Every initiation aims at uniting us with the World and with the Deity."

Plotinus describes the initiate transcending his limited sense of himself as a separate ego and experiencing mystical union with God: "As if borne away, or possessed by a god, he attains to solitude in untroubled stillness, nowhere deflected in his being and unbruised with self, utterly at rest and become very rest. He does not converse with a statue or image but with Godhead itself. And this is no object of vision, but another mode of seeing, a detachment from self, a simplification and surrender of self, a yearning for contact, and a stillness and meditation directed towards transformation. Whoever sees himself in this way has attained likeness to God; let him abandon himself and find the end of his journeying." No wonder the initiate Sopatros poetically mused, "I came out of the Mystery Hall feeling like a stranger to myself."

THE SACRED SPECTACLE AT ELEUSIS

What were these ancient Mysteries that could inspire such reverent awe and heartfelt appreciation? The Mystery religion was practiced for thousands of years, during which time it spread throughout the ancient world, taking on many different forms. Some were frenzied and others meditative. Some involved bloody animal sacrifice, while others were presided over by strict vegetarians. At certain moments in history the Mysteries were openly practiced by whole populations and were endorsed, or at least tolerated, by the state. At other times they were a small-scale and secretive affair, for fear of persecution by unsympathetic authorities.

Central tail of these forms of the Mysteries, however, was the myth of a dying and resurrecting godman. The Greek Mysteries celebrated at Eleusis in honor of the Great Mother goddess and the godman Dionysus were the most famous of all the Mystery cults. The sanctuary of Eleusis was finally destroyed by bands of fanatical Christian monks in 396 CE, but up until this tragic act of vandalism the Mysteries had been celebrated there for over 11 centuries. At the height of their popularity people were coming from all over the then known world to be initiated: men and women, rich and poor, slaves and emperors -- even a Brahmin priest from India. Each year some 30,000 Athenian citizens embarked on a 30-kilometre barefoot pilgrimage to the sacred site of Eleusis on the coast to celebrate the autumn Mysteries of Dionysus. For days they would have been preparing for this important religious event by fasting, offering sacrifices and undergoing ritual purification.

As those about to be initiated danced along the 'Sacred Way' to Eleusis, accompanied by the frenzied beat of cymbals and tambourines, they were accosted by masked men who abused and insulted them, while others beat them with sticks.

At the head of the procession was carried the statue of Dionysus himself, leading them ever onward. After ritual naked bathing in the sea and other purification ceremonies the crowd reached the great doors of the Telesterion, a huge purpose-built initiation hall. Only the chosen few who were already initiated or about to be initiated into the secret Mysteries could enter here.

What awesome ceremony was held behind these closed doors that touched the great philosophers, artists, statesmen and scientists of the ancient world so deeply? All initiates were sworn to secrecy and held the Mysteries so sacred that they kept this oath. From large numbers of hints and clues, however, we know that they witnessed a sublime theatrical spectacle. They were awed by sounds and dazzled by lights. They were bathed in the blaze of a huge fire and trembled to the nerve-shattering reverberations of a mighty gong. The Hierophant, the high priest of the Mysteries, was quite literally a 'showman' who orchestrated a terrifyingly transformative dramatic reenactment of sacred myth. He himself was dressed as the central character - the godman Dionysus.

A modern scholar writes: "A Mystery Religion was thus a divine drama which portrayed before the wondering eyes of the privileged observers the story of the struggles, sufferings, and victory of a patron deity, the travail of nature in which life ultimately triumphs over death, and joy is born of pain. The whole ritual of the Mysteries aimed especially at quickening the emotional life. No means of exciting the emotions was neglected in the passion-play, either by way of inducing careful predispositions or of supplying external stimulus.

Tense mental anticipations heightened by a period of abstinence, hushed silences, imposing processions and elaborate pageantry, music loud and violent or soft and enthralling, delirious dances, the drinking of spirituous liquors, physical macerations, alternations of dense darkness and dazzling light, the sight of gorgeous ceremonial vestments, the handling of holy emblems, auto-suggestion and the promptings of the Hierophant -- these and many secrets of emotional exaltation were in vogue." This dramatization of the myth of Dionysus is the origin of tragedy and theatre. But the initiates were not a passive audience.

They were participants who shared in the passion of the godman whose death and rebirth symbolically represented the death and spiritual rebirth of each one of them. As a modern authority explains: "Dionysus was the god of the most blessed ecstasy and the most enraptured love. But he was also the persecuted god, the suffering and dying god, and all whom he loved, all who attended him, had to share his tragic fate." By witnessing the awesome tragedy of Dionysus, the initiates at Eleusis shared in his suffering, death and resurrection, and so experienced a spiritual purification known as 'catharsis.' The Mysteries did not offer religious dogmas to simply be believed, but a myth to be entered into. Initiation was not about learning something, but about experiencing an altered state of awareness.

Plutarch, a Pagan high priest, confesses that those who had been initiated could produce no proof of the beliefs that they acquired. Aristotle maintains, "It is not necessary for the initiated to learn anything, but to receive impressions and to be put in a certain frame of mind." The philosopher Produs talks of the Mysteries as evoking a "sympathy of the soul with the ritual in a way that is unintelligible to us and divine, so that some of the initiates axe stricken with panic, being filled with divine awe; others assimilate themselves to the holy symbols, leave their own identity, become at home with the gods, afford experience divine possession."

Why did the myth enacted by the Mysteries have such a profound effect?

*** *** ***

ENCODED SECRET TEACHINGS

In antiquity the word mythos did not mean something 'untrue as it does (for us today. Superficially a myth was an entertaining story, but to the initiated it was a sacred code that contained profound spiritual teachings. Plato comments, "It looks as if those also who established rites of initiation for us were no fools, but that there is a hidden meaning in their teachings."

He explains that it is "those who have given their lives to true philosophy" who will grasp the "hidden meaning" encoded in the Mystery myths, and so become completely identified with the godman in an experience of mystical enlightenment.

The ancient philosophers were not so foolish as to believe that the Mystery myths were literally true, but wise enough to recognize that they were an easy introduction to the profound mystical philosophy at the heart of the Mysteries. Sallustius writes: "To wish to teach all men the truth of the gods causes the foolish to despise, because they cannot learn, and the good to be slothful, whereas to conceal the truth by myths prevents the former from despising philosophy and compels the latter to study it." It was the role of the priests and philosophers of the Mysteries to decode the hidden depths of spiritual meaning contained within the Mystery myths. Heliodorus, a priest of the Mysteries, explains: "Philosophers and theologians do not disclose the meanings embedded in these stories to laymen but simply give them preliminary instruction in the form of a myth. But those who have reached the higher grades of the Mysteries they initiate into clear knowledge in the privacy of the holy shrine, in the light cast by the blazing torch of truth."

The Mysteries were divided into various levels of initiation, which led an initiate step by step through ever deepening levels of understanding. The number of levels of initiation varied in different Mystery traditions, but essentially the initiate was led from the Outer Mysteries, in which the myths were understood superficially as religious stories, to the Inner Mysteries, in which the myths were revealed as spiritual allegories. First the initiate was ritually purified. Then they were taught the secret teachings on a one-to-one basis.

The highest stage was when the initiate understood the true meaning of the teachings and finally experienced what Theon of Smyrna calls "friendship and interior communion with God."

*** *** ***

THE INTERNATIONAL MYSTERIES

The Mysteries dominated the Pagan world. No other deity is represented on the monuments of ancient Greece and Italy as much as Dionysus, godman of the Eleusinian Mysteries. He is a deity with many names: Iacchos, Bassareus, Bromios, Euios, Sabazius, Zagreus, Yhyoneus, Lenaios, Eleuthereus, and so the list goes on. But these are just some of his Greek names! The godman is an omnipresent mythic figure throughout the ancient Mediterranean, known in different ways by many cultures.

Five centuries before the birth of Christ, the Greek historian Herodotus, known as 'the father of history', discovered this when he traveled to Egypt. On the shores of a sacred lake in the Nile delta he witnessed an enormous festival, held every year, in which the Egyptians performed a dramatic spectacle before "tens of thousands of men and women," representing the death and resurrection of Osiris.

Herodotus was an initiate into the Greek Mysteries and recognized that what he calls "the Passion of Osiris" was the very same drama that initiates saw enacted before them at Eleusis as the Passion of Dionysus. The Egyptian myth of Osiris is the primal myth of the Mystery godman and reaches back to prehistory. His story is so ancient that it can be found in pyramid texts written over 4,500 years ago!

In traveling to Egypt Herodotus was following in the footsteps of another great Greek.

Before 670 BCE Egypt had been a closed country, in the manner of Tibet, or Japan more recently, but in this year she opened her borders and one of the first Greeks who traveled there in search of ancient wisdom was Pythagoras.

History remembers Pythagoras as the first 'scientist' of the Western world, but although it is true that he brought back many mathematical theories to Greece from Egypt, to his contemporaries he would have seemed anything but 'scientific' in the modern sense. A wandering charismatic sage dressed in white robes and crowned with a gold coronet, Pythagoras was part scientist, part priest and part magician. He spent 22 years in the temples of Egypt, becoming an initiate of the ancient Egyptian Mysteries. On returning to Greece he began to preach the wisdom he had learned, performing miracles, raising the dead and giving oracles.

Inspired by Pythagoras, his disciples created a Greek Mystery religion modeled on the Egyptian Mysteries. They took the indigenous wine god Dionysus, who was a minor deity all but ignored by Hesiod and Homer, and transformed him into a Greek version of the mighty Egyptian Osiris, godman of the Mysteries.

This initiated a religious and cultural revolution that was to transform Athens into the centre of the civilized world. The followers of Pythagoras were models of virtue and learning, regarded as puritans by their neighbors. Strict vegetarians, they preached non-violence towards all living things and shunned the temple cults that practiced the sacrifice of animals.

This made it impossible for them to participate in the traditional Olympian religion of Athens. Forced to live on the fringes of acceptability, they often organized themselves into communities that shared all possessions in common, leaving them free to devote themselves to their mystical studies of mathematics, music, astronomy and philosophy.

Nevertheless, the Mystery religion spread quickly amongst the ordinary people and within a few generations the Egyptian Mysteries of Osiris, now the Mysteries of Dionysus, inspired the glory of Classical Athens.

In the same way that Osiris was synthesized by the Greeks with their indigenous god Dionysus to create the Greek Mysteries, other Mediterranean cultures which adopted the Mystery religion also transformed one of their indigenous deities into the dying and resurrecting Mystery godman.

So, the deity who was known as Osiris in Egypt and became Dionysus in Greece was called Attis in Asia Minor, Adonis in Syria, Bacchus in Italy, Mithras in Persia, and so on. His forms were many, but essentially he was the same perennial figure, whose collective identity was referred to as Osiris-Dionysus.

Because the ancients recognized that all the various Mystery godmen were essentially the same mythic being, elements from different myths and rites were continually combined and recombined to create new forms of the Mysteries.

In Alexandria, for example, a charismatic sage called Timotheus consciously fused Osiris and Dionysus to produce a new deity for the city called Serapis.

He also gave an elaborate account of the myth of the Mystery godman Attis. Lucius Apuleius received his initiation into the Mysteries from a high priest named after the Persian godman Mithras. Coins were minted with Dionysus represented on one side and Mithras on the other? One modern authority tells us that "possessed by the knowledge of his own secret rites," the initiate of the Mysteries "found no difficulty in conforming to any religion in vogue."

Like the Christian religion which superseded it, the Mysteries reached across national boundaries, offering a spirituality which was relevant to all human beings, regardless of their racial origins or social status. Even as early as the fifth century CE philosophers such as Diogenes and Socrates called themselves "cosmopolitans' -- "citizens of the cosmos" -- rather than of any particular country or culture, which is testimony to the international nature of the Mysteries. One modern scholar, commenting on the merging and combining of different mystery traditions, writes: "This went a long way towards weaning the minds of men from the idea of separate gods from the different nations, and towards teaching them that all national and local deities were but different forms of one great Power. But for the rise of Christianity and other religions, there can be little doubt but that the whole of the Greco-Roman deities would continually have merged into Dionysus."

*** *** ***

OSIRIS-DIONYSUS AND JESUS CHRIST

> Osiris-Dionysus had such universal appeal because he was seen as an 'Everyman' figure who symbolically represented each initiate. Through understanding the allegorical myth of the Mystery godman, initiates could become aware that, like Osiris-Dionysus, they were also 'God made flesh.' They too were immortal Spirit trapped within a physical body. Through sharing in the death of Osiris-Dionysus initiates symbolically 'died' to their lower earthly nature. Through sharing in his resurrection they were spiritually reborn and experienced their eternal and divine essence.

This was the profound mystical teaching that the myth of Osiris-Dionysus encoded for those initiated into the Inner Mysteries, the truth of which initiates directly experienced for themselves. Writing of the Egyptian Mystery godman Osiris, Sir Wallis Budge, who was keeper of antiquities in the British Museum, explains:

"The Egyptians of every period in which they are known to us believed that Osiris was of divine origin, that he suffered death and mutilation at the hands of the power of evil, that after great struggle with these powers he rose again, that he became henceforth the king of the underworld and judge of the dead, and that because he had conquered death the righteous might also conquer death. "He represented to men the idea of a man who was both God and man, and he typified to the Egyptians in all ages the being who by reason of his sufferings and death as a man could sympathies with them in their own sickness and death. The idea of his human personality also satisfied their cravings and yearnings for communion with a being who, though he was partly divine, yet had much in common with themselves. Originally they looked upon Osiris as a man who lived on the earth as they lived, who ate and drank, who suffered a cruel death, who by help of certain gods triumphed over death, and attained unto everlasting life. But what Osiris did they could also do."

These are the key motifs that characterize the myths of all the Mystery godmen. What Budge writes of Osiris could equally be said of Dionysus, Attis, Adonis, Mithras and the rest. It also describes the Jewish dying and resurrecting godman Jesus Christ. Like Osiris-Dionysus, he is also God Incarnate and God of the Resurrection. He also promises his followers spiritual rebirth through sharing in his divine Passion.

CONCLUSION

The Mysteries were clearly an extremely powerful force in the ancient world. Let's review what we've discovered about them:

- The Pagan Mysteries inspired the greatest minds of the ancient world. - They were practiced in different forms by nearly every culture in the Mediterranean.
- They comprised Outer Mysteries which were open to all and secret Inner Mysteries known only to those who had undergone a powerful process of mystical initiation.
- At the heart of the Mysteries was the myth of a dying and resurrecting godman - Osiris-Dionysus.
- The Inner Mysteries revealed the myths of Osiris-Dionysus to be spiritual allegories encoding spiritual teachings.

The question which intrigued us was whether the Mysteries could have somehow influenced and shaped what we have inherited as the "biography" of Jesus? Unlike the various Pagan Mystery godmen, Jesus is traditionally viewed as an historical rather than a mythical figure, literally a man who was an incarnation of God, who suffered, died and resurrected to bring salvation to all humankind. But could these elements of the Jesus story actually be mythical stories inherited from the Pagan Mysteries?

We began investigating the myths of Osiris-Dionysus more closely, searching for resemblances with the Jesus story. We were not prepared for the overwhelming number of similarities that we uncovered.

*** *** ***

Diabolical Mimicry

"Having heard it proclaimed through the prophets that the Christ was to come and that the ungodly among men were to be punished by fire, the wicked spirits put forward many to be called Sons of God, under the impression that they would be able to produce in men the idea that the things that were said with regard to Christ were merely marvelous tales, like the things that were said by the poets." Justin Martyr

Although the remarkable similarities between the myths of Osiris-Dionysus and the supposed "biography" of Jesus Christ are generally unknown today, in the first few centuries CE they were obvious to Pagans and Christians alike. The Pagan philosopher and satirist Celsus criticized Christians for trying to pass off the Jesus story as a new revelation when it was actually an inferior imitation of Pagan myths. He asks: "Are these distinctive happenings unique to the Christians -- and if so, how are they unique? Or are ours to be accounted myths and theirs believed?

What reasons do the Christians give for the distinctiveness of their beliefs? In truth there is nothing at all unusual about what the Christians believe, except that they believe it to the exclusion of more comprehensive truths about God."

The early Christians were painfully aware of such criticisms. How could Pagan myths which predated Christianity by hundreds of years have so much in common with the biography of the one and only savior Jesus? Desperate to come up with an explanation, the Church fathers resorted to one of the most absurd theories ever advanced.

From the time of Justin Martyr in the second century onwards, they declared that the Devil had plagiarized Christianity by anticipation in order to lead people astray? Knowing that the true Son of God was to literally come and walk the Earth, the Devil had copied the story of his life in advance of it happening and created the myths of Osiris-Dionysus.

281

The Church father Tertullian writes of the Devil's "diabolical mimicry" in creating the Mysteries of Mithras: "The devil, whose business is to pervert the truth, mimics the exact circumstances of the Divine Sacraments. He baptizes his believers and promises forgiveness of sins from the Sacred Fount, and thereby initiates them into the religion of Mithras. Thus he celebrates the oblation of bread, and brings in the symbol of the resurrection. Let us therefore acknowledge the craftiness of the devil, who copies certain things of those that be Divine." Studying the myths of the Mysteries it becomes obvious why these early Christians resorted to such a desperate explanation. Although no single Pagan myth completely parallels the story of Jesus, the mythic motifs which make up the story of the Jewish godman had already existed for centuries in the various stories told of Osiris-Dionysus and his greatest prophets. Let's make a journey through the 'biography' of Jesus and explore some of these extraordinary similarities.

*** *** ***

SON OF GOD

Despite Christianity's claim that Jesus is the "only begotten Son of God." Osiris-Dionysus, in all his many forms, is also hailed as the Son of God. Jesus is the Son of God, yet equal with the Father. Dionysus is the "Son of Zeus, in his full nature God, most terrible, although most gentle to mankind." Jesus is "Very God of Very God." Dionysus is "Lord God of God born." Jesus is God in human form. St John writes of Jesus as "the Word made flesh." St. Paul explains that "God sent his own Son in the likeness of sinful flesh? Dionysus was also known as Bacchus, hence the title of Euripides' play The Bacchae, in which Dionysus is the central character. In this play, Dionysus explains that he has veiled his "Godhead in a mortal shape" in order to make it "manifest to mortal men.. He tells his disciples, "That is why I have changed my immortal form and taken the likeness of man."

Like Jesus, in many of his myths the Pagan godman is born of a mortal virgin mother. In Asia Minor, Attis' mother is the virgin Cybele. In Syria, Adonis' virgin mother is called Myrrh. In Alexandria, Aion is born of the virgin Kore. In Greece, Dionysus is born of a mortal virgin Semele who wishes to see Zeus in all his glory and is mysteriously impregnated by one of his bolts of lightning.

It was a popular tradition, recorded in the most quoted non-canonical text of early Christianity, that Jesus spent only seven months in Mary's womb. The Pagan historian Diodorus relates that Dionysus' mother Semele likewise was said to have also had only a seven-month pregnancy. Justin Martyr acknowledges the similarities between Jesus' virgin birth and Pagan mythology, writing: *"In saying that the Word was born for us without sexual union as Jesus Christ our teacher, we introduce nothing beyond what is said of those called the Sons of Zeus."* Nowhere was the myth of the 'Son of God' more developed than in Egypt, the ancient home of the Mysteries.

Even the Christian Lactantius acknowledged that the legendary Egyptian sage Hermes Trismegistus had "arrived in some way at the truth, for on God the Father he had said everything, and on the Son." In Egypt, the Pharaoh had for thousands of years been regarded as an embodiment of the godman Osiris and praised in hymns as the Son of God. As an eminent Egyptologist writes, *"Every Pharaoh had to be the Son of God and a human mother in order that he should be the Incarnate God, the Giver of Fertility to his country and people."* In many legends the great prophets of Osiris-Dionysus are also portrayed as saviors and sons of God. Pythagoras was said to be the son of Apollo and a mortal woman called Parthenis, whose name derives from the word parthenos, meaning "virgin." Plato was also posthumously believed to be the son of Apollo. Philostratus relates in his biography of Apollonius that the great Pagan sage was regarded as the "Son of Zeus." Empedocles was thought to be a godman and savior who had come down to this world to help confused souls, becoming "like a madman, calling out to people at the top of his voice and urging them to reject this realm and what is in it and go back to their own original, sublime, and noble word."

Mythic motifs from the Mysteries even became associated with Roman Emperors who, for political reasons, cultivated legends about their divine nature which would link them to Osiris-Dionysus.

Julius Caesar, who did not himself even believe in personal immortality, was hailed as "God made manifest, the common savior of human life."

His successor, Augustus, was likewise the "savior of the universal human race." and even the tyrannical Nero is addressed on an altar piece as "God the deliverer for ever."

In 40 BCE, drawing on Mystery myths, the Roman poet and initiate Virgil wrote a mystical 'prophesy' that a virgin would give birth to a divine child. In the fourth century CE Literalist Christians would claim that it foretold the coming of Jesus, but at the time this myth was interpreted as referring to Augustus, said to be the "Son of Apollo," preordained to rule the Earth and bring peace and prosperity.

In his biography of Augustus, Suetonius offers a cluster of 'signs' that indicated the Emperor's divine nature. One modern authority writes: "They include some striking points of similarity to the gospel narratives of the birth of Christ. The senate is supposed, with ludicrous implausibility, to have decreed a ban on rearing male Roman babies in the year of Augustus' birth because of a portent indicating that a king of Rome had been born. On top of this slaughter of the innocents, we are offered an Annunciation: his mother Aria dreamed during a visit to the temple of Apollo that the god had visited his favor on her in the form of snake; Augustus was born nine months later."

An inscription written around the time that Jesus is supposed to have lived reads: "This day has given the earth an entirely new aspect. The world would have gone to destruction had there not streamed forth from him who is now born a common blessing. Rightly does he judge who recognizes in this birthday the beginning of life; now is that time ended when men pitied themselves for being born. From no other day does the individual or the community receive such benefit as from this natal day, full of blessing to all. The Providence which rules over all has filled this man with such gifts for the salvation of the world as designate him as savior for us and for the coming generations; of wars he will make an end, and establish all things worthily. By his appearing are the hopes of our forefathers fulfilled; not only has he surpassed the good deeds of earlier times, but it is impossible that one greater than he can ever appear. The birthday of God has brought to the world glad tidings that are bound up in him. From his birthday a new era begins."

But this is not a Christian celebration of the birth of Jesus. It is not even a eulogy to the Mystery godman. It is in honor of Augustus. These mythic motifs were clearly so common by the first century BCE that they were used to fabricate legends politically helpful to a living Emperor. Celsus catalogues numbers of figures to whom legend similarly attributes divine parentage and a miraculous birth, and accuses Christianity of clearly using Pagan myths "in fabricating the story of Jesus' virgin birth." He is disparaging of Christians who interpret this myth as historical fact and regards the notion that God could literally father a child on a mortal woman as plainly absurd.

*** *** ***

284

CONCLUSION

Either the Devil really has perfected the art of diabolical mimicry or there is a mystery to solve here. Let's review the evidence:

- Jesus is the savior of mankind, God made man, the Son of God equal with the Father; so is Osiris-Dionysus.
- Jesus is born of a mortal virgin who after her death ascends to heaven and is honored as a divine being; so is Osiris-Dionysus.
- Jesus is born in a cave on 25 December or 6 January, as is Osiris-Dionysus.
- The birth of Jesus is prophesied by a star; so is the birth of Osiris-Dionysus.
- Jesus is born in Bethlehem, which was shaded by a grove sacred to Osiris-Dionysus.
- Jesus is visited by the Magi, who are followers of Osiris-Dionysus.
- The Magi bring Jesus gifts of gold, frankincense and myrrh, which a sixth-century BCE Pagan tells us is the way to worship God.
- Jesus is baptized, a ritual practiced for centuries in the Mysteries.
- The holy man who baptizes Jesus with water has the same name as a Pagan god of water and is born on the summer solstice celebrated as a Pagan water festival.
- Jesus offers his followers elemental baptisms of water, air and fire, as did the Pagan Mysteries.
- Jesus is portrayed as a quiet man with long hair and a beard; so is Osiris-Bionysus.
- Jesus turns water into wine at a marriage on the same day that Osiris-Dionysus was previously believed to have turned water into wine at a marriage.
- Jesus heals the sick, exorcises demons, provides miraculous meals, helps fishermen make miraculous catches of fish and calms the water for his disciples; all of these marvels had previously been performed by Pagan sages.
- Like the sages of the Mysteries, Jesus is a wandering wonder-worker who is not honored in his home town.
- Jesus is accused of licentious behavior, as were the followers of Osiris-Dionysus
- Jesus is not at first recognized as a divinity by his disciples, but then is transfigured before them in his glory; the same is true of Osiris-Dionysus.
- Jesus is surrounded by 12 disciples; so is Osiris-Dionysus.

285

- Jesus rides triumphantly into town on a donkey while crowds wave branches, as does Osiris-Dionysus. Jesus is a just man unjustly accused of heresy and bringing a new religion, as is Osiris-Dionysus.

- Jesus attacks hypocrites, stands up to tyranny and willingly goes to his death predicting he will rise again in three days, as do Pagan sages.

- Jesus is betrayed for 30 pieces of silver, a motif found in the story of Socrates.

- Jesus is equated with bread and wine, as is Osiris-Dionysus.

- Jesus' disciples symbolically eat bread and drink wine to commune with him, as do the followers of Osiris-Dionysus.

- Jesus is hung on a tree or crucified, as is Osiris-Dionysus.

- Jesus dies as a sacrifice to redeem the sins of the world; so does Osiris-Dionysus.

- Jesus' corpse is wrapped in linen and anointed with myrrh, as is the corpse of Osiris-Dionysus.

- After his death Jesus descends to hell, then on the third day resurrects before his disciples and ascends into heaven, where he is enthroned by God and waits to reappear at the end of time as a divine judge, as does Osiris-Dionysus.

- Jesus was said to have died and resurrected on exactly the same dates that the death and resurrection of Osiris-Dionysus were celebrated.

- Jesus' empty tomb is visited by three women followers; Osiris-Dionysus also has three women followers who visit an empty cave. - Through sharing in his passion Jesus offers his disciples the chance to be born again, as does Osiris-Dionysus.

Discounting the 'diabolical mimicry' argument, as all sane people must, how are we to explain these extraordinary similarities between Pagan myth and the story of Jesus? (Sources Professor Darrell J. Doughty, Timothy Freke, Peter Gandy, Drew University)

*** *** ***

58-Do You Believe Everything Sitchin Has Said?

The Answer

Note from the Editorial Board: We (The editorial Board of Mr. de Lafayette's Books and Encyclopedias) have received so many letters accusing us of being "disturbed people", "blind", "Pro Sitchin", and "fooling the uninformed", and not giving the "logical" and "serious" archeologists and historians a platform for their "solid" opinions in our books. The truth is, Mr. de Lafayette never advanced any theory, nor has he passed any judgment. In fact, he never took a stand or proposed any thesis. In many of his books, he candidly stated that he is just reporting what the brightest minds (pros and cons) have said, and/or proposed. Just to prove to the cynical minds that we are not biased, blind, or po-Sitchin, we are hereby presenting the opinions of writers and researchers who are on the other side of the fence. Please bear in mind, that pro or con theories, assumptions and criticism do not necessarily reflect the opinion of our editors, nor those of Mr. de Lafayette.

The Whole Story
Sitchin Reexamined?
Criticism and Claims: Sitchin's account of the creation of Earth can easily be shown to be entirely wrong.

*** *** ***

Like so many 'fringe' writers, Zecharia Sitchin assumes that ancient texts are inherently trustworthy, straightforward accounts by disinterested observers. In his view, Sumerian mythological tracts are historical and scientific texts, which he alone has interpreted correctly. The Twelfth Planet, Sitchin's first book, was published in 1976; it forms the first part of a series known as *The Earth Chronicles*. Not only is Sumerian mythology treated as a straightforward account of the remote past, but the Bible is equally presented as a treatise full of references to an ancient and lost science.

Subsequent books (*The Stairway to Heaven*, 1980, *The Wars of Gods and Men*, 1985 and *The Lost Realms*, 1990) build on this story.

Sitchin presents his work as erudite and scholarly, with a compendious knowledge of Sumerian myth.

He regards the astronomical knowledge of the various peoples of Mesopotamia as being much more complex and accurate than is usually assumed to be the case.

288

In particular, he reads a number of texts as indicating that there were originally twelve separate planets in our solar system: the Sun (*Abzu*), Mercury (*Mummu*), Venus (*Lahamu*), Mars (*Lahmu*), Tiamat (a planet then orbiting in what is now the asteroid belt), Jupiter (*Kishar*), Saturn (*Anshar*), Pluto (*Gaga*, which was then in a closer orbit), Uranus (*An*), Neptune (*Enki*), Nibiru (*Marduk*) and its satellite *Kingu*. The formation of Earth is part of a complex cosmic drama that can only be summarised here.

According to Sitchin's interpretation of a text known as *The Epic of Creation*, Nibiru was the home planet of being called the Anunnaki. Originally, the Earth and Moon were not present in the solar system, although there was an extra planet (Tiamat) where the asteroid belt now sits, between Mars and Jupiter.

According to his reading of the Epic, Nibiru was originally from outer space, entering our solar system on a retrograde path and passed close to Neptune; the gravity of Neptune bent its trajectory so that it entered the solar system on a retrograde path and pulled a bulge in its side. Passing Uranus, the bulge ripped open and several lumps were pulled out of Nibiru to become its moons. Once again, the gravity of Uranus drew Nibiru ever closer to the centre of the solar system.

As it pulled on Gaga, a planet orbiting between Saturn and Uranus, Gaga was swept out of its orbit, eventually to settle down as Pluto. Missing Saturn and Jupiter, Nibiru approached Tiamat and its gravity began to tear away bits of the planet. Tiamat was cracked but remained whole. Nibiru then swept past the sun, swinging into an orbit that took it back out into deep space past Neptune. Having been pulled into an eccentric orbit around the sun, Nibiru returned thousand of years later, when it destroyed Tiamat. Half of it became the asteroid belt, while the other half was knocked closer to the sun by one of Nibiru's satellites and became the Earth. Kingu, one of Tiamat's satellites, accompanied the broken half and became the Moon. Nibiru continues in this highly eccentric orbit, which takes it out beyond Neptune and back into the asteroid belt in a retrograde orbit that takes 3,600 years to complete. The reason that Sumerian and Babylonian astronomers continued to regard the Moon as a planet, not a satellite of Earth, was that it had originally been a planet in its own right.

In his version of the Sumerian myths, beings from Nibiru much later created humans from apes by genetic engineering. This was possible because although life had originally developed on Nibiru, its collision with Tiamat had seeded some of the genetically identical molecules on what was to become Earth, so the beings of both planets share a common genetic ancestry. Modified eggs were implanted into the Anunnaki women about 450,000 years ago (which is part of the thesis of von Däniken's second book, *Return to the Stars*).

The created humans were intended to be slaves for the Anunnaki, who needed minerals from the Earth to maintain their own civilisation.

The Anunnaki continued to direct events on Earth until about 13,000 years ago. All trace of the civilisation of the Anunnaki on Earth was destroyed in a Deluge caused by part of the Antarctic ice cap breaking off and falling into the ocean about 13,000 years ago. To escape the resulting flood, the Anunnaki retreated into space, while all their millennia of engineering efforts were destroyed. Enki had taken pity on the humans and allowed a small group of them to build an Ark to ride out the floodwaters, so after the Deluge, the Anunnaki returned to Earth and taught them the basics of agriculture and animal husbandry.

The Anunnaki built a spaceport in Sinai that was destroyed in a nuclear war 4,000 years ago. For reasons that Sitchin does not make clear, they decided to abandon their mining operations on Earth and to return only occasionally to help out humanity. A large part of Sitchin's thesis is given to an explanation about why civilisation developed where and when it did. According to Sitchin, *"most scholars now admit in frustration, by all data Man should still be without civilization"*.

This is not a view that forms part of mainstream archaeology. Most of the orthodox archaeologists who have worked on the question of the origin of civilisation seem pretty much agreed that it develops in those societies where an unusual degree of cooperation between communities is required, for whatever reason. In many parts of the world, such as Mesopotamia, the Indus Valley, Egypt, the Vale of Mexico, the Yangtse Valley and so on, the early civilisations are all basically 'hydraulic'; in other words, these communities all require large-scale water works for agriculture.

Sitchin believes the Sumerians to have invented a host of technological accomplishments, including writing, printing, metallurgy, a written law, medical technology and so on. He describes Sumerian religion in his own way. According to him, An was the chief god; the problem here is that although the original sources make him the god of the heavens, they nowhere suggest that he outranks the other gods. Indeed, it is usually Enlil, the god of the air, who is usually portrayed as the leader of the gods. Going further, he then claims that twelve gods made up a ruling council of the gods; no ancient or modern sources to agree with this interpretation, although a group of seven deities who decree fate are mentioned (the deities in question being An, Enki, Enlil, Inanna, Nanna-Sin, Ninhursag and Utu). Other documents talk of fifty great gods, who are never named but who seem to be the Anunnanki, the children of An. To make up his list of twelve ruling gods, Sitchin adds some of the sons of Enki and Enlil to the list of the seven who decree fate.

Much of Sitchin"s work depends on the reinterpretation of various words found in ancient texts. One of his key words, *shem*, is translated by orthodox Sumerian scholars as 'name" or 'reputation"; he prefers to see in it a word meaning 'sky chamber" and, by extension, 'spaceship'.

Another is the term *Anunnaki*, which he translates as 'those who have come down from the Heavens to Earth'. Once again, orthodox linguists translate the term rather differently, as 'the descendants of the monarch". Nevertheless, he suggests that the Biblical term *Nephilim* is a Hebrew equivalent of *Anunnaki*, allowing him to draw parallels between various Sumerian texts and parts of the Bible.

A genius?

According to his admirers, Zecharia Sitchin is a top-of-the-line linguist, maybe the greatest historian of all time and the creator of the most mind-stretching cosmology to date. Furthermore, it appears academically unchallengeable to his followers. Sitchin also claims to be a Sumerian, whose research has been to prepare us, the human race, for the return of our creators. Zecharia Sitchin's interpretations of ancient writings are eccentric, to say the very least. The Anunnaki are known from Sumerian mythology, where they are the children of the god of the heavens and the seven judges of the underworld. It is thought that they were originally regarded as fertility deities, something that makes sense in the context of the first agricultural civilisation on earth. They recur in Assyro-Babylonian mythology. None of the ancient texts seems to treat them as anything other than divinities: there is no suggestion that they are physical visitors to this world. Moreover, Sitchin does not seem to have discovered previously unknown meanings of ancient words and then uncovered the scenario he proposes for the origins of the earth and humanity: rather, he seems to have come up with his thesis first and then looked for new ways of translating key texts to support it, the reverse of normal academic practice.

Sitchin's account of the creation of Earth can easily be shown to be entirely wrong. The chemical composition of the Moon and Earth, for instance, demonstrate that they both originally formed as a single astronomical body that was town apart early in its history.

Sitchin's reconstruction of Sumerian mythology and his highly speculative account of the family relationships between the gods, makes An a remote figure who, as the overlord of the gods, visited the Earth only when Nibiru entered the inner solar system every 3,600 years. This return was a time of great rejoicing and activity. Earth was ruled directly by An's eldest son, Enki, who acted as a viceroy. Eventually, Enki's position was usurped by Enlil, who was An's son by his own half sister. This led to a blood feud between the descendants of the half brothers, which continued through many generations. His reconstruction of the family relationships of the Sumerian gods is what has allowed him to work out the stages in the ensuing war, but it is a reconstruction that does not match the results of orthodox scholars.

Sitchin and von Däniken

There are parts of Sitchin's account that clearly derive from von Däniken: we have the story of Etana and the Eagle (which von Däniken wrongly makes a part of *The Epic of Gilgamesh*), in which the eagle carrying Etana flies higher and higher, allowing the narrator to give an 'accurate' description of the earth from space. We also get the supposition that the Ark of the Covenant was "principally a communications box".

Sitchin believes that "evolution cannot account for the appearance of Homo Sapiens, which happened virtually overnight in terms of the millions of years which evolution requires, and with no evidence of the earlier stages which would indicate a gradual change from Homo Erectus". This is utter nonsense.

The evolution from African Homo Erectus (which some palaeoanthropologists now prefer to call Homo Ergaster) to archaic forms of Homo Sapiens took place something like 200,000 years ago and does not involve as huge a change as Sitchin seems to believe.

Ironically, many creationists will insist that Homo Erectus fossils are the remains of modern humans! (Sources: Keith Fitzpatrick-Matthews and James Doeser)

Another Contra Attitude...

Sitchin's Cosmology and Planet X

By Ian Lawton

The Mesopotamians' 'Twelve Planets'

We have already seen that Sitchin's starting point is to ask who were the Nefilim or Anunnaki. Convinced that they were capable of space travel (which theme we will examine in the next paper), he turns his attention to identifying the planet from which they came. He examines the evidence for the Mesopotamians having astronomical knowledge far in excess of that attributed to them by orthodox scholars, and then quotes extracts from a number of astronomical texts for which he, for once, provides references[1] and which, he suggests, indicate that the Mesopotamians considered our solar system to be made up of *twelve* planets. This would presuppose that not only did they know of Mercury, Venus, Earth, Mars, Jupiter, Saturn, Uranus, Neptune and Pluto (the latter three only being discovered in modern times since 1781); not only did they typically count the Sun and the Moon as 'planets'; but also they knew of the existence of an additional *twelfth planet*.

He suggests that it is this factor which determined the number of gods in the supreme pantheon which he regards as being made up of twelve members. Further, he argues that they used this number twelve in a variety of contexts as a result - for example, dividing the heavens into twelve signs of the zodiac, the year into twelve months, and the day into two sets of twelve hours.[2]

I have not investigated the astronomical texts to which Sitchin refers for reasons which will become obvious. However it is worth considering the main piece of pictorial evidence he cites - a six-pointed star surrounded by eleven spheres of varying size, which forms part of an Akkadian seal. For once this is not a hand-drawn reproduction but a photograph, and surprisingly we are once again given a source - we are told that it is in the *Vorderasiatische Abteilung* of the State Museum in East Berlin, and even given the catalogue number - VA / 243. However we should not hold our breath.

Sitchin goes on to blow up the relevant section with a drawing and compare it to a representation of what our solar system would look like if the planets were placed to scale in a circle around the Sun, in order, rather than in linear fashion as we normally depict them.[3]

This reconstruction requires so much imagination and assumption that I could devote pages just to this one piece of analysis, but we do not have the time and it is not that interesting. Suffice to say that in the real version, the centres of the 'planets' are shown at varying distances from the centre of the 'Sun', for no apparent reason even if a simple circular rather than linear representation is indeed what the artist intended; and the relative sizes of the 'planets' are hopelessly inaccurate in most cases - Mercury, the Moon and Pluto being much too large, while Jupiter and Saturn are way too small. The foregoing could be dismissed as inaccuracies in knowledge or simply artistic licence, since this is only a relatively rough engraving on a stone seal. However if Sitchin's analysis has any basis, Mercury is effectively shown as a satellite of Venus (with Venus lying directly between it and the Sun, just as the Earth is shown lying between the Moon and the Sun) - and this point is completely ignored by Sitchin.[4] Further Pluto is shown out of position between Saturn and Uranus - a point which Sitchin attempts to reconcile with events in the *Epic of Creation* (see below). Despite all the foregoing, Sitchin uses this seal as a major foundation for the existence of a 'twelfth' planet; for its position relative to the others - arguing that its orbit brings it between Mars and Jupiter; for its relative size - apparently smaller than Jupiter and Saturn, but significantly larger than Mars and the Earth; and for its role in the creation of Earth (see below). In my view this supposedly major piece of primary evidence is weak, and its interpretation selective and inconsistent.

The Creation of Earth

Sitchin places a highly literal interpretation on the *Epic of Creation*. This is another of the major pieces of evidence which apparently persuades him that this 'twelfth' planet was primarily referred to as Nibiru, and was the planet from which the Anunnaki came. Ignoring for the moment whether he has any grounds for such a literal interpretation, let us review the principal elements of his analysis.[5] (Note that in the main his interpretation requires the names of gods to be substituted for those of the planets, and these are provided in brackets where appropriate.)

In brief, he suggests that originally our solar system consisted of, in order of orbit: the Sun (Abzu), Mercury (Mummu), Venus (Lahamu), Mars (Lahmu), Tiamat (a planet then orbiting in what is now the asteroid belt), Jupiter (Kishar), Saturn (Anshar), Pluto (Gaga, which was then in a closer orbit - see above), Uranus (An) and Neptune (Enki).

He argues that the planet Nibiru (Marduk) came from outer space on a retrograde path (i.e., moving in the opposite direction from the rest of the planets in our solar system), was attracted by the gravitational pull of the outer planets into an ever tighter orbit around the Sun, caused a variety of initial disruptions, and then on its second pass collided with Tiamat which split into two - one half forming the Earth which proceeded into a tighter orbit inside that of Mars, the other breaking up to form the asteroid belt. The Moon (Kingu), a satellite of Tiamat, was at the same time shunted into an orbit of the Earth (and because it had originally been a planet on its own before becoming a satellite of Tiamat and then the Earth, the Moon continued to be regarded as a planet in its own right.)

There are primarily two angles from which this interpretation should be judged. First, does his interpretation hold up under the scrutiny of modern scientific understanding? Although I am no cosmologist, my research reveals that there are a number of objections to his theories[6].

1. It would require an extraordinary series of coincidences for even one of the Earth, Moon, Pluto and Nibiru to stabilise in a different orbit after a collision without additional accelerative stimuli. It is therefore highly unlikely that they could all benefit from such an unlikely sequence of events.

2. Sitchin's view of gravity and its effects is hopelessly inadequate. For example, he has Nibiru being affected by the pull of Neptune and Uranus, but there is no contra effect on them; gravity works both ways, especially since Nibiru is supposed to be of similar size to them, and yet their orbits remain to this day more circular than that of the Earth. Similarly, he suggests that the gravitational pull of other planets could cause 'bulges' in Nibiru sufficient to cause satellites to be ripped out of it; this is an idiotic view of how gravity works.

3. Nibiru had to make at least two orbital passes to tear Tiamat in half - and yet on the second pass it came back in roughly the same orbit, despite all the gravitational interactions it must have suffered on the first pass which should have altered its orbit considerably. From the opposite perspective, one might also ask why Nibiru managed to cause so much devastation on these first two passes, and yet cause none on the myriad of passes it has supposedly made subsequently.

4. As a corollary to the above, Sitchin uses another supposed text (unnamed) to suggest that Nibiru's orbital plane is inclined at 30 degrees to the ecliptic.[7] I am inclined to ask how, if this is the case, did it manage to come so close to so many of the planets in our solar system on its first two devastating passes?

295

Or is he suggesting that once more unknown forces forced it to stabilise in this non-aligned orbit thereafter?

5. Nowadays the asteroid belt does not contain anything like enough mass to make up a planet the size of the Earth (i.e., the other half of Tiamat). However it must be appreciated that Jupiter would have acted like a giant suction cleaner on any debris from an exploding planet (a possibility that still cannot be written off, even if Sitchin's interpretations are wrong), and other factors would have reduced the extent of the debris remaining over time.

6. Bodes law predicts that not only should a planet have originally formed between Mars and Jupiter as Sitchin asserts (but which many astronomers believe never formed due to the gravitational effects of the massive Jupiter, leaving the asteroid belt only), but also that a planet should always have been where the Earth is now. Yet according to Sitchin the latter's position was achieved subsequent to the original formation of our solar system, so originally this space must have been empty. This law supports him in one sense but at the same time undermines him in another - although at one point he does produce what appears to be somewhat contrived evidence, involving simplification of Bode's Law, to refute this claim[8]. (However in fairness it should be appreciated that Bodes Law is not as foolproof as it sounds, and is in reality only another 'theory' about how the solar system was formed.)

7. The idea that the Moon was originally a planet in its own right is not supported by modern discoveries; the latest thinking appears to be that, most likely, it split off from the Earth after the impact of a Mars-sized body.

8. Sitchin's initial evidence for Nibiru having a retrograde orbit appears to be purely based on the order in which it encounters the outer planets - according to him, Neptune then Uranus. Given that the relative position of these two to each other must change as they orbit the Sun at different speeds, it appears to me that this argument is pretty insubstantial. I would have thought that in a sense it could just as easily have passed them in this order while travelling in a conventional direction of orbit.

9. In *Genesis Revisited* Sitchin goes to some lengths in attempting to prove that modern scientific analysis of the Earth and its crust, the theory of continental drift, and the study of plate tectonics all support his claim that the Earth as we now know it was formed by a huge impact.[9] This may be so, but in my view his analysis does not support his theory of the Earth being formed by the splitting in two of another planet any better than it supports the more conventional idea of the Moon being split off from the Earth.

The second approach is to question the extent to which it is reasonable for Sitchin to even attempt to place a literal interpretation on this most enigmatic of texts. We have already seen that one of the motives of this relatively late Akkadian work is political - to elevate the late-emerging Babylonian god Marduk from local to national status. When criticising Sitchin's interpretation, some of the orthodox scholars tend to place most of the emphasis on this factor - suggesting that this is the text's primary purpose. While this is undoubtedly true, the issue is far more complex.

Sitchin himself acknowledges the political influence, but argues that the text has far earlier Sumerian origins. In this he appears to be supported by many of the scholars, despite the fact that no Sumerian version has yet been discovered (apart from similarities in isolated passages). Furthermore the common practice of amalgamating originally separate texts and tacking on new passages is probably at work; for example, Marduk's establishment of Babylon and the extensive listing of his epithets in Tablets V to VII are likely to be late additions, while a brief version of the creation of man story is stuck in the middle of all this. Since Tablets II and III deal mainly with the search for a champion to fight Tiamat - in which role Marduk finally offers himself - this leaves us with the likelihood that it is primarily Tablets I and IV, if any, which reflect important earlier tales.

Concentrating on Tablet IV, Marduk's battle with Tiamat - who represents primeval 'watery chaos' - in which he splits her in two to create heaven and earth and restore order to the universe, is clearly a basic creation theme which ties in closely with that of many other ancient civilisations. Alexander Heidel points out that in Egyptian legends 'the air-god Shu separated heaven and earth by lifting the sky-goddess Nut from the earth-god Geb and placing himself between the two', and that the Phoenician and Vedic legends both contain the concept of 'the cosmic egg being split to create heaven and earth'.[10] Meanwhile Sitchin is quite right to draw parallels with *Genesis* 1:6-8:

And God said, Let there be a firmament in the midst of the water, and let it divide the waters from the waters. And God made the firmament and divided the waters which were under the firmament from the waters which were above the firmament: and it was so. And God called the firmament Heaven.

***   ***   ***

297

Sitchin goes on to argue that the Hebrew word *Tehom*, used in *Genesis* to denote the 'watery deep', stems from the word *Tiamat*, and also that the *firmament* which was called 'heaven' is in the original Hebrew 'rakia', which translates as 'hammered bracelet', and therefore argues that it actually refers to the asteroid belt.[11] However we have already that his etymological work is often flawed, and in any case I have little doubt that all these texts should be interpreted from an esoteric rather than a literal viewpoint. This factor, combined with the blatant cosmological flaws in his theory, in my view utterly refute his interpretation of the *Epic of Creation.*

Visitors from Elsewhere?

Even if Sitchin's account of the creation of Earth is fatally flawed, is he nevertheless right to infer that the Anunnaki were indeed visitors from elsewhere? I can find precious little evidence to support Sitchin's repeated claim that the Mesopotamian texts state that the planet Nibiru is where the Anunnaki originated. In Stephanie Dalley's translation of the *Epic of Creation* it is directly mentioned only in the brief passage which is quoted below, while the remaining references are all to Marduk - and it is only Sitchin's creativity which links the two. Furthermore I have found no reference to Nibiru in any of the other literary texts. With no supporting argument Sitchin suggests that the multiple versions of a 'winged globe', which are indeed found in great numbers on a variety of reliefs from Mesopotamia and elsewhere, represent Nibiru[14], but most enlightened commentators recognise this as a universal esoteric archetypal symbol. He goes on to suggest that various Babylonian astronomical texts[15] and biblical passages foretell of the events which accompany each return of Nibiru,[16] but as I have previously indicated I have not consulted these in detail because of the evident weaknesses in the other aspects of his argument.

It is in fact Sitchin's interpretation of the words Nefilim and Anunnaki which appear to provide most support for this assertion. We have already noted his argument that the Hebrew word has the Semitic derivative 'nafal' or 'nfl' which he suggests means 'to fall, come down, descend' - although, after quoting supposed backing from the 19th century Jewish biblical commentator Malbim, he exaggerates this somewhat in his books into 'those who were cast down upon Earth', and 'those who have come down, from the Heavens to Earth'.[17]

As for the Sumerian term - which he translates similarly without any detailed explanation - there is no doubt that the separate word *An* is not only the name of the chief deity, but also translates as 'heaven'; similarly the word *Ki* as 'earth'. However as we have seen this does not mean that when they are combined the syllables can be neatly deconstructed to suit one's purpose, and in any case I can find no support for the remaining syllables (un.na) providing the necessary meaning of 'fall' or 'come down'.

The only attempts at translation of the entire term that I have found are by John Heise[18] in which he breaks it down as A.nun.nak and translates it as 'the semen/descendants of the monarch (nun)', and by Thorkild Jacobsen who translates it similarly as 'the sons of princes'.[19]

It should also be noted that orthodox commentators suggest the alternative term Igigi is of unknown origin and meaning, while Sitchin insists it means 'those who observe and see'[20] - which ties in with his theory that they remained in orbit, and is possibly backed up to the extent that one of the meanings of the Sumerian word *igi* is 'to see'. However, even if Sitchin's interpretation is correct in this instance, it hardly represents overwhelming evidence of visitors from elsewhere.

Sitchin produces a variety of other examples of interpretations of words and reproductions of statues and stelae to support this argument. They are too numerous to be analysed individually, but suffice to say that there is strong reason to believe that they suffer from the same inadequacies as evidence as those we have already considered here and in previous papers. However he does produce one other piece of evidence that at least at first sight appears quite enigmatic, sufficiently so for us to consider it here. It is a most interesting circular clay tablet which was found in the ruins of Nineveh, and is now in the British Museum (exhibit WAK 8538). Although about 50 per cent of the surface is worn away, it is divided into eight equal triangular segments, and clearly contains an assortment of cuneiform signs along the dividing lines and elsewhere which are often repeated. More curious still are the 'arrowed' lines which appear in several places, along with at least two diagrams which look very much like constellations. Although Sitchin's copy is hand drawn,[21] Alan Alford has reproduced a photograph which allows us to establish that Sitchin's blown-up drawing is reasonably accurate[22] (some of the cuneiform signs appear slightly different, but the scale makes it difficult to be sure of this). Sitchin quotes a number of turn of the century studies of this tablet in which a consensus that it is a planisphere of some sort appears to have developed. However these early scholars seemed to have struggled with the interpretation of what they considered, given its location and age, to be Akkadian cuneiform signs - which in this language made no sense.

He contends that it was only when he attempted to read these signs in Sumerian that they started to make sense, and revealed a 'Celestial Route Map' which records how the Anunnaki travelled to Earth via the outer planets. If he is right about the language used, based on the fact that this is a copy of an older Sumerian tablet, his interpretations of the words thereon are still open to question. Here are some examples: we have *sham* (not *shem*) translated as 'rocket', an interpretation we have already dismissed in detail; *na* translated as 'high', when the word *an* is the normal Sumerian term (because of the association with An), so this is perhaps a casual and inappropriate juxtaposition of letters; and *apin* translated as 'where the right course is set', when every use of the word that I can find clearly indicates it means 'plough'.

Sitchin's further interpretation of this tablet is a hotch-potch of ideas which mixes, for example, supposedly technical flight direction details with mundane issues such as stocking up with grain for the return journey; personally I find it unlikely that the two would be combined on one diagram of such supposed importance. Furthermore I fail to see how such a technical set of instructions would be expressed using such unspecific terms as 'high', 'sky', 'mountain', 'set', 'change' and 'glide', which according to Sitchin are repeated numerous times apparently without further detail, and which in any case *may* be distorted translations of the cuneiform signs.

Despite the fact that I do not believe this tablet supports his contention that space travel was at one time familiar to the Ancient Mesopotamians, I would accept that this enigmatic disc - which as far as I am aware appears relatively unique - deserves further study by experts.

Planet Nibiru

Let us briefly review the remainder of the points Sitchin makes about Nibiru itself. First, he provides further evidence (in addition to that in the diagram on the seal mentioned above) that Nibiru's (retrograde) orbit takes it between Jupiter and Mars. His support for this comes in the form of extracts from the *Epic of Creation*, in which Nibiru supposedly 'holds the central position' (i.e., he suggest that it divides the other planets, excluding the Sun, into two groups of five) and 'in the midst of Tiamat keeps crossing' (i.e., it returns to the original position of Tiamat); and also of 'astronomical texts' (unnamed) which 'list the planets in their celestial order'.[23]

It is worth noting that at least the first of these, the extract from Tablet VII of the *Epic of Creation* which relates to several of Marduk's epithets, is, as so often, somewhat at odds with Dalley's version:[24]

> Nibiru: he does indeed hold the crossings of heaven and earth. Neither up nor down shall they cross over; they must wait on him. Nibiru is his star which is bright in the sky. He *controls the crossroads*; they must look to him, saying: 'He who *kept crossing inside Tiamat* without respite, shall have Nibiru as his name, grasping her middle.'

All we can say is that Dalley does accept the translation of Nibiru as 'crossing place', which seems to support Sitchin's 'planet of the crossing' and his assertion that its pictographic sign is a cross (which, he claims, is the same as that for An) - although Dalley identifies it with Jupiter itself.[25]

Second, in answering the question as to why we have not yet observed such a large planet in the inner solar system, Sitchin uses a variety of textual references to suggest that it has a highly elliptical orbit which takes it deep into space at its apogee (furthest point from the Sun).[26] These are as follows: From the *Epic of Creation*, he quotes that Marduk 'established an outstanding abode' - this is so innocuous that I have not even traced it to check its accuracy against Dalley's version. From *Job* 26:10 he suggests that 'Upon the Deep he (the Lord) marked out an orbit; where light and darkness merge is his farthest limit', whereas the Authorised King James Version says 'He hath compassed the waters with bounds, until the day and night come to an end' - not much similarity there, so perhaps this is yet another of his creative translations, this time of the original Hebrew Old Testament.

Finally from *Psalms* he suggests 'From the end of heavens he (the Lord) emanates, and his circuit is to their end' - I could not even trace this passage, but it is hardly conclusive even if the rendering is anywhere near accurate. Altogether then, not convincing evidence in itself.

Third, one of the chief units of Mesopotamian time measurement was the 3600-year 'sar', and Sitchin suggests that this measure derives from the periodic return of Nibiru from its deep-space orbit (because its appearance held so much significance for the Ancients that, having recorded its orbital period over many millennia and measured it at 3600 years, they designated the Sar to represent this number).

301

He further cites the apparent fact that this number was written as a large circle, and that the similar word *shar* was an epithet for the word *planet* which translates as 'perfect circle' or 'completed cycle'. Of course this could represent a piece of brilliant intuition, but somehow I doubt it.

It would be a mercy to leave this analysis of Sitchin's cosmology here and return to something more constructive. However, because Sitchin and his supporters make such a song and dance about it[27], we must turn our attention to some recent findings which appear at first sight to support his claims of Nibiru's existence: a number of modern astronomers have in fact gathered evidence - most of which came out after *The Twelfth Planet* was published - which suggests to them that what is in reality an additional *tenth* planet (if one ignores the Sun and Moon) might indeed exist in our solar system...

The Search for 'Planet X'

Neptune was only discovered in 1846 after astronomers had noticed perturbations in the orbit of Uranus.

Similarly Pluto was only discovered in 1930 after its existence had been postulated because of irregularities in the orbit of Neptune. However observation of continued irregularities in the orbits of primarily Uranus and Neptune remained a puzzle to astronomers. It was originally believed they were caused by Pluto itself, but the discovery of its moon Charon at the US Naval Observatory in Washington in 1978 indicated that Pluto was too small to have the necessary influence on the other planets.

In fact back in 1972 discrepancies in the orbit of Halley's comet had already caused one astronomer to suggest that a tenth planet may exist - dubbed 'Planet X' to reflect the number ten and its unknown status.

The later revelations about Pluto, combined with theories regarding the gravitational force required to have so disrupted Neptune's satellite system that, for example, Triton was forced into a retrograde orbit, led to a renewed search for Planet X spearheaded by two astronomers at the US Naval Observatory - Robert Harrington and Tom Van Flandern. They commenced with computer simulations which have been constantly updated, but observation was also attempted when NASA linked up with them in 1982 and announced that one of the objectives of the Infrared Astronomical Satellite (IRAS) would be to scan the skies for Planet X.

Sitchin and his supporters attached great weight to subsequent announcements made in the press, and two in particular. The first was reported in the *Washington Post* of 30 December 1983 (the italics in this and subsequent quotes are mine):[28]

> A heavenly body possibly as large as the giant planet Jupiter and possibly so close to Earth that it would be part of this solar system has been found in the direction of the constellation of Orion... [by IRAS]... *astronomers do not know if it is a planet, a giant comet, a protostar... or a distant galaxy... 'All I can tell you is that we don't know what it is,'* said Gerry Neugebauer, chief IRAS scientist... Conceivably it could be the tenth planet that astronomers have searched for in vain.'

A proper reading of this announcement reveals it was hardly conclusive proof that Planet X had been found. However in his 1990 book *Genesis Revisited* Sitchin put what he termed the 'official denials' down to a government conspiracy to withhold information which was in fact shaping the end of the cold war, as the two superpowers combined to ward of the threat of imminent extra-terrestrial invasion. He also inferred that his own theories were ignored by the establishment as part of a cover-up, and used an assortment of contrived argument insists that although the multitude of satellites and probes launched in recent years and planned for the future had been officially searching for planets in neighbouring solar systems, in reality they were concentrating closer to home. However, as we will see, many teams of astronomers were involved in reviewing the IRAS data, and have written about it at great length. This does not smack of a cover-up to me.

The second announcement was reported in *Newsweek* of 13 July 1987:

> NASA held a press conference last week to make a rather strange announcement: an eccentric 10th planet may - *or may not* - be orbiting the Sun. John Anderson, a NASA research scientist who was the principal speaker, has a *hunch* Planet X is out there, though nowhere near the other nine.

Hunch is the right word! On further investigation[29] we find that what Anderson had done was observe the *lack* of gravitational effects on the Pioneer 10 and 11 craft - which were by then well into the outer reaches of our solar system - and from this *negative* evidence postulated the *possibility* of a tenth planet which *would have to have* a highly elliptical and inclined orbit to produce no effect. Since this was only a supplement to the fact that he had recently become converted to the idea of a tenth planet by the theoretical 'irregular orbit' argument (having previously been a sceptic), this is about as unconvincing as 'evidence' gets.

Returning to Harrington and Van Flandern, both have been courted assiduously by Sitchin and his supporters because of the scientific backbone their work supposedly gives to his theories, and he quotes their work as if the existence of Planet X is almost a foregone conclusion. In addition to the 'announcements' reviewed above, Sitchin detailed numerous predictions about Planet X - culminating in his suggestion that by 1990 Harrington's team believed 'that the tenth planet is about five times larger than Earth and about three times farther from the Sun than Neptune or Pluto', and that they had initiated all manner of searches of the skies, providing detailed instructions on where to look. Yet if you read Van Flandern's own book, *Dark Matter, Missing Planets and New Comets*, published three years later in 1993, you obtain a rather different picture:[30][31]

> Certainly if such a 'Planet X' *were to be discovered* in a highly inclined and eccentric orbit that approached Neptune's orbit at perihelion and has a mass near the interesting range of 2-to-5 Earth masses, its existence would argue strongly for the essential correctness of the whole scenario [of the development of Neptune's satellite system] just described.
>
> A planet in the two-to-five Earth-mass range... *could* explain the observed irregularities in the planet orbits if it were presently located 50 to 100 times further from the Sun than the Earth's orbit.

This is as explicit as Van Flandern got in his book, and hardly suggested the definitive distance, size, and orbital plane which Sitchin would have had us believe; as far as the orbital period was concerned, all the studies seemed to work on the basis of something like 500-1000 years, substantially lower than Sitchin's 3600.

Moreover Van Flandern indicated that further study of the orbits of a number of comets beyond Neptune - and possibly detailed changes to the laws of gravity - would be required before the mathematical calculations could properly predict the location in which observational searches for Planet X should concentrate 'if it exists'. Primarily because of this dissatisfaction with the theoretical data at that point, Van Flandern did not mention the IRAS observational programme at all. By contrast Harrington remained somewhat sceptical about the orbital irregularity data, and was therefore more inclined to use the 'brute force' mass computation and observational method, although with in his own words 'nothing to show for my efforts'.[32]

We should also recognise that a number of other groups have been engaged in the search for a tenth planet in recent decades. All have pursued different logic and come up with different conclusions, some convergent, some divergent. These studies were thoroughly described by Mark Littmann, former director of the Hansen Planetarium in Salt Lake City, in his 1988 book *Planets Beyond: Discovering the Outer Solar System*.[33]

In particular, Littmann at the time quoted a number of experts who feel that reliance on the apparent deviations in the orbits of Uranus and Neptune to predict the existence of a tenth planet is misguided. He himself argued that the deviations are extremely small, and their analysis relies on data which has been gathered over several centuries; since it is highly likely that the older data - which has been collected using many different reference systems and has to be converted to a common reference frame - suffers from many potential inaccuracies, he suggests it is incorrect to rely on them to draw such conclusions. E. Myles Standish, Jr. of the Jet Propulsion Laboratory even discovered that these older observations suggest irregularities in the orbits of *all* the planets, and asks: 'Did Planet X visit each one on a grand tour'?[34] However, in fairness we should stress that Van Flandern based his beliefs not only on orbital irregularities but also on the idiosyncrasies of the Neptunian planetary system.

Continuing our perusal of Van Flandern's book, we find that although he supported Sitchin's ideas of a 'dynamic' evolution of our solar system - whereby collisions and interactions continually form or change the roles of planets and satellites - his own theory of the creation of the solar system was completely at odds with Sitchin's in the detail. For example he appeared to support the commonly-held view that the Moon was formed by splitting off from the Earth, and argued that the Earth itself was one of the original members of our solar system.[35]

Furthermore he argued that there is evidence that a planet that has nothing to do with Planet X exploded between Mars and Jupiter about three million years ago, and - in a self-acknowledged departure into pure speculation in a book which is otherwise highly rigorous and scientific - suggested that *this* was the home planet of the gods who, knowing their imminent fate, escaped to Earth, created mankind and passed on their knowledge.[36] Again this was totally at odds with Sitchin: he was talking about a totally different planet (one which exploded), the timescales were about 2.5 million years too early, and his gods died out early on, unable to live long-term on Earth due to its different environment.

Intriguingly none of these discrepancies were mentioned in the book.

Although more work has been performed in the last few years since I conducted the bulk of the research for this paper,[37] I nevertheless believe we can draw only one valid conclusion. Planet X may indeed exist, as for that matter may Planet XI and others. But it has not yet been definitively discovered and observed. Furthermore the huge variety of theoretical postulations concerning its properties do not lend great credence to Sitchin's claims that its orbital eccentricity, plane, and period are so well defined that they confirm the details of what the Sumerians were recording 6000 years ago.

Furthermore, there remains an essential aspect of this debate which we have so far ignored: *it is only if an additional planet could support life that its existence or otherwise would be of any real relevance to Sitchin's theme...*

Life on Planet X?

In considering this question, let us first see what Sitchin himself has to say:[38]

> The notion that the only source of energy and heat available to living organisms is the Sun's emissions has been discarded. Thus, the spacecraft Pioneer 10 discovered that Jupiter, though much farther away from the Sun than Earth, was so hot that it must have its own sources of energy and heat. A planet with an abundance of radioactive elements in its depths would not only generate its own heat; it would also experience substantial volcanic activity. Such volcanic activity provides an atmosphere. If the planet is large enough to exert a strong gravitational pull, it will keep its atmosphere almost indefinitely. Such an atmosphere, in turn, creates a hothouse effect: it shields the planet

from the cold of outer space, and keeps the planet's own heat from dissipating into space.

What are we to make of this? For many years cosmologists had assumed that the planets in the outer reaches of the solar system would be mainly gaseous. Sitchin is right to point out that data collated by various probes over the last thirty years has proved this to be incorrect - most notably in the cases of Uranus and Neptune. Although hardly an expert, I can find no obvious fault with his assertion that distant planets can generate their own internal heat and atmosphere. However, remember that we are attempting to assess whether a race of beings who are virtually identical to ourselves (since they created us 'in their own image') could have evolved on such a planet. And in my view there are two *fundamental* objections to this.

First, both Sitchin and certain of the astronomers he cites are united in their belief that Planet X has such an elliptical orbit that at its apogee it is an extremely long distance from the Sun. Consequently, even if its core did provide sufficient heat to unfreeze the surface, *it would be in complete darkness for most of its orbit.*[39] Second, *the chances of its atmosphere being of similar composition to Earth's when it has such different circumstances are highly remote.*

Two further sources are worthy of mention. First, the apparent opinions of Harrington and Van Flandern themselves, as reported by Littmann:[40]

> He [Harrington] and Van Flandern still agree that Planet 10 should be a frozen methane, ammonia, and water world somewhat like Uranus and Neptune...

Second, the following report which appeared in the *Sunday Times* of 27 October 1996:

> A new planet with an egg-shaped orbit has been discovered by American astronomers. It orbits Cygni B, a star resembling our own sun. William Cochrane, the head of the team that discovered the new planet, is baffled. 'We don't understand how it could have formed like this' he says. 'The new planet has a *wildly changeable temperature as it swoops close to the star*, then moves out into the far reaches of its solar system.' This elliptical orbit is similar to that postulated for Planet X by astronomers such as Tom Van Flandern. Its 'discovery' is mathematical rather than visible, which places it in exactly the same category as Planet X.

The phrase which I have highlighted in italics surely indicates that, even if it had its own internal heat source, Planet X itself would suffer from similar wild fluctuations in temperature as its orbital position in relation to the Sun varied by enormous amounts - having a massive impact on any life-forms which might inhabit it.

Once again a vital piece of Sitchin's jigsaw appears not to fit at all.

Summary

- The Mesopotamians *may* have been aware of the existence of all nine currently-discovered planets in our solar system.

- They *may* also have been aware of the existence of a tenth (or to them 'twelfth') planet, which they called Nibiru - although there is minimal support for this in the *literary* works.

- Sitchin's theory of the creation of Earth, and of the role Nibiru supposedly played in it, is most certainly incorrect - both from a theoretical standpoint, and because it is far too literal an interpretation of the *Epic of Creation.*

- An additional 'Planet X' *may* yet be proved to exist by modern astronomers who are searching for it based on *theoretical* evidence.

- This planet has *not been discovered* as yet, and theories about its orbital properties vary widely. Therefore even if it is discovered it is highly unlikely to support Sitchin's detailed theories.

- If this planet exists, for it to remain undiscovered by modern technology it must have a highly eccentric orbit, or an extremely remote circular one. Either would dictate that human-like life could not have evolved and prospered there. It could not therefore be the 'planet of the gods'.

*** *** ***

Source References:

1.For those who would like to investigate further, the works Sitchin quotes are:
Charles Virolleaud, *L'Astrologie Chaldeenne*, 1903-1908.
Ernst F. Weidner, Der Tierkreis und die Wege am Himmel, (date unspecified).
S. Langdon, Babylonian Menologies and the Semitic Calendar, (date unspecified).
Fritz Hommel, *Die Astronomie der alten Chaldaer*, (date unspecified).
Charles F. Jean, *Lexicologie Sumerienne*, (date unspecified).
F. Thureau-Dangin, *Rituels Accadiens*, 1921.

These all appear to be relatively old studies; however since they do not necessarily concentrate on literary works but on perhaps lesser-studied astronomical ones, and since at least some of these authors are scholars whose work is recognised even by myself, we must not assume that their age necessarily renders them obsolete. Whether or not Sitchin's quoting from them is accurate is of course another matter - and is something I have not investigated, for reasons that will become clear.

2. These arguments are contained in Sitchin, *The Twelfth Planet* (Bear & Co, 1991), Chapters 6-7, pp. 184-188.

3. Ibid., Chapter 7, p. 189, Figures 99-101.

4. Interestingly, astronomer Tom Van Flandern (of whom more later) suggests that Mercury may indeed have been a satellite of Venus during the early development of our solar system. However this does not affect my overall impression of the evidence.

5. Sitchin, *The Twelfth Planet*, Chapter 7, pp. 191-213. Sitchin's analysis is highly detailed, and again for reasons which will become clear I have provided a brief summary only. Note also that, although I do not compare them in any detail, the many extracts from the *Epic of Creation* which he quotes are very much his own interpretations, and differ substantially from Dalley's.

6. The bulk of this information comes from a posting by Rob Hafernik, who has a degree in Aerospace Engineering and worked as a government contractor for NASA on the Space Shuttle for three years.

7. Sitchin, *The Twelfth Planet*, Chapter 8, pp. 222-3.

8. Sitchin, *Genesis Revisited* (Avon, 1990), Chapter 2, p. 39.

9. Ibid., Chapter 5.

10. Heidel, *The Babylonian Genesis* (2nd Edition, University of Chicago Press, 1951), p. 115.

11. Sitchin, *The Twelfth Planet*, Chapter 7, pp. 208-9.

12. Sitchin, *Genesis Revisited*, Chapter 3, p. 46.

13. Ibid., Chapter 1.

14. Sitchin, *The Twelfth Planet*, Chapter 8, pp. 217-8.

15. Apparently translated by R. Campbell Thompson in *Reports of the Magicians and Astronomers of Nineveh and Babylon*.

16. Sitchin, *The Twelfth Planet*, Chapter 8, pp. 218-221.

17. Taken from Sitchin, ibid., Chapter 6, p. 161, and *Genesis Revisited*, Chapter 1, p. 19.

18. Heise is a senior scientist in the High Energy Astrophysics Division of the Space Research Organization Netherlands, whose high quality Internet site indicates that Assyriology must be a serious hobby for him.

19. Jacobsen, *The Harps that Once... Sumerian Poetry in Translation* (Yale University Press, 1987), p. 240, Note 10.

20. Sitchin, *Genesis Revisited*, Chapter 4, p. 87.

21. Sitchin, *The Twelfth Planet*, Chapter 9, pp. 246-251.

22. Alford, *Gods of the New Millennium* (Hodder & Stoughton, 1997), Plate 41.

23. Sitchin, *The Twelfth Planet*, Chapter 8, pp. 215-6.

24. Dalley, *Myths from Mesopotamia* (Oxford University Press, 1989), pp. 272-3.

25. Ibid., Glossary, p. 325.

26. Sitchin, *The Twelfth Planet*, Chapter 8, pp. 216-7.

27. Sitchin, *Genesis Revisited*, Chapter 13.

28. Sitchin, ibid., Chapter 13, pp. 319-321. This is an abbreviation of Sitchin's extract, which is itself abbreviated.

29. See Mark Littmann, *Planets Beyond: Discovering the Outer Solar System* (Wiley and Sons, 1988), Chapter 13, p. 204.

30. Van Flandern, *Dark Matter, Missing Planets and New Comets* (North Atlantic Books, 1993), Chapter 17, p. 312.

31. Ibid., Chapter 18, p. 322.

32. Quoted in Littmann, op. cit., Chapter 13, p. 198.

33. Ibid., Chapter 13 and the Chronological Table on p. 258.

34. Ibid., Chapter 13, pp. 216-9.

35. Van Flandern, op. cit., Chapter 19, pp. 332-6.

36. Ibid., Chapter 19, pp. 340-2.

37. Hence my repeated use of the past tense in this section. For example, see Alan Alford's summary of Van Flandern's current 'Exploded Planet Hypothesis (it should be emphasised that Alford is now following this theory from an entirely non-Sitchinesque viewpoint). Also Van Flandern's own Meta Research organisation's web page (and again it should be emphasised that a new edition of his book has been published which I have not consulted).

38. Sitchin, *The Twelfth Planet*, Chapter 8, p. 229.

39. Again I am indebted to Rob Hafernik (see Note 6) for pointing this out—even though it should perhaps be obvious common sense!

40. Littmann, op. cit., Chapter 13, p. 199.

59-Were The Sumerians Or The Phoenicians The First Human Race Created By The Anunnaki?
Did Dr. Sitchin Cover All The Anunnaki Territories?

The Answer

Were The Sumerians Or The Phoenicians The First Human Race Created By The Anunnaki? Did Dr. Sitchin Cover All The Anunnaki Territories?

*** *** ***

UfoCenter, UK claimed that "Most of Sitchin's work is based on his reading of ancient texts in obscure languages. How Sitchin came by his mastery of these languages is not clear. There is no evidence that he ever underwent formal schooling in them. Since so few people know these languages, it is also difficult for others to critique Sitchin's work. One linguistic scholar who has reviewed Sitchin's claims, however, believes his interpretations of the ancient texts are profoundly wrong and that Sitchin's knowledge of the languages in which the texts are written is rudimentary at best."

A few linguists from Ivy League universities in the United States reported that Dr. Sitchin's translations of the Sumerian texts were not accurate at all. Those academicians claimed that he took liberty in the translation and added his own interpretations and personal views which are not substantiated by historical, linguistic and archeological facts. In other words, Dr. Sitchin made up the whole thing! I found their attitude to be sarcastic and their statements not totally honest to say the least.

I have studied the ancient languages of the Near and Middle East, and various regional tribal dialects, and the origin of writing going back in history as far as the dawn of the Phoenician Alphabet, for almost twenty five years...this could give me certain knowledge in the field and a justification to come forward and state without hesitation that the majority of the work of Dr. Sitchin is reliable, accurate and stimulating.

I have studied those languages in college and ON LOCATION for approximately 15 years.

Yes, some descendants of the Sumerians and Babylonians still speak these vanished languages at home, and in their very small communities in Iraq, Syria, Turkey, and Lebanon.

I met many of them, and exchanged information and compared historical and linguistic notes. My direct rapports with them and the in-depth investigative studies of those ancient languages convinced me that Dr. Sitchin's work is most authoritative.

In my opinion, Dr. Sitchin is a pioneer in the field. Of course, not all his theories are hundred per cent correct, and most certainly, some of his translations of the Sumerian texts (Few passages) were not totally accurate. Nevertheless, Dr. Sitchin shed a bright light on a multitude of possibilities regarding the genetic origin of mankind, the human race-extraterrestrials connection, and chronology of humanity development. Although he is not a "professional" linguist or a certified translator of ancient languages, particularly Sumerian, Babylonian and Akkadian, Dr. Sitchen's work remains the primordial, paramount and most authoritative source of reference on the direct link between the Sumerians and the Anunnaki. There is no doubt about it.

You can't evaluate and criticize the literary wealth and beauty of the poetry of Victor Hugo if you don't know French.

And you can't fully absorb and sense the mesmerizing musical beauty, and breathtaking linguistic imageries of Abu Tib Al Mutanabi if you did not study Arabic literature in Arabic. Of course, you can still study Hugo and Al Mutanabi in English or even in Chinese, but it will never be the same, and you will never grasp the nuances, flair and cache of the original texts, no matter how accurate and comprehensive were the translations.

Same principle applies to the scenario of Dr. Sitchin's translations.

Those who have criticized Dr. Sitchin and questioned the accuracy and validity of his translations and interpretations of the ancient Sumerian texts have their own reasons, and motives, and frankly, their criticism did not solve any problem, nor enriched our understanding of the Sumerian civilization. Consequently, we should not spend more time on this subject.

98% of the readers will never know who is right and who is wrong (Sitchin or his critics) unless and until they become well-versed in Sumerian, and this is not going to happen in the near future. It is more likely that they could become prolifically experts in new computer programs languages than in Sumerian or ancient languages of vanished civilizations of the Middle and Near East.

Then, major questions arise:

- Did Dr. Sitchin cover all the Anunnaki territories by exclusively focusing on Sumerian texts?
- In other words, were the Sumerians de facto the first and only human race who knew the Anunnaki? Were they the first contactees?

- What about academic and historic claims that other civilizations in the region such as the Phoenicians were the first human race to be genetically created by the Anunnaki?
- Could we conclude from ancient Phoenicians texts and tablets found in Carthage, Island of Arwad, Amrit, Ugarit, Bijjeh, Amchit, Byblos, Antioch, Tyre, Sidon, Tartous, Lattakieh, Batroon, Baalbeck, Crete, and even in Sicily, that The Phoenicians were Anunnaki's first "human creation"?

And the answer is: Absolutely Yes!

> Long, longtime before the Anunnaki landed in Summer, and centuries before the Anunnaki-Sumerian texts were written, the Phoenicians had direct contacts with the Anunnaki, as well as with other extraterrestrial races. The Phoenician civilization is much older than the Sumerian civilization. And The Phoenician language gave birth to all the known languages on earth (except Chinese, Korean and Japanese), including Greek, Latin, Aramaic, Hebrew, Egyptian, and Romance languages. Even the name of the deities supreme gods and goddesses, rulers of the earth, angels, demons, demi-gods, and early prophets in the Bible in the Habiru tradition, in the Egyptian pantheon and scriptures were derived from the Phoenician language.

*** *** ***

In the beginning, at the very dawn of religions in the Near East, and the Middle East (Lebanon known as Phoenicia, Syria, Palestine/Israel, Isle of Arwad, Cyprus, Jordan, Iraq, Sinai), the Mother Goddess (Ishtar, Ashtaroot in Phoenician, and Inanna in Sumerian) was considered the life giver and the creator of all life-forms, including mankind. The world, the planets, animals and all humans were created by a woman; a Phoenician Mother Goddess, NOT Sumerian. And this goddess was worshiped by the Phoenicians, Canaanites, Hebrews, Akkadians, Hittites, Babylonians, Sumerians, Egyptians et al...But later on in history, two things happened:

- 1-Religions became dominated by male gods. Nevertheless, female goddesses remained extremely important, and played a paramount role in the daily life of humans. The supreme deity became a male god called "EL" and "Baal" in Phoenician; in Aramaic, it is "El", and "Eli" and means "first, ultimate, god, power"; in early Hebrew, it is "Elohi", and "Adonai" (Taken from the Phoenician Adon, another major Phoenician god) and it means "origin, my master, my lord, number one, and god of gods"; In Arabic, it is "Ilahi", and "Allah".

314

- 2-The early Phoenician accounts of initial contacts between the inhabitants of Phoenicia and the Lyrans and the Anunnaki vanished, and were substituted by Sumerian texts found in Iraq. But later, those precious Phoenician scriptures resurfaced and were preserved by the Ulema, The Knights of St. John Order of Malta, "The Templars", The Cathars", The "Serpent Society" of Island of Arwad, etc…but it was too late for the Phoenician accounts to be re-examined and considered as the first texts and evidence on contacts between mankind and extraterrestrials. Instead, the Sumerian texts, thanks to the translations of Dr. Sitchin became the most accepted and authoritative source of information and evidence in the field.

*** *** ***

Titans and Extraterrestrial Gods Were Phoenicians

We find in the Phoenician cosmogony that the Titans (Rephaim) derive their origin from the Phoenician gods Agrus and Agrotus.

This connects the Phoenicians with that island in the remote west, in the midst of ocean, where, according to the Greeks, the Titans dwelt. According to Sanchoniathon, *Ouranos* was the son of Autochthon, and, according to Plato, Autochthon was one of the ten kings of Atlantis. He married his sister Ge. He is the Uranos of the Greeks, who was the son of *Gaea* (the earth), whom he married.

The Phoenicians tell us, "Ouranos had by Ge four sons: Ilus (El), who is called Chronos, and Betylus (Beth-El), and Dagon, which signifies bread-corn, and Atlas (Tammuz?)." Here, again, we have the names of two other kings of Atlantis. These four sons probably represented four races, the offspring of the earth. The Greek Uranos was the father of Chronos, and the ancestor of Atlas.

The Phoenician god Ouranos had a great many other wives: his wife Ge was jealous; they quarreled, and he attempted to kill the children he had by her. This is the legend which the Greeks told of Zeus and Juno.

In the Phoenician mythology Chronos raised a rebellion against Ouranos, and, after a great battle, dethroned him. In the Greek legends it is Zeus who attacks and overthrows his father, Chronos. Ouranos had a daughter called Astarte (Ashtoreth), another called Rhea. "And Dagon, after he had found out bread-corn and the plough, was called Zeus-Arotrius."

We find also, in the Phoenician legends, mention made of Poseidon, founder and king of Atlantis.

Chronos gave Attica to his daughter Athena, as in the Greek legends. In a time of plague be sacrificed his son to Ouranos, and "circumcised himself, and compelled his allies to do the same thing." It would thus appear that this singular rite, practised as we have seen by the Atlantidae of the Old and New Worlds and the red men of America, dates back, as we might have expected, to Atlantis.

*** *** ***

Phoenicians Connected to Atlantis Extraterrestrial Civilization

"Chronos visits the different regions of the habitable world."

He gave Egypt as a kingdom to the god Taaut, who had invented the alphabet. The Egyptians called him Thoth, and he was represented among them as "the god of letters, the clerk of the under-world," bearing a tablet, pen, and palm-branch.

This not only connects the Phoenicians with Atlantis, but shows the relations of Egyptian civilization to both Atlantis and the Phoenicians. There can be no doubt that the royal personages who formed the gods of Sumer and Greece were also the gods of the Phoenicians.

We have seen the Autochthon of Plato reappearing in the Autochthon of the Phoenicians; the Atlas of Plato in the Atlas of the Phoenicians; the Poseidon of Plato in the Poseidon of the Phoenicians; while the kings Mestor and Mneseus of Plato are probably the gods Misor and Amynus of the Phoenicians.

Sanchoniathon tells us, after narrating all the discoveries by which the people advanced to civilization, that the Cabiri set down their records of the past by the command of the god Taaut, "and they delivered them to their successors and to foreigners, of whom one was Isiris (Osiris), the inventor of the three letters, the brother of Chua, who is called the first Phoenician."[1]

This would show that the first Phoenician came long after this line of the kings or gods, and that he was a foreigner, as compared with them; and, therefore, that it could not have been the Phoenicians proper who made the several inventions narrated by Sanchoniathon, but some other race, from whom the Phoenicians might have been descended.

And in the delivery of their records to the foreigner Osiris, the god of Egypt, we have evidence that Egypt derived her civilization from Atlantis and Phoenicia.

316

Max Müller says: "The Semitic languages also are all varieties of one form of speech. Though we do not know that primitive language from which the Semitic dialects diverged, yet we know that at one time such language must have existed; but we can well understand how both may have proceeded from one common source. They are both channels supplied from one river, and they carry, though not always on the surface, floating materials of language which challenge comparison, and have already yielded satisfactory results to careful analyzers."[2]

There was an ancient tradition among the Persians that the Phoenicians migrated from the shores of the Erythraean Sea, and this has been supposed to mean the Persian Gulf; but there was a very old city of Erythia, in utter ruin in the time of Strabo, which was built in some ancient age, long before the founding of Gades, near the site of that town, on the Atlantic coast of Spain. May not this town of Erythia have given its name to the adjacent sea? And this may have been the starting-point of the Phoenicians in their European migrations. It would even appear that there was an island of Erythea. In the Greek mythology the tenth labor of Hercules consisted in driving away the cattle of Geryon, who lived in the island of Erythea, "an island somewhere in the remote west, beyond the Pillars of Hercules."[3] Hercules stole the cattle from this remote oceanic island, and, returning drove them "through Iberia, Gaul, over the Alps, and through Italy."[4] It is probable that a people emigrating from the Erythraean Sea, that is, from the Atlantic, first gave their name to a town on the coast of Spain, and at a later date to the Persian Gulf--as we have seen the name of York carried from England to the banks of the Hudson, and then to the Arctic Circle. The builders of the Central American cities are reported to have been a bearded race.

The Phoenicians, in common with the Indians, practised human sacrifices to a great extent; they worshipped fire and water, adopted the names of the animals whose skins they wore--that is to say, they had the totemic system--telegraphed by means of fires, poisoned their arrows, offered peace before beginning battle, and used drums.[5]

The extent of country covered by the commerce of the Phoenicians represents to some degree the area of the old Atlantean Empire.

Their colonies and trading-posts extended east and west from the shores of the Black Sea, through the Mediterranean to the west coast of Africa and of Spain, and around to Ireland and England; while from north to south they ranged from the Baltic to the Persian Gulf. They touched every point where civilization in later ages made its appearance.

Strabo estimated that they had three hundred cities along the west coast of Africa. When Columbus sailed to discover a new world, or re-discover an old one, he took his departure from a Phoenician seaport, founded by that great race two thousand five hundred years previously. This Atlantean sailor, with his Phoenician features, sailing from an Atlantean port, simply re-opened the path of commerce and colonization which had been closed when Plato's island sunk in the sea. And it is a curious fact that Columbus had the antediluvian world in his mind's eye even then, for when he reached the mouth of the Orinoco he thought it was the river Gihon, that flowed out of Paradise, and he wrote home to Spain, "There are here great indications suggesting the proximity of the earthly Paradise, for not only does it correspond in mathematical position with the opinions of the holy and learned theologians, but all other signs concur to make it probable."

Sanchoniathon claims that the learning of Egypt, Greece, and Judaea was derived from the Phoenicians. It would appear probable that, while other races represent the conquests or colonizations of Atlantis, the Phoenicians succeeded to their arts, sciences, and especially their commercial supremacy; and hence the close resemblances which we have found to exist between the Phoenicians and the people of America.

Upon the Tsurian sea the people live
Who style themselves Phoenicians...
These were the first great founders of the world--
Founders of cities and of mighty states--
Who showed a path through seas before unknown.
In the first ages, when the sons of men
Knew not which way to turn them, they assigned
To each his first department; they bestowed
Of land a portion and of sea a lot,
And sent each wandering tribe far off to share
A different soil and climate. Hence arose
The great diversity, so plainly seen,
'Mid nations widely severed.

Dyonysius of Susiana, A.D. 3

Sources:
1.Lenormant and Chevallier, "Ancient History of the East," vol. ii., p. 228.
2."Outlines of Philosophy of History," vol. i., p. 475.
3.Murray's "Mythology," p. 257.
4.Ibid.
5.Bancroft's "Native Races," vol. v., p. 77.
6.Text: Phoenicaorg.

I have established the link between the Anunnaki and the Phoenicians, and provided ample information and historical data on the subject in two books I wrote: "Anunnaki Encyclopedia", and "Anunnaki Greatest Secrets Revealed By The Phoenicians."Please refer to.

*** *** ***

Also in these two books, I provided information related to the origin of early Christians in Anatolia, Asia Minor, Syria, Iraq and Lebanon, and their DNA relation - to/with - the Phoenicians as the descendants and remnants of the Anunnaki on earth.

My studies and research in this context were based upon ancient Phoenician tablets, The Rama-Dosh Book, Greek texts, and several early Christian writings by founding fathers of the Church in the Eastern world, most notably, Bishop Eusebius of Caesarea (260 - 341 AD). Eusebius Pamphili was the Bishop of Caesarea in Palestine. He is considered the "Father of Church History"; the scriptures of Sanchuniathon of Berytus (Beirut) or Sakkun-yathon; Philo of Byblius (Byblos) or Herennios Philon of Byblos (64 - 141 AD). He was a Phoenician scholar and Roman citizen, born in Byblos, and representative of the Roman Consul Herennius Severus; Porphyry Malchus of Tyre (223 - 309 AD) was born in Tyre and studied in Athens, before joining the Neoplatonic group of Plotinus in Rome were he studied philosophy; my studies of ancient Phoenicians tablets and texts on location.

*** *** ***

60-The Parallel Universes And Other Dimensions:
Do They Exist? Where?

The Answer

The Parallel Dimensions And Other Universes: Do They Exist? Where?

YES! According To Science

Supersymmetry and Parallel Dimensions...Beyond our visible world...

Harvard Professor, Dr. Lisa Randall believes the answer to what physicists call the hierarchy problem may lie outside our visible world. Gravity may be weak compared to forces such as electromagnetism, because it is concentrated in another dimension. Along with Raman Sundrum of Johns Hopkins University, she published two papers in 1999 that have changed how physicists think about the structure of space. Randall proposed that the universe has more than four dimensions (three of space and one of time) and that these extra dimensions could be infinitely large. Randall who has influenced string theorists, also claim that extra dimensions exist. String theory is a model of physics in which building blocks are one-dimensional objects called strings instead of zero-dimensional particles like electrons.

Extra dimensions could be hidden and infinitely large

Until now, string theorists have accounted for the fact that we can detect only three dimensions by claiming that the extra dimensions are curled up into infinitesimal loops and thus imperceptible. Randall claims that these dimensions could be infinitely large provided that space has a warped geometry. In effect, we could be living in a three-dimensional pocket of higher dimensional space. Randall refers to these pockets in space as branes. Like a bead on a wire that can only move along one dimension, a brane may restrict our motion to three dimensions although other dimensions exist.

With branes, Randall discovered a way to explain how extra dimensions could be hidden and infinitely large.

Because the math behind her theory works, theoretical physicists have paid close attention to her research. In trying to better understand supersymmetry, Randall discovered that extra dimensions of space could solve its problems.

If other dimensions exist, then it becomes possible to separate particles and to prevent unwanted interactions.

Randall's theory of extra dimensions also would answer the hierarchy problem.

With the help of Andreas Karch of the University of Washington, Randall found that gravity could be concentrated somewhere in an extra dimension.

The force's strength becomes exponentially weaker further from the gravity brane. "Gravity is so strongly peaked near the brane that gravity doesn't leak away," Randall says. "If you are anywhere except the brane where gravity is concentrated, you would see gravity as very weak." (Source: HarvardCrimson)

*** *** ***

Other Dimensions

The idea of another dimension - or more than one other dimension - has been theorized for many years, and is a cornerstone of many religions. Indeed, even Albert Einstein speculated about the possibility of the existence of a parallel universe. A scientific article entitled "The Universe's Unseen Dimensions," released in August, 2000, postulates that we may actually have scientific proof of other dimensions within the next 10 years! Proof such as this will not only rock the scientific community, but will undoubtedly also shed new light on many currently unexplainable paranormal events.

Psychics and paranormal researchers have long suspected one or more parallel universes, and have often speculated that there may be doorways or "portals" in certain areas that allow entities to travel into our dimension.

These entities may be spirits, demons, extraterrestrials, or something we have never even imagined.

Well-known hauntings, that persist over long time spans, are likely candidates as portals - as opposed to sites that have been the location of an isolated or otherwise unconnected violent death or tragic accident to which the haunting can be fairly easily traced.

Many old Indian burial grounds seem to act as portals, for reasons unknown, other than the Indians consciously located their burial grounds in places that they felt were close to the after-death realm.

How they determined which sites fit this criteria is lost knowledge, but a disproportionate number of these "sacred burial grounds" are known hotspots for paranormal activity. Other non-Indian cemeteries are also suspected portal sites, probably for the same reasons - either consciously or unconsciously, the site chosen for the burials was already the site of a portal.

It appears that portals are at fixed places all over the world, and that they don't move or drift from place to place. Whether new portals open up from time to time is unclear, but this definitely warrants further study.

Controlled studies done around suspected portals have revealed that there are definite temperature fluctuations in the vicinity of the site. Photographs taken at suspected sites often produce amazing results, and reveal mists, orbs, light streaks, figures, and even saucer-shaped objects - all of which are unseen by the bystanders at the scene, though many do report feeling cold chills.

People who are more sensitive report that they get a feeling of "magnetism" at suspected portal sites, and often report that they sense large numbers of entities passing back and forth - which is unusual in an ordinary haunting.

One might wonder why we, as humans, don't seem to be able to pass through these doorways into other dimensions. It appears that the reason is that we are hindered by our physical bodies.

However, in meditation or an astral projection situation, it does seem that we may have the capabilities to pass through and explore these realms, and at this writing we are in the process of seeking out reports from people who think they have actually experienced this. (Source: Mystical Blaze)

*** *** ***

Extraterrestrials, and "entities from higher spheres" allegedly explained to contactees, and even to prominent scientists working in secret military bases in the United States, that there is an absolute and an infinite space with multiple dimensions independent of time In this absolute world, cosmic energy exists in a variety of forms, both matter, and anti-matter. Each with its own logic, reason, geometry, dimensions, beyond space-time properties, and physical parameters. Those parallel universes are the universes of multidimensional and vibrational extraterrestrials. And they exist with or without relations to other worlds, including Earth.

To us, these concepts are incomprehensible. They defy our laws of physics and perhaps terrestrial common sense. One ufologist said: "The origin of the absolute space and the origin of the energy is unknown even to the aliens. They believe it always existed." It seems like magic and astral mythology. Also, it is hard to believe or disbelief those concepts and theories because humans have not yet explored those dimensions and the frontiers of space-time. The Anunnaki live in those dimensions, as well as in spheres similar to earth. Perhaps, mainstream, as well ad avant-garde science could explain these hypotheses and theories. Here are some of the most mind-boggling views of leading scientists, and excerpts from fascinating articles on the subject…

*** *** ***

How do we know we live in a four-dimensional universe?
On Gravity, Oreos and a Theory of Everything

The portal to the fifth dimension, sadly, is closed. There used to be an ice cream parlor in the student center at the Massachusetts Institute of Technology. And it was there, in the summer of 1998, that Lisa Randall, now a professor of physics at Harvard and a bit of a chocoholic, and Raman Sundrum, a professor at Johns Hopkins, took an imaginary trip right out of this earthly plane into a science fiction realm of parallel universes, warped space and otherworldly laws of physics.

They came back with a possible answer to a question that has tormented scientists for decades, namely why gravity is so weak compared with the other forces of nature: in effect, we are borrowing it from another universe. In so doing, Dr. Randall and Dr. Sundrum helped foment a revolution in the way scientists think about string theory - the vaunted "theory of everything" - raising a glimmer of hope that coming experiments may actually test some of its ineffable sounding concepts.Their work undermined well-worn concepts like the idea that we can even know how many dimensions of space we live in, or the reality of gravity, space and time. The work has also made a star and an icon of Dr. Randall.

The attention has been increased by the recent publication to laudatory reviews of her new book, "Warped Passages, Unraveling the Mysteries of the Universe's Hidden Dimensions," A debate broke out on the physics blog Cosmic Variance a few weeks about whether it was appropriate, as a commentator on NPR had said, to say she looked like Jodie Foster.

"How do we know we live in a four-dimensional universe?" she asked a crowd who filled the Hayden Planetarium on a stormy night last week."You think gravity is what you see. We're always just looking at the tail of things."

Although it is the unanswerable questions that most appeal to her now, it was the answerable ones that drew her to science, especially math, as a child, the middle of three daughters of a salesman for an engineering firm, and a teacher, in Fresh Meadows, Queens. "I really liked the fact that it had definite answers," Dr. Randall said.

At Stuyvesant High School, where she was in the same class as Brian Greene, the future Columbia string theorist and best-selling author, she was the first girl to serve as captain of the school's math team, and she won the famous Westinghouse Science Talent Search competition with a project about complex numbers. She went on to Harvard where she stayed until 1987 when she emerged with a Ph.D. in physics. Those were heady times in physics. Fired by the dream of a unified theory of everything, theorists flocked to string theory, which envisioned the fundamental elements of nature as tiny wriggling strings. Dr. Randall, however, resisted this siren call, at least for a while. For one thing, physicists thought it would take a particle accelerator 10 million billion times as powerful as anything on earth to produce an actual string and test the theory.

String theory also stubbornly requires space-time to have 10 dimensions, not the 4 (3 of space and 1 of time) that we experience. Preferring to stay closer to testable reality, Dr. Randall was drawn to a bottom-up approach to theoretical physics, trying to build models that explain observed phenomena and hoping to discover principles with wider application. But Dr. Randall and string theory had their own kismet.In the mid-90's, theorists discovered that the theory was even richer than its founders had thought, describing not just strings but so-called branes, as in membranes, of all dimensions. Our own universe could be such a brane, an island of three dimensions floating in a sea of higher dimension, like a bubble in the sea. But there could be membranes with five, six, seven or more dimensions coexisting and mingling like weird cosmic soap bubbles in what theorists sometimes call the multiverse."The stuff we're really famous for was really lucky in a way,"

Dr. Randall said.In the summer of 1998, after postdoctoral stints at Harvard and the University of California, Berkeley, she was a tenured M.I.T. professor ready to move to Princeton. She wondered then whether parallel universes could help solve a vexing problem with a favorite theories of particle physicists.

That theory, known as supersymmetry, was invented in turn to solve another problem - the enormous gulf known as the hierarchy problem between gravity and the other forces. Naïve calculations from first principles suggest, Dr. Randall said, that gravity should be 10 million billion times as strong as it is. You might find it hard to imagine gravity as a weak force, but consider, says Dr. Randall, that a small magnet can hold up a paper clip, even though the entire earth is pulling down on it. But there was a hitch with the way the theory worked out in our universe.

It predicted reactions that are not observed. Dr. Randall wondered if the missing reactions could be explained by positing that some aspects of the theory were quarantined in a separate universe.

She called up Dr. Sundrum, who was then a fellow at Boston University and happy to collaborate, having worked with her before. A lot of physics is taste, he explained, discerning, for example, what is an important and a potentially soluble problem. Dr. Randall's biggest strength, he said, is a kind of "unworldly" instinct. "She has a great nose," Dr. Sundrum said. "It's a mystery to those of us - hard to understand, almost to the point of amusement - how she does it without any clear sign of what led her to that path," he continued. "She gives no sign of why she thinks what she thinks."They began by drawing pictures and making crude estimates over ice cream and coffee in that ice cream parlor, which is now a taqueria. What they drew pictures of was a kind of Oreo cookie multiverse, an architecture similar to one first discovered as a solution of the string equations by Edward Witten of the Institute for Advanced Study and Petr Horava, now at Berkeley. Dr. Randall and Dr. Sundrum's model consisted of a pair of universes, four-dimensional branes, thinly separated by a five-dimensional space poetically called the bulk.

When they solved the equations for this setup, they discovered that the space between the branes would be warped. Objects, for example, would appear to grow larger or smaller and get less massive or more massive as they moved back and forth between the branes. Such a situation, they realized to their surprise, could provide a natural explanation for the hierarchy problem without invoking supersymmetry. Suppose, they said, that gravity is actually inherently as strong as the other forces, but because of the warping gravity is much much stronger on one of the branes than on the other one, where we happen to live. So we experience gravity as extremely weak. "You can be only a modest distance away from the gravity brane," Dr. Randall said, "and gravity will be incredibly weak." A result was a natural explanation for why atomic forces outgun gravity by 10 million billion to 1. Could this miracle be true? Crazy as it sounded, they soon discovered an even more bizarre possibility. The fifth dimension could actually be infinite and we would not have noticed it.

In this case, there would be only one brane, ours, containing both gravity as we know it and the rest of nature. But it would warp space in the same way as in the first model, trapping gravity nearby so that we would experience space-time as four-dimensional. This new single brane model did not solve the weak gravity problem, Dr. Randall admitted, but it was a revelation, that an infinite ocean of space could be sitting next to us undetected.

"So when we wrote this paper, what we were concentrating on was this amazing fact that really had been overlooked for 100 years - well, years, whatever - that you can have this infinite extra dimension," she said. "I mean it was quite wild."This was not the first time that theorists had tinkered with the extra dimensions of string theory, dimensions that had been presumed to be coiled out of sight of experiment, into tight loops so small that not even an electron could enter. In 1998, three theorists - Nima Arkani-Hamed of Harvard, Gia Divali of New York University and Savas Dimopoulos of Stanford (a group known in physics as A.D.D.) - had surprised everybody by suggesting that if one or two of the curled-up extra dimensions had sizes as big as a tenth of millimeter or so (gigantic on particle physics scales), gravity would be similarly diluted and weakened. When Dr. Randall and Dr. Sundrum published their first paper, describing the two-brane scheme, in 1999, she said that many physicists did not recognize it as a new idea and not just an elaboration on the large extra dimensions of the A.D.D. group. In fact, she said, the extra dimensions don't have to be very large in the two-brane theory, less than a millionth of a trillionth of a trillionth of an inch. When they published their second paper, about the infinite dimension, she said, even some of their best friends, reserved judgment.

But by the time a long-planned workshop on strings and particle physics at the Kavli Institute for Theoretical Physics in Santa Barbara rolled around that fall, string theorists were excited about the Randall-Sundrum work and the earlier A.D.D. proposal.The reason was simple: If they were very lucky and one of these versions of string theory was the one that nature had adopted, it could actually be tested in the Large Hadron Collider, the giant particle accelerator due to go into operation at CERN near Geneva in 2007.

Colliding beams of protons with a combined energy of 14 trillion electron volts, the collider could produce particles like gravitons going off into the fifth dimension like billiard balls hopping off the table, black holes or even the illusive strings themselves.

"If this is the way gravity works in high-energy physics, we'll know about it," Dr. Randall said. Although physicists agree that these theories are a long shot, the new work has captured their imaginations and encouraged them to take a fresh look at the possibilities for the universe and their new accelerator.

Dr. Greene of Columbia said, "Sometimes it takes an outsider to come into a field and see what is being missed, or taken for granted."

At first the idea that extra dimensions could be bigger than any of us had thought was shocking, he said. Andrew Strominger, a Harvard string theorist, said: "Before A.D.D. we believed there was no hope of finding evidence for string theory at the Large Hadron Collider, an assumption that was wrong. It shows how unimaginative and narrow-minded we are. I see that as cause for optimism. Science and nature are full of surprises, we never see what's going to happen next."

It was shortly before a conference that Dr. Randall had organized during the Kavli workshop that she had her own experience with gravity: she fell while rock climbing in Yosemite, breaking several bones. Only a day before, she said, she had completed a climb of Half Dome and was feeling cocky. Another symptom of gravity's weakness is that a rope is sufficient to hold a human body up against earth's pull, but Dr. Randall was still on the first leg of her climb and hadn't yet attached it to the rock.. She woke up in a helicopter. For a long time, she said, new parts kept hurting as old ones healed. "I was very much not myself. I didn't even like chocolate and coffee."

Since she was the conference organizer, her ordeal was more public than she would have liked. "In some ways you sort of want to do this in private," Dr. Randall said. "On the other hand people were really nice." After two years at Princeton, Dr. Randall returned to M.I.T. in 2000, but then a year later moved to Harvard, by then a powerhouse in string theory. She was the third woman to get tenure in physics there. Dr. Randall, 43 and single, prefers not to talk about "the women in science thing," as she calls it. That subject that gained notoriety earlier this year when Harvard's President Larry Summers famously ventured that a relative lack of women in the upper ranks of science might reflect innate deficiencies, but Dr. Randall said it had been beaten to death. Asked if she would rather be a woman in science than talk about women in science, Dr. Randall said, "I'd rather be a scientist." She did say that part of the reason she had written her book was to demonstrate that that there were women out there doing this kind of science. "I did feel extra pressure to write a good book," she said, adding that the response in reviews and emails from readers had been much greater than she had expected. She was particularly pleased that some of her readers were attentive and studious enough to catch on to various puns and games she had inserted in the book, like the frequent references to Alice in Wonderland, which, she said, is a pun on "one-d-land." Dr. Randall is intrigued by that fact that her results, as well as other results from string theory seem to paint a picture of the universe in which theories with different numbers of dimensions in them all give the same physics? She and Andreas Karch of the University of Washington have found, for example, that the fifth dimension could be so warped that the number of dimensions you see would depend on where you were. Our own universe might just be a three-dimensional "sinkhole," she says. "It's not completely obvious what gravity is, fundamentally, or what dimensions are, fundamentally," she said over lunch. "One of these days we'll understand better what we mean, what is the fundamental thing that's given us space in the first place and dimensions of space in particular." She held out less hope for time, saying, "I just don't understand it. "Space we can make progress with."

Is time an illusion? "I wish time were an illusion," she said as she carved up the last of her chocolate bread pudding, "but unfortunately it seems all too real." (Sources: 1-Denis Overbye; 2-New York Times)

The Universe Duplicates Itself According To The Anunnaki!

Is the universe -- correction: "our" universe -- no more than a speck of cosmic dust amid an infinite number of parallel worlds? asked a science writer at Agence Press in Paris. According to the Anunnaki, Earth is a small dot on the map of the universe. In fact, there are many worlds, many universes, many dimensions, and each one of them is different from the other. And several different laws of physics govern each separate world. For instance, you are 175 pounds on earth and you walk very normally. In other dimension, you become 50 pounds and barely you could move, yet, in a fifth dimension, you become 300 pounds and you will be able to fly. How our sane mind can explain these phenomena?

Another scenario; on earth, it would take an aeroplane taking off from New York 7 hours to reach Paris, roughly. On another dimension or other world, the same aeroplane will land in Paris in 2 minutes, considering that there are Paris and New York in that dimension. Well, the Anunnaki explain that in fact, there are manyNew Yorks and other Parises in many dimensions. And speed changes considerably in other worlds, because speed is no longer regulated by time. And why is that?

Because, in those dimensions, time does not exist, and copies of everything occurring on a physical plane could and would exist somewhere else on other planets or dimensions.

The universe duplicates itself. Now, try to figure out this dilemma?

These phenoma have disturbed and intrigued so many hard-nosed scientists, physicists, astronomers, mathematicians, cosmic explorers, and cosmologists too.

The Anunnaki-Ulema also said that in other dimensions, you can visit your friend and by the same token, leave yourself at home. They meant that, in fact you will be visiting your friend in blood and flesh, but an identical copy of yourself (Also blood and flesh) stays at home, because you can separate yourself from time, space, and matter. On earth, avant-garde quantum physicists seem to accept this idea.

According to them, a human being can duplicate and reduplicate himself/herself infinitely in other dimensions, because the newly created body will not occupy two spots in the same place.

This explanation is more confusing than the Anunnaki-Ulema theory.

But apparently, advocates of the multiple universes theories, M Theory, String Theory, Singularity Theory, and the Everything Theory, talk about these astonishing concepts all the time, and broadcast their revolutionary ideas on the air.

330

The History Channel and the Science Channel in the United States regularly invite those scientists to explain their views which are highly welcomed by the scientific community, but leave the inquisitive viewers - who after having watched the televised show for two hours - remain in a state of total confusion and perplexity. Science writers at Agency Press said: "We may not be able -- at least not yet -- to prove they exist, many serious scientists say, but there are plenty of reasons to think that parallel dimensions are more than figments of eggheaded imagination.

The specter of shadow worlds has been thrown into relief by the release of "The Golden Compass," a Hollywood blockbuster adapted from the first volume of Philip Pullman's classic sci-fi trilogy, "His Dark Materials". In the film, an orphaned girl living in an alternate universe goes on a quest, accompanied by an animal manifestation of her soul, to rescue kidnapped children and discover the secret of a contaminating dust said to be leaking from a parallel realm." Talking bears and magic dust aside, the basic premise of Pullman's fantasy is not beyond the scientific pale."The idea of multiple universes is more than a fantastic invention -- it appears naturally within several scientific theories, and deserves to be taken seriously," said Aurelien Barrau, a French particle physicist at the European Organization for Nuclear Research (CERN), hardly a hotbed of flaky science.

The multiverse is no longer a model, it is a consequence of our models," explained Barrau, who recently published an essay for CERN defending the concept. There are several competing and overlapping theories about parallel universes, but the most basic is based on the simple, if mind-boggling, idea that if the universe is infinite then logically everything that could possibly occur has happened or will happen.

Try this on for size: a copy of you living on a planet and in a solar system like ours is reading these words just as you are. Your lives have been carbon copies up to now, but maybe he or she will keep reading even if you don't, says Max Tegmark, a cosmologist at MIT in Boston, Massachusetts.

The existence of such a doppleganger "does not even assume speculative modern physics, merely that space is infinite and rather uniformly filled with matter as indicated by recent astronomical observations," Tegmark concluded in a study of parallel universes published by Cambridge University.

"Your alter ego is simply a prediction of the so-called concordance model of cosmology," he said.

Another type of multiverse arises with the theory of chaotic inflation, which tells us that all these parallel worlds are expanding so rapidly -- stretching further and further in to space -- that they remain out of reach even if one could travel at the speed of light forever.

Things get even stranger when one brings the often counter-intuitive laws of quantum physics into the picture, these experts say.

In a landmark paper published in 1957 while he was still a graduate student at Princeton University, mathematician Hugh Everett showed how quantum theory predicts that a single classical reality should gradually split into separate but simultaneously existing realms. "This is simply a way of trusting strictly the fundamental equations of quantum mechanics," says Barrau. "The worlds are not spatially separated, but exist as kinds of 'parallel' universes." The borderline between physics and metaphysics is not defined by whether an entity can be observed, but whether it is testable, pointed out Tegmark. There are many phenomena -- black holes, curved space, the slowing of time at high speeds, even a round and rotating Earth -- that were once rejected as scientific heresy before being proven through experimentation, even if some remain beyond the grasp of observation, he said. He concluded that it was becoming increasingly clear that multiverse models grounded in modern physics could be empirically testable, predictive and disprovable. (Source: Agence Press.)

This leads us to this question: **Is time-travel possible?**

According to the Ulemas, yes, you can! They said, humans and non-physical entities can travel back in time, and zoom into the future via many means and "techniques" such as, to name a few:

1-The Duplication Process;
2-Bending time by escaping the cosmic net;
3-Reducing distances by traveling faster than the speed of light;
4-Self-Projection through the cosmic monitor called in their language, the "Miraya";
5-Defragmenting molecules;
6-Substance Transmutation;
7-Via a wormhole;
8-Via the Anunnaki "Ba'abs"; Stargates.

Ironically and fortunately for mankind, many of our world-famous avant-garde quantum physics theorists like Dr. Michio Kaku, and Dr. John Schwarz prophets of the Superstring Theory, said yes, we can travel back in time, because there are no laws of physics that contradict this possibility. Many of their assumptions find fertile soil in the explanations given by the Ulemas and the Anunnaki.

One more time: Is time-travel possible? Asked Dr. Randy Inmerganson. And he answered: That depends (as Mr. Clinton might say) on what you mean by "time-travel." In a sense, we're all "time-travelers," since we experience time flowing while we travel from our past to our future.

That's the normal, boring sense of time-travel. But can we zip forward hundreds or thousands of years into our future? Thanks to Einstein, all physicists agree that the answer is yes. All you need is a very fast rocket-ship that can get you up to almost lightspeed. With that, you can go as far into the future as you want. That's an exciting prospect, but...**Can you travel backward in time?**

In theory, you could, via a wormhole. In Einstein's classical theory of general relativity, that is. But quantum mechanics might destabilize it, preventing you from actually going through the wormhole. As of now, the question is not quite decided, but it looks like quantum mechanics may be a show-stopper. So maybe nature has really made the universe "safe for historians," as Stephen Hawking put it. Still, it's a lot of fun to think about, isn't it? After all, if you could go back in time, maybe you could change something. If so, what would you do? Take advantage of yesterday's stock fluctuations? Bet on last year's Super Bowl? Kill the infant Hitler? There are a ton of books out there that explain the ideas of modern physics in more or less simple terms. I'd like to say I've read 'em all, but I haven't; there are just too many of the varmints. Here is a list of those I've read that deal most directly with time-travel. The following links will take you down the page to the appropriate review. (Ingermanson) Michio Kaku is a well-known theoretical physicist who's made a number of important contributions to elementary particle theory and superstring theory. He also writes very well, and has a knack for storytelling.

In Hyperspace, Kaku dives into the mysteries of the universe. Modern superstring theories are embedded in a ten-dimensional hyperspace. Theorists hope to incorporate all of physics in these theories. Kaku breaks the book into two parts. In Part I, he breaks the reader into the notion of higher dimensions by discussing a five-dimensional universe. (The usual three spatial dimensions, plus time as the fourth dimension, plus a strangely-curled up fifth dimension that accounts for light.) He tells some of the history of mathematics and physics, with stories of Gauss, Riemann, Einstein, and other great mathematicians and physicists.

In Part II, Kaku begins with an explanation of quantum mechanics, then plunges into the arcane world of supergravity and superstrings. Without a deep background in math, it's impossible to really understand these theories, but Kaku makes a valiant effort, and he certainly captures the main ideas.

Next, he moves on to cosmology, black holes, and wormholes. Check out his sketches of a wormhole on pages 229 and 230! He has some fun discussing the paradoxes of backwards time-travel. He

Kip Thorne is a Caltech professor and one of the world's leading experts on Einstein's theory of general relativity. In the late 1980s, he and his students created a new cottage industry studying wormholes -- portals through space and time. It wasn't even really Thorne's idea; Carl Sagan prompted it by asking for a "scientific" way to travel quickly through the universe. Sagan was working on his novel Contact at the time. Thorne wound up discovering many new ideas in wormhole theory. This book is his highly personal account of those discoveries.

It's an amusing book, full of interesting anecdotes about many physicists. Thorne spends the early chapters talking about gravity, relativity, warped spacetime, black holes, white dwarfs -- the usual suspects in modern astronomy and cosmology. There's quite a bit of overlap with Michio Kaku's book Hyperspace, reviewed above. And that's just as well, because most people need to hear this stuff several times before it starts sinking in. And that includes most physicists.

For our time-travel interests, chapter 14 is a jewel. There, Thorne gets into the details of wormholes (the logical details, not the mathematical ones) and shows that backward time-travel through wormholes causes some unexpected logical problems. And not just the usual "can I go back in time and kill my own grandfather" paradoxes. In the presence of wormholes, it

also gets into the recent developments in wormhole theory pioneered by Kip Thorne and his students at Caltech (and inspired by Carl Sagan's novel Contact).

becomes impossible to predict the trajectory of even simple things like billiard balls. An infinite number of possible trajectories are allowed! Poor Isaac Newton would turn over in his grave.

You'll be amused to see Thorne's picture of a wormhole on page 500 and even more amused to see that it looks very different from the picture in Kaku's book. Thorne's is more accurate; it shows the light-diffusing properties of a wormhole.

Paul J. Nahin is a professor in the Electrical and Computer Engineering Department of the University of New Hampshire.

You might imagine that an electrical engineer wouldn't know much about Einstein's general relativity.

You would be wrong. Professor Nahin knows more about the subject than most physicists. He very much would like to see a time machine built. This book is about that dream. The book is organized into four exceedingly long chapters.

The chapters are a very weird and delightful mix of hard physics, philosophy, and summaries of science fiction stories. Nahin seems to have read practically every time-travel story ever written, and he can illustrate practically any good (or bad) idea with half a dozen stories using that idea.

Chapter 1 gives an overview of time travel, and it's a very broad overview. Nahin is most interested in the possibility of backwards time-travel, and so he needs to resolve the paradoxes.

Is it logically possible to go back in time? If so, then can one change the past? And if time-travel will eventually be discovered, then where are all the "time-tourists" from the future? Nahin doesn't solve these issues in this chapter, but he brings them all up and promises to wrestle with them later in the book. Chapter 2 discusses the nature of time, spacetime, and the universe. Is time real? Does the past exist somewhere? What about the future? Is the universe like a giant "block" that God (or some other person "outside" of spacetime) could observe all at once?

Can God be omniscient?

What does that do to free will? These are interesting questions, and philosophers have given an amazingly wide range of answers. Nahin has his own opinions about who's right and who's wrong and he examines some of these questions in detail. Chapter 3 moves on to the question of the direction of time. Why does time seem to flow in only one direction? Can there be backward causation? What does "now" mean? Could you imagine a universe in which time flowed backward? What does that mean? What about multidimensional time? Chapter 4 gets to the really fun stuff, the paradoxes of time-travel. Can we change the past? Nahin doesn't believe we can. Since he hopes that time-travel is possible, this leads him to conclude that time-travelers to the past can affect the past but not change it. That is, their actions may certainly influence the past, but only in such a way as to bring about the past that actually occurred. In other words, the past must be consistent.

Nahin goes on to discuss the grandfather paradox in this light. Why can't you go back in time and kill old Grandad? You could, but you won't, because you didn't. If you had, then you wouldn't be here in the first place.

Causal loops are even more intriguing. Suppose you read a book on how to build a time machine. You build the machine, go back in time, and publish the book -- which later gets read by a younger version of you living in the future. OK, fine, this is all self-consistent. But where did the knowledge of how to build the time-machine come from? Apparently from nowhere. Nahin sees no problem with this kind of paradox, in which something happens without a cause. Big-bangers believe in a Big Bang without a cause, he argues. Quantum mechanics tells us that radioactive decay has no cause.

Theologians argue that God has no cause. So where's the paradox with a little book explaining how to travel back in time? You may not buy his argument, but have fun trying to refute it.

Then there are sexual paradoxes. The most elegant of these is given in Robert Heinlein's short story, "All You Zombies -- ". The story is too long to summarize here, but the upshot is that "Jane" is her own mother, father, lover, and daughter.

Bizzare! Where did Jane come from? If you're technical, you'll enjoy the appendices in Nahin's book. They start out easy and get progressively more difficult until only specialists will follow it all. Enjoy yer meal! It's all good fun and it stretches your mind, so where's the harm? The ultimate proof of time-travel will come when somebody builds a time machine. Until then, we'll wonder. (Source: Dr. Randy Inmerganson)

Extraterrestrials and Anunnaki Speed of Light, Time Travel and Other Dimensions Concepts Can Be Explained By Scientists...

The quest for a theory linking all matter and all forces led physicists deep into hyperspace, where they got horribly lost. But suddenly the way ahead has become clear, says superstring theorist, Dr. Michio Kaku. Is there a Final Theory in physics? Will we one day have a complete theory that will explain everything from subatomic particles, atoms and supernovae to the big bang? Einstein spent the last 30 years of his life in a fruitless quest for the fabled unified field theory. His approach has since been written off as futile. In the 1980s, attention switched to superstring theory as the leading candidate for a final theory. This revolution began when physicists realised that the subatomic particles found in nature, such as electrons and quarks, may not be particles at all, but tiny vibrating strings. Superstring theory was a stunning breakthrough. It became one of the fastest growing and most exciting areas of theoretical physics, generating a feverish outpouring of thousands of papers. Then, in the early 1990s, progress seemed to grind to a halt. People became discouraged when they failed to find the answers to two key questions: where do strings come from, and is our Universe among the many solutions of superstring theory? But now the Internet is buzzing again as papers pour in to the bulletin board at Los Alamos National laboratory in New Mexico, the official clearing house for superstring papers.

The trigger for this excitement was the discovery of "M-theory", which may answer those two vital questions about superstrings. "I may be biased on this one, but I think it is perhaps the most important development not only in string theory, but also in theoretical physics at least in the past two decades," says Harvard physicist Cumrun Vafa. M-theory led John Schwarz of Caltech, one of the founders of superstring theory, to proclaim a "second superstring revolution". And it inspired a spellbinding three-hour lecture by another leading exponent, Edward Witten of the Institute for Advanced Study at Princeton, New Jersey.

The aftershocks of the breakthrough have spread to other disciplines, too. "The excitement I sense in the people in the field and the spin-offs into my own field of mathematics...have really been quite extraordinary," says Phillip Griffiths, director of the Institute for Advanced Study." I feel I've been very privileged to witness this first hand."

In one dazzling stroke, M-theory has come close to solving superstring theory's two long-standing questions , leaving many theoretical physicists (myself included) gasping at its power. M-theory, moreover, may even force string theory to change its name because, although many features of M-theory are still unknown, it does not seem to be a theory purely of strings. Other strange beasts seem to emerge, including various types of membranes. Michael Duff of Texas A&M University is already giving talks with the title "The theory formerly known as strings".

"Nature shows us only the tail of the lion. But I do not doubt that the lion belongs to it even though he cannot at once reveal himself because of his enormous size" - Albert Einstein

M-theory does not prove the final correctness of superstring theory. Not by any means. Proving or disproving its validity may take years more.

But it still marks an astonishing breakthrough. Remember that some of the finest minds of this century have been stumped by the problem of creating a "Theory of Everything".

Einstein summed up the problem when he said: Nature shows us only the tail of the lion. But I do not doubt that the lion belongs to it even though he cannot at once reveal himself because of his enormous size."

The tail" is what we see in nature, which can be described by the four fundamental forces gravity, electromagnetism and the strong and weak nuclear forces. The lion is the ultimate theory that will unify them in one short equation. Today, physicists believe that the first force, gravity, can be described by Einstein's general relativity, based on the smooth warping of the fabric of space- time.

This is an elegant theory that describes the macroscopic world of black holes, quasars and the big bang. But gravity has stubbornly refused to unite with the other three forces, which are described by quantum theory. Here, instead of the smooth fabric of space-time, we have the discrete world of packets of energy, or quanta.

The form of quantum theory that goes furthest in describing matter and its interactions is the Standard Model, which is based on a bizarre bestiary of particles such as quarks, leptons and bosons. The Standard Model may be one of the most successful theories in science, but it is also one of the ugliest. Its inadequacy is betrayed by some 19 arbitrary constants not derived by any kind of theory that have to be put in "by hand" to make the equations work.

Capturing the "lion", which unites these two great theories, would be a crowning achievement for physics. But while Einstein was first to set off on this noble hunt, tracking the footprints left by the lion, he ultimately lost the trail and wandered off into the wilderness.

Crazy departure: Today, however, physicists are following a different trail-the one leading to superstring theory. Unlike previous proposals, it has survived every blistering mathematical challenge ever hurled at it. Not surprisingly, the theory is a radical-some might say crazy-departure from the past, being based on tiny strings vibrating in 10-dimensional space-time.

"The subatomic particles we see in nature are nothing more than different resonances of the vibrating superstrings"

To understand how going to higher dimensions can help to unify lower dimensions, think back to how the Romans used to fight wars. Without radio communications and spy planes, battles were horribly confused, raging on many fronts at the same time. That's why the Romans always leapt into "hyperspace"- the third dimension-by seizing a hill-top. From this vantage point, they were able to survey the two-dimensional battlefield as a single, unified whole. Leaping to higher dimensions can also simplify the laws of nature. In 1915, Einstein changed completely our notion of gravity by leaping to the extra dimension of time. In 1919, the German mathematician Theodor Kaluza added a fifth dimension and in so doing unified space-time with Maxwell's equations for electromagnetism. This triumph was largely forgotten amid the frenzy of interest generated by quantum mechanics. Only in the 1980s did physicists return to this idea to create superstring theory.

In superstring theory, the subatomic particles we see in nature are nothing more than different resonances of the vibrating superstrings, in the same way that different musical notes emanate from the different modes of vibration of a violin string. (These strings are very small-of the order of 10^{35} metres.) Likewise, the laws of physics -the forces between charged particles, for example-are the harmonies of the strings; the Universe is a symphony of vibrating strings. And when strings move in 10-dimensional space-time, they warp the space-time surrounding them in precisely the way predicted by general relativity. So strings simply and elegantly unify the quantum theory of particles and general relativity. Better still, gravity is not an inconvenient add-on. "Unlike conventional quantum field theory, string theory *requires* gravity," Witten has said. "I regard this fact as one of the greatest insights in science ever made."

But, of course, all this takes place in 10 dimensions. Physicists retrieve our more familiar 4-dimensional Universe by assuming that, during the big bang, 6 of the 10 dimensions curled up (or "compactified") into a tiny ball, while the remaining four expanded explosively, giving us the Universe we see. What has consumed physicists for the past ten years is the task of cataloguing the different ways in which these six dimensions can compactify. Their task has been especially difficult because mathematicians have not worked out the topology and properties of these higher-dimensional universes. The physicists have had to blaze the trail and invent entirely new areas of mathematics. These efforts have revealed millions of compactifications, each of which yields a different pattern of quarks, electrons and so on.

As we have seen, the first frustrating problem with superstring theory is that physicists do not understand where strings come from. To make matters worse, there are five string theories that unify quantum theory with relativity.

This is an embarrassment of riches. Each competing theory looks quite different from the others. One, called Type 1 string theory, is based on two types of strings: "open strings", like short strands with two ends, and "closed strings", in which the ends meet to form a ring. The other four have only closed strings. Some, such as Type 2b, generate only left- handed particles, which spin in only one direction Others, such as Type 2a, have left and right-handed particles.

Today's excitement has grown from the finding that if we postulate the existence of a mysterious M-theory in 11 dimensions we can show that the five competing string theories are actually different versions of the same thing. Like a Roman general surveying the battlefield from the third dimension, physicists today stand on the hilltop of the 11th dimension and see the five superstring theories below, unified into a simple, coherent picture, representing different aspects of the same thing.

Tracking lion: The first step towards this advance came two years ago when Witten and Paul Townsend of the University of Cambridge showed that Type 2a string theory in 10 dimensions was equivalent to M-theory in 11 dimensions with one dimension curled up.

Since then, all five theories have been shown to be equivalent. So at last physicists know where superstrings come from: they originate in the 11th dimension from M-theory.

M-theory also predicts that strings coexist with membranes of various dimensions. For example, a particle can be defined as a zero-brane (zero-dimensional object).

A string is a one-brane; an ordinary membrane like a soap bubble is a two-brane, and so on. (Using p to represent the dimension of the object, one wag dubbed this motley collection "p-branes") When these p-branes vibrate or pulsate, they create new resonances, or particles, which were missed in earlier formulations of superstrings. The name "M-theory" was coined by Witten: M perhaps stands for "membrane" or the "mother of all strings", or possibly "mystery" Take your pick. To see how this all fits together, imagine three blind men hot on the trail of Einstein's lion. Hearing it race by, they give chase and desperately grab at it. Hanging onto the tail for dear life, one feels its one-dimensional form and loudly proclaims, "It's a string. The lion is a string." The second man grabs the lion's ear. Feeling a two-dimensional surface, he calls out "No, no, the lion is really a two-brane." The third blind man, hanging on to the lion's leg, senses a three-dimensional solid, and shouts, "You're both wrong. The lion is a three- brane!" They are all right. Just as the tail, ear and leg are different parts of the same lion, the string and various p-branes appear to be different limits of M-theory. Townsend calls it "p-brane democracy".

The acid test for any theory is that it must fit the data. No matter how original and elegant superstring theory is, it will stand or fall on whether it describes the physical Universe.

Either it is a Theory of Everything, as its advocates hope, or it is a theory of nothing. There is no in-between. So theoretical physicists must answer the second question: is our Universe, with its strange collection of quarks and subatomic particles, among the solutions of superstring theory? This is where it runs into an embarrassing problem, which is that physicists have been unable to find all its four-dimensional solutions. The mathematics have been fiendishly difficult- too hard for anyone to solve completely.

In general, there are two types of solutions. So far, only the first class, called "perturbative" solutions have been found. Across all branches of physics, theorists faced by an equation they cannot solve reach for well-established ways to find approximate solutions. In superstring theory, millions of these perturbative solutions have been catalogued. Each one corresponds to a different way in which to curl up 6 of the 10 dimensions.

However, none of them precisely reproduces the pattern of quarks, leptons and bosons in the Standard Model, although some come close.

"M-theory solves entire classes of problems that were previously thought to be unsolvable. It even gives us valuable details of quantum effects in black holes"

So, many believe that the Standard Model may be found among the second class of solutions, the "non-perturbative" solutions. But non-perturbative solutions are generally among the most difficult of all solutions in physics. Some physicists despaired of ever finding non- perturbative solutions of superstring theory. After all, even the non-perturbative solutions of simple four-dimensional theories are completely unknown, let alone those of a complicated 10-dimensional theory.

How does M-theory help to solve this intractable problem? The answer lies in a startling tool called "duality". Simply put, in M-theory there is a duality, or simple mathematical relationship, between the perturbative and non-perturbative regions. This allows us at last to take a peek at this "forbidden zone". To see how duality works, consider Maxwell's theory of electricity and magnetism, for example. Physicists have known for decades that if they interchange the electric field E and magnetic field B in Maxwell's equations, and also swap the electric charge e and magnetic charge g, then the equations stay the same. That is, nothing happens to Maxwell's theory if we make the dual transformation: $E«B$ and $e«g$.

Hidden theories: In fact, in Maxwell's theory, the product e time's g is a constant: so small e corresponds to large g. This is the key. Suppose an equation includes a mathematical function that depends on g^2 and which cannot be solved exactly. The standard mathematical trick is to approximate a solution with a perturbation expansion: $g^2 + g^4 + g^6$... and so on. So long as g is less than 1, each successive term in the series is smaller than the last, and the overall value converges on a single figure.

But if g is greater than 1 then the total gets larger and larger, and the approximation fails. This is where duality comes in. If g is large, then e is less than 1. Using perturbation, we get the series $e^2 + e^4 + e^6$ which gives a sensible value. Ultimately, this means that using perturbation on e can solve problems in the non-perturbative region of g.

Duality in Maxwell's theory is rather trivial. But in M-theory, we find another duality: $g \ll 1/g$. This relationship, though simpler, turns out to be incredibly powerful. When I first saw it, I could hardly believe my eyes. It meant that a string theory defined for large g, which is usually impossible to describe using present-day mathematics, can be shown to be equivalent to another type of string theory for small g, which is easily described using perturbation theory.

Thus, two different string theories can be dual to each other. In the non-perturbative region of string theory was another string theory. This is how, in fact, we prove the equivalence of all five string theories. Altogether, three different types of duality called S, T and U have been discovered, which yield an intricate web of dualities linking string theories of various dimensions and types. At an incredible pace, physicists have now mapped almost all the solutions and dualities that exist in 10, 8 and 6 dimensions. Before M-theory, finding the non-perturbative solutions in these dimensions would have been considered impossible. Now the problem is trivial. For example, let us say that two theories A and B are dual to each other in 10 dimensions. If we compactify both theories in the same way, then we obtain theories A' and B'. But now we know something new: that A' is also dual to B'. Thus, the non-perturbative behaviour of A' is given by B'. By elaborating this process, we get an almost complete understanding of the different possible universes down to 6 dimensions. Thus, M-theory solves entire classes of problems that were previously thought to be unsolvable. It even gives us valuable new details about quantum effects in black holes.

But there are many loose ends. For example, what precisely is M-theory? So far, we only know fragments of the theory (the low-energy part). We are still waiting for someone to come up with a full description of M-theory Last year, Vafa shocked physicists by announcing that there may be a 12-dimensional theory lurking out there, which he called "F-theory" (F for father).

More important, we are still far from mapping all the dualities of four dimensions. If everything works out as hoped, we should find that one of these four-dimensional universes contains the Standard Model and thus describes the known Universe. But there are millions of these solutions, so sifting through them to find the one we are after will take many years.

So will the final theory be in 10, 11 or 12 dimensions? According to Schwarz, the answer may be none of these. He feels that the true theory may not have a fixed dimensionality, and that 11 dimensions only emerge once we try to solve it. Townsend takes a similar view, saying, "The whole notion of dimensionality is an approximate one that only emerges in some semiclassical context."

So does this means that the end is in sight that some day soon we will be able to work out the Standard Model from first principles? When I put this question to some leading physicists in this field they were still cautious. Townsend likened our present state of knowledge to the old quantum era of the Bohr atom, just before the full elucidation of quantum mechanics. "We have some fruitful pictures and some rules," he says. "But it's also clear that we don't have a complete theory."

Witten, too, believes we are on the right track. But he says we will need a few more "revolutions" like the present one to finally solve the theory. "I think there are still a couple more superstring revolutions in our future, at least," says Witten. "If we can manage one more superstring revolution a decade, I think that we will do all right." From Harvard, Vafa adds: "I hope this is the light at the end of the tunnel'. But who knows how long the tunnel is?" Personally, I am optimistic. For the first time, we can see the outline of the lion, and it is magnificent. One day, we will hear it roar. (Sources: Dr. Michio Kaku; Fortune City)

61-Physical World, Biological World, And Extraterrestrial World Face To Face

The Answer

The Physical World...The Biological World...The Extraterrestrial World

There are millions, and millions and millions of different types and categories of extraterrestrial civilizations and universes in the known and unknown cosmos.

According to ufologists, earth has been visited by at least 47 different extraterrestrial races. Also included in the far-fetched literature of ufology, an infinite number of aliens' types and species inhabiting planets, stars, physical and non-physical worlds, in the astral, on earth, underground and underwater. And if we add all the spatio-spiritual messages received by channelers and mediums, we probably end up gaining a few hundreds more; aliens of all sorts, types, shapes and sizes!!

But how do we know about all these extraterrestrial species?

Their characteristics?

Their shapes?

Their sizes?

Where do they live?

Their bizarre physiognomies, reptilian appearances, shape-shifting, and habitat?

For sure? Hundred per cent? We don't.

Any person who claims to know the answers is an ignoramus, a fool par excellence! However, we have some clues, reports by credible scientists who allegedly worked with advanced alien races in United States military bases...we have also very ancient texts and tablets from Phoenicia, Sumer, Peru, Guatemala, Mexico, Egypt, Syria, Brazil, and other regions of the globe that have provided information and accounts about the origin, nature and spaceships' drawings of extraterrestrial races who landed on earth at the dawn of the history of the humanity, and who have interacted with the early human races.

Even, the Bible could serve as an extraterrestrial reference tool –to a certain degree -

Very few records and accounts provided information on the habitable worlds of extraterrestrials and alien life beyond our solar system, such as:

1-The Book of Rama-Dosh;

2-The Ulema Book: Code and Language of the World Beyond;

3- Edgar Cayce's séances and readings;

4-Contactees' accounts based on their telepathic conversations with aliens;

5-Channeling here and there;

6-Accounts given by bona fide scientists with advanced degrees in the field who allegedly worked on alien reverse technolohy;

7-Military men reports and public statements based on "what aliens told them" in secret military installations in the United States;

8-Accounts of contactees who have visited aliens' planets as guests of the extraterrestrials;

9-The formidable revelations of Victoria; a hybrid woman (Half Anunnaki half human) (Note: With Dr. Ilil Arbel, I wrote a book about Victoria and the Anunnaki's life on Nibiru "Revelations of an Anunnaki's Wife).

*** *** ***

Now, the two big questions are: What to believe and what to discredit?

Who or what is the credible souce and the fake/fantasmagoric source? Hard to tell!

However, I do strongly believe that some of the reports of top scientists and military men who worked with extraterrestrials at Hangar 18, S4, Andrews Air Force Base Underground facilities, Area 51, Dulce Base, and few other secret military bases in Nevada and Arizona could be seriously considered.

But as of today, the most credible information and descriptive data came from Victoria's revelations and the Ulema book.

The question of life beyond our home planet, has exercised human imagination, and sometimes stirred irrational fears, since the ancient Greeks. These fears were in part responsible for the spectacle that took place almost exactly 400 years ago, on February 17, 1600, when Giordano Bruno was summoned from his Inquisition prison cell in Castel San Angelo across the Tiber from the Vatican, marched to the Campo dei Fiori, and burned at the stake in large part for his belief in an infinite number of inhabited worlds. So anathema was the subject of other worlds that even historians of science avoided it until the 1970s.

Are Extraterrestrials Physical, Biological or Simply Extraterrestrial?

Dr. Steven J. Dick said: "I well remember when I proposed to write the history of the extraterrestrial-life debate as a doctoral dissertation in the History of Science Department at Indiana University, I was initially told there were two problems: it wasn't science, and it had no intellectually significant history! To the department's credit, I was allowed to proceed with the dissertation anyway, and thirty years, several dozen planetary systems, and some thousands of pages of history later, both of those stumbling blocks have been largely removed.

There is no doubt now that the subject has an intellectually significant history, although a few still argue about whether or not it is a science. One still hears the phrase that exobiology is a science without a subject."

*** *** ***

The Known Universe To Mankind: "Is that all there is?"

It is possible that in addition to astronomy's three related and evolving kingdoms there is a fourth great kingdom, that in addition to planets, stars, and galaxies-lurks the kingdom of universes, or the "multiverse" as Sir Martin Rees and Lee Smolin have recently put it. Their contention is that there may be more than one universe, where "universe" is defined as everything we have seen, or can see. (This is a remarkable revival of the Greek concept of a plurality of *kosmoi*, isolated ordered systems that originated the Greek plurality of world's tradition.) Such a claim has emerged over the last few years after pondering the fact that our universe seems to be finely tuned for life. If the gravitational constant were different by an extremely small amount, there would be no stars to warm any planets, and more to the point, no planets at all. If the value for the strong nuclear force were different, there could be no atoms.

There are many parameters of this type. The fact that the universe seems to be fine tuned for life (which is not equivalent to saying that life is prevalent) has been given the elegant misnomer of "anthropic principle." It is a misnomer because it is relevant to the existence of life (not just humanity) in the universe, and therefore is not anthropic. But how does one explain this fine tuning of the physical constants? Why should the physical constants of the universe be fine tuned for life? One answer is that we would not be here to ask the question if they were not fine tuned. Another answer is that God did it. But a third answer-more in the realm of science-is that perhaps our universe is only one of many, some of which have physical constants attuned for life, and others that do not. Lucky for us, we happen to live in a universe fine tuned for life, and thus can ask "Why?"

Magnificent as the physical universe is, we are drawn to ask, "is that all there is?" Or does cosmic evolution frequently, almost as a matter of course, end in life, mind, and intelligence as it did on Earth?

In short, is the universe in its essence-perhaps via the anthropic principle-a biological universe?

And if so, are there universal laws of biology yet to be discovered?

348

Here we enter the realm of bioastronomy (as the astronomers like to call it), exobiology (as many biologists refer to it), or astrobiology, the programmatic name for the discipline for which the National Aeronautics and Space Administration (NASA) Ames Research Center has now taken the lead.

The very existence of a biological universe is much more difficult to determine than the details of the physical universe, because we cannot yet observe extraterrestrial biology or its effects. We can send Viking landers to Mars, we can listen patiently for artificial radio signals from putative extraterrestrial intelligence, we can perform suggestive experiments on the origin of life, or analyze the occasional Mars rock on Earth, and recently we have confirmed some three dozen planets around other stars. But in a cosmological sense the biological universe is not nearly as amenable to direct probing as is the physical universe. The realm of biology is also immensely more complex than astronomy; a humble insect is more complex than a star, and animal behavior, human psychology, and social behavior are much more so, to the extent that we might despair of ever understanding them at all.

Nevertheless, we can tackle the problem of the biological universe in the same way as the physical universe by discussing its extent, its content, and its evolution. Its extent as confirmed by science is summed up in one word: "terrestrial."

I need hardly say that even the tiniest microbe has not been found beyond the Earth, notwithstanding claims of Martian fossils. A blade of grass found on Mars would be the greatest discovery in the history of science, and great pains are being taken with hazard protocols for the Mars sample return mission, not only because of concerns for contamination of Earth, but also for contamination of Mars, a possibly irretrievable blunder in either case. So the extent of the *proven* biological universe is at present limited to one planet in the universe: Earth.

This is not for lack of trying. The history of ideas about the possible biological universe is now well known, stretching from the ancient Greeks, through Galileo and Kepler, Descartes and Newton, to the present. It is a fascinating history because it tells us about the limits of science when addressing a problem of compelling human interest, it tells us about the cultures of science, it is a remarkable example of a developing scientific discipline, or "protoscience," and it holds great cultural significance.

But it tells us nothing about whether or not the biological universe exists.

Perhaps life on Earth is the entire extent of life in the universe. If this is the case, the biological universe would be disproven, we would remain in a significant biological and moral sense the center of the universe, and the Copernican revolution would have had its boundaries defined. But we must address the question of the extent of the biological universe by asking what is the evidence for life beyond the Earth?

EXTRATERRESTRIAL LIFE

Here I wish to make a large distinction that has not been made often enough in discussions of extraterrestrial life: a weak version of the biological universe and a strong version. The weak version is that *low forms of life* are common throughout the universe, in forms analogous to bacteria or archaea on Earth. The strong form is that *intelligence* is common throughout the universe. The NASA astrobiology program today assumes only the weak version, but all SETI (Search for Extraterrestrial Intelligence) programs assume the strong version. The strong version would be considerably more interesting, but perhaps not as likely. So we have now refined our question: what is the evidence for the weak version and for the strong version of the biological universe?

Here are five empirical arguments often given in the literature, listed in order of those I consider strongest:

1-The argument from the origin of life on Earth.

The historical record of the origin of life on Earth indicates that microbial life originates fairly easily, or at least fairly quickly. The Earth is some 4.5 billion years old, and already some 3.8 billion years ago low forms of life existed, immediately after the heavy bombardment of asteroidal bodies ceased impacting the Earth. But certainly a relevant fact is that microbial life dominated the Earth for 3 billion years. Complex life is only about 600 million years old, especially with the Cambrian explosion of body types. And intelligent life, by almost any definition beyond mere consciousness, is less than 2 million years old, with the rise of the genus *homo*. So this argument favors the weak biological universe-one full of microbes.

2-The discovery of life on Earth thriving under extreme conditions, known as "extremophiles."

This discovery indicates that microbial life can live in a much wider range of extraterrestrial environments than previously believed. It greatly expands the idea of an "ecosphere" or "habitable zone." This argument again favors only the weak biological universe.

3-The history of Mars and the current state of the Jovian moon Europa.

Spacecraft observations of Mars clearly indicate the existence of past channels with flowing water. The famous claim in 1996 of possible fossils in Martian meteorite ALH 84001, while unproven, points to the possibility of fossil life on Mars. The consensus that Europa is a body covered with water ice, and that it likely contains oceans under this ice, shows that conditions favorable for life may still exist in our solar system beyond Earth. The evidence that the conditions for life existed on Mars in the past, and may exist on Europa at present, lends credence again to at least a weak biological universe.

4.-The existence of complex organic molecules in interstellar molecules, meteorites, and comets.

Though a long way from life, this observation favors a weak biological universe in the sense that the precursors for life are plentiful in the universe.

5-Principle of Mediocrity.

The philosophical argument, sometimes referred to as the "principle of mediocrity," whereby the Copernican principle dictates the Earth should not be regarded as unique. This has been proven for the physical universe in terms of our non-central location, and the existence of other planetary systems. But it is the very thing we are trying to prove under the name of the biological universe, and so cannot be assumed. This argument is only weakly empirical in the sense that we have observed the Copernican principle works for the physical universe, and that the universe provides a vast scope for possible life. But it is the driving force for many scientists and the public, and it is one of the few arguments that bears on the strong biological universe-that extraterrestrial intelligence should exist. These arguments leave the *extent* of the biological universe very much an open question.

And if its extent is problematic, the possible *content* of the biological universe must be even more speculative. Our confirmed knowledge of that content must begin with what we know of terrestrial life. One of the most astonishing properties of life on Earth is its diversity; Harvard naturalist E. O. Wilson and his colleagues estimate the number of *known* species of plants, animals and microorganisms on Earth at 1.4 million. They also estimate this is less than one tenth of those actually living on Earth, so there may be 15 million species of terrestrial life. Similarly, diversity is likely to be a property of any extraterrestrial life.

What we know of this life on Earth is best summarized by biological taxonomies devised over the last three centuries. Until recently systematists divided all life on Earth into five kingdoms, but following the work of Carl Woese, Norman Pace, and others on evolutionary relationships as established by gene sequencing, most microbiologists (if not most zoologists) now divide life on Earth into three kingdoms, or "domains:" archaea, bacteria, and eukaryotes, the latter incorporating the animals, plants, and fungi of the previous "five kingdoms" system. The evolutionary diagram of biology's three kingdoms, shown in Figure 25, is sometimes called "the universal tree of life."

In our present context, it is well to remember that it may be no such thing; it is more prudently called "the terrestrial tree of life."

Our understanding of the terrestrial tree of life, and the very existence of three kingdoms, took centuries of observations to develop. Even Aristotle could catalog the incredible variety of life visible to the naked eye, the macroscopic life now classified as the eukaryote kingdom. In a parallel to Galileo opening a new world for astronomy with the telescope in 1610, the English scientist Robert Hooke and the Dutch scientist Antoni van Leeuwenhoek opened biology's second kingdom, the microscopic world of bacteria, some fifty-sixty years later. But only in the late twentieth century has life been discovered in extreme environments, revealing an entire new kingdom of life.

The so-called "extremophiles" were first found in hot springs in the 1970s, and are now known to exist at temperatures exceeding the boiling point of water (thermophiles), at pressures of more than a thousand atmospheres (barophiles), and at conditions of extreme saltiness (halophiles) and acidity (acidophiles).

One hardy microbe reported in the journal *Science* a few weeks ago exists in the depths of an abandoned copper mine at a pH near zero, some of the most acidic waters on Earth. These are the archaea, and because of their primitive and hardy nature, many biologists believe they are related to the origin of life.

While there is great diversity in terrestrial biology's three kingdoms, it is very unlikely that the content of the biological universe is similar to life on Earth, for the extension of Darwinian natural selection to other planets dictates that any life will depend on its environment.

This brings us to the third problem of the biological universe (after its extent and content): its *evolution*. Whether or not microbial life evolves to more complex life, including intelligence, immediately raises a variety of deep philosophical problems, including the role of chance and necessity in the evolution of life. This problem, already present in the origin of life, is immensely magnified in the realm of complex and intelligent life. We simply do not know what is contingent and what is necessary in the evolution of life, what are the "universals" are what are the "parochials." The lessons of life on Earth in this connection, particularly in the form of the Burgess shale and the Cambrian explosion of life, are ambiguous: Stephen Jay Gould's Wonderful Life: The Burgess Shale and the Nature of History *and Simon* Conway Morris's The Crucible of Creation: The Burgess Shale and the Rise of Animals draw very different conclusions about macroevolution and the role of contingency. Many evolutionary biologists, such as George Gaylord Simpson and Ernst Mayr, seeing the great complexity of life and its evolution on the way to human intelligence, are very skeptical about the existence of intelligence in the universe. Many astronomers, seeing the vast universe and imbued with the Copernican principle, are less skeptical.

The only way to resolve the dispute over the strong biological universe is the Search for Extraterrestrial Intelligence

The only way to resolve the dispute over the strong biological universe (short of interstellar travel) is the Search for Extraterrestrial Intelligence, observational programs that employ radio and optical telescopes to search for artificial signals from putative civilizations. Needless to say, these programs have had no success to date. The proponents emphasize they have only searched an extremely small fraction of our own Galaxy, and only at certain frequencies. Still, it is a valid question how much longer such observations should continue. The central icon of SETI is the Drake Equation, a concatenation of astronomical, biological, and social factors that purports to estimate N, the number of communicative technological civilizations in the Galaxy. All we can say now is that the number ranges between one and one hundred million. If the five arguments enumerated earlier fall short of proof of the weak (microbial) biological universe, they certainly leave a universe full of intelligence problematic.

The five "strongest arguments" elaborated above are not necessarily strong in an absolute sense. Lest you think all scientists have adopted the biological universe you should read Peter Ward and Donald Brownlee's recent book *Rare Earths*. While even they agree that microbial life may be common in the universe, they argue that complex life is extremely rare. Such books offer a proper antidote to undue optimism. In my view, the jury is still out, and I believe only two conclusions are warranted by the evidence at this stage:

1. If it exists, life beyond Earth will be astonishingly diverse
2. The abundance of extraterrestrial life will be inversely proportional to its complexity, i.e., microbial life will be more abundant, intelligent life less abundant.

At the end of the twentieth century we are left with twoworld views-the physical universe and the biological universe-neither one proven. Despite the cogency of some of the arguments against extraterrestrial life, the general populace has been "captured by aliens" in Joel Achenbach's felicitous phrase. Why? The reasons are as complex as human behavior. Darwin's defender, T. H. Huxley, perhaps articulated a primary reason 150 years ago when he said, "The question of questions for mankind-the problem which underlies all others, and is more deeply interesting than any other-is the ascertainment of the place which Man occupies in nature and of his relations to the universe of things." This sentiment explains why we search; more complex reasons must be invoked for why we hope to find life, especially intelligent life.

Whatever the reasons, in pursuit of the biological universe, two great disciplines, biology and astronomy-one descriptive and the other mathematical-have begun the fascinating process of merging at certain points to address an issue of great scientific and cultural importance. NASA, in the form of its Origins and Astrobiology programs, is the flagship patron of this merger, which enjoys considerable public support.

The passionate nature of the ongoing debate derives from the fact that much more is at stake than new facts or theories: as in the seventeenth century, two world views now hang in the balance, their fate to be decided in the twenty-first century. We are now well into *our* "dialogue on the two chief world systems."

Implications Of The Two Modern World Systems

Just as the two chief world systems of the 17th century had profound implications for the humanity, so too will our modern two chief world systems. And the implications of the two world views are very different. If we live in a physical universe where the ultimate product of cosmic evolution is planets, stars, and galaxies, it may be human destiny to populate the universe rather than to interact with extraterrestrials. Humanity would eventually *become* the extraterrestrials. It would be the universe of Isaac Asimov's *Foundation* series rather than the universe of Arthur C. Clarke's *Childhood's End* and *2001: A Space Odyssey*.

A biological universe would be considerably more interesting, and perhaps this is one of the psychological reasons that many favor it. In discussing its implications we must again distinguish the weak from the strong version.

By curious Congressional mandate, NASA's astrobiology program concentrates only on microbial life. Perhaps we can all agree that the discovery of microbes will have less effect than the discovery of intelligence. Barring an *Andromeda Strain* scenario, in the weak biological universe there will be no *Close Encounters of the Third Kind*, no *Independence Day*, no *ET*, and no *Contact*. Any *Star Wars* will be limited to humanity's descendants. One might argue that, because even the discovery of possible Martian fossils raised a great debate at all levels of society worldwide, so should the discovery of microbial life. But I believe that the discovery of fossils or microbes derives much of its impact from the fact that it is the first step on the road to intelligence, though longer than most people think. It would have great scientific interest, but might not necessitate the realignment of theologies and world philosophies.

Nonetheless, a microbial universe has its own set of consequences; the three fundamental questions in NASA's astrobiology program (the origin and evolution of life, the existence of extraterrestrial life, and the future of life on Earth and beyond) have important cultural implications that social scientists should address.

The problem of the implications of the strong biological universe has been considered in some detail, notably by a NASA team in the early 1990s, and can be subjected to systematic inquiry.

One approach to the implications of extraterrestrial intelligence has been general historical analogies, especially physical culture contacts on Earth, which usually end in disaster. But many consider physical culture contact unlikely (at least in the form of UFOs if not probes or microprobes), and in any case it is only one scenario among many that might be considered.

355

Perhaps more suitable is the analogy of the transmission of knowledge from Greece to the Latin West via the Arabs. Such encounters-which historian Arnold Toynbee called "encounters between civilizations in time" resulted in a renaissance of learning in Europe in the twelfth century, and so offer quite a different scenario than physical culture contact.

Psychologist Albert Harrison has pioneered another approach to extraterrestrial contact by applying living systems theory. This also is a kind of analog approach, relying on a systems theory in which what we know about organisms, societies and supranational systems on Earth is used to discuss the outer space analogs of aliens, alien civilizations and the galactic club. It offers the promise of bringing the social sciences into SETI in a substantive way. Considering the biological universe as a world view, as we have in this paper, also offers a variety of advantages to the study of implications of contact with extraterrestrials.

First, comparing like entities we can analyze the reception of past world views and ask how this might apply to the reception of the biological universe.

One must always use analogs cautiously, but they are a starting point, and I have argued elsewhere that all world views undergo similar stages, ranging from their first motivation through elaboration, opposition, exploration of implications, and general acceptance or rejection. Just as the Copernican Revolution had its Galileo, Kepler and Newton, as well as its detractors, so will the biological universe.

Whereas the heliocentric theory took some 150 years for widespread acceptance after Copernicus's arguments were presented, paradoxically we have the curious situation today of widespread acceptance of the biological universe before any solid evidence has been presented. In this regard, the exploration of implications is certainly an important stage in the life of any world view.

To take only one, a primary lesson of past world views is that they harbor uncharted theological implications.

The course of theological controversies for the Copernican theory and for Darwinian evolution, for example, form a rich literature in the history of science.

They have a history already in the context of the extraterrestrial life debate, and the possibility of a "Cosmotheology" is receiving increasingly serious attention from scholars.

A second advantage of the biological universe as world view is that elements of the debate make more sense when seen in the context of exploration of implications. I would suggest that UFOs and science fiction are two ways of working out the biological universe world view in popular culture.

Although I do not see any evidence in favor of the extraterrestrial hypothesis of UFOs, the idea has undeniably had a significant impact on popular culture.

As for science fiction, a full range of scenarios has been explored with greater or lesser degrees of intelligence and foresight. H. G. Wells's *The War of the Worlds* (1898) expressed one stunning possible outcome of this world view. The works of Olaf Stapledon and Arthur C. Clarke, including *Star Maker* (1937), *Last and First Men* (1930), *Childhood's End* (1953), and *2001: A Space Odyssey* (1968) play out the opposite outcome.

The Polish science fiction author Stanislaw Lem represents yet a third choice: in *Solaris* (1961) and *His Master's Voice* (1968) he argues that we may be unable to comprehend, much less communicate, with extraterrestrials. By the late twentieth century these themes had been elaborated in ever more subtle (and sometimes not so subtle) form.

Maria Doria Russell's *The Sparrow* (1996) and *Children of God* (1998) raise powerful theological questions in an extraterrestrial context. am sympathetic with Lem's view that extraterrestrial communication may be much more challenging than we think.

Needless to say, this has important consequences for SETI searches. In the final analysis, the problem reduces to a question of extraterrestrial epistemology, or ways of knowing.

There are 3 cases in comparative terrestrial-extraterrestrial epistemology: no overlap, partial overlap, and complete overlap between human and non-human knowledge.

SETI researchers usually assume complete overlap when they search for artificial transmissions. But with no overlap between human and alien minds, there would be no communication; with partial overlap the form of communication might be very different, perhaps mediated by other civilizations.

Far from being an intractable problem, extraterrestrial epistemology should receive more attention in the future. The whole idea of socially constructed science in a strong sense of allowing no objective knowledge seems to me to be extremely unlikely in a purely terrestrial context. There are no Chinese laws of gravity, no Islamic laws of thermodynamics, no Egyptian theory of relativity. Only one law "works" in nature, and it is to the credit of all humanity when it is discovered. The universe began in only one way, and we either have knowledge of it now, or will in the future.

But when applied to extraterrestrial knowledge, social constructionism in an interspecies sense raises a more profound question: as data is filtered through many sensory systems, will alien knowledge be the same as human knowledge? Do Locke's *Essay on Human Understanding*, Hume's *Treatise on Human Nature*, and Kant's *Critique of Pure Reason* apply to extraterrestrials? If not, in the end there may be many world systems, as many as there are cognitive systems among extraterrestrials, and some day we may have an *Essay on Non-Human Understanding*. On the question of objective knowledge, perhaps the social constructionists were ahead of their time; a century or millennium from now, perhaps our descendants will be discussing "extraterrestrial constructionism!"

In many ways a strong biological universe is more interesting. We would not be able to contemplate extraterrestrial epistemology in a universe full of bacteria. Others might be fearful that extraterrestrials would upset their current world view; they have no need of that hypothesis. Neither did religions have a need for Copernicanism, but they eventually had to adjust, though not without the tragic episodes of Bruno and Galileo, and a long and fruitless battle between science and religion. In the end, interest, need, and desire may well serve religion, but they are no criteria of truth. And although the truth about Galileo's two chief world systems is now known, the truth of the two modern world systems remains a mystery. This is precisely my point: that we teeter on the brink of a new world view that may change everything in its strong version, and a great deal even in its weak version. Even the disproof of the biological universe may have its effect. As we stand on the threshold of a new millennium, we may conjecture that 1,000 years from now we will have had our answer to this age-old question. Humanity 3000 will know whether or not it is alone in the universe, at least within our galaxy. Olaf Stapledon's vision of "Interplanetary Humanity" fifty years ago will be extended to "Interstellar Humanity," in which our philosophy, religion, and science are much more attuned to the cosmos. By then we will know if we live in a physical or a biological universe, and we may even have traveled to the nearest stars. Extraterrestrial life is humanity's great secular meditation on the other. It is a search for the universal laws of biology as opposed to the elaborate natural history of life on Earth that we now possess. It is becoming a new window on traditional theological concerns, as scholars broach the subject of "Cosmotheology." And, if the biological universe is proven true in the strong sense it has the potential to become much more than that: the universal system of thought of which our science, our art, religion, philosophy and history-in short, our knowledge and belief-are but specific instances of the manifestations of intelligence in the universe. In short, the biological universe will affect our world view at many levels, no less than the geocentric cosmos did for Dante's contemporaries, and the heliocentric cosmos did for Galileo's, even though the full scope of the Copernican revolution was unfulfilled then, and remains so today. (Source Dr. Steven J. Dick)

62-THE ENUMA ELISH

Enuma Elish ('When on High') is the name given to the Babylonian Epic of Creation, which was composed circa 1000 BC. To orthodox scholars, *Enuma Elish* is almost totally beyond comprehension. But, the Epic makes complete logical sense when viewed as an exploded planet myth. It is worth outlining one particular theory, advocated by the American author Zecharia Sitchin, which has gained some popularity in recent years (it was borrowed without credit, for example, by the writers D.S. Allan and J.B. Delair in their book 'Cataclysm', alias 'When the Earth Nearly Died').

Sitchin's interpretation of *Enuma Elish* focuses on the battle between Marduk and Tiamat. In his view, Marduk originates from the abyss of space as an intruder planet, and proceeds to undergo various encounters with the outer planets of our solar system, followed by a climactic and catastrophic encounter with a planet named Tiamat. According to Sitchin's interpretation, the scarred planet Tiamat was then shifted by the impact of Marduk's satellites into a new orbit to become the Earth, acquiring in the process a Moon (named Kingu) which was previously the satellite of Tiamat. Marduk, meanwhile, sailed off into space to begin a vast elliptical orbit which would bring it back to the site of the celestial battle every 3,600 years.

As he has pointed out in his book 'The Phoenix Solution', the magnificent author, linguist and researcher, Alan Alford stated: "Sitchin's scenario is totally contrary to the laws of celestial dynamics, and cannot possibly represent a scientific record of the history of the solar system. But beyond that, his reading of *Enuma Elish* is based on a highly subjective interpretation. In this context, Mr. Alford presents and explains his personal interpretations…

Enuma Elish – The Exploded Planet Interpretation According to Author Extraordinaire, Alan Alford

The opening lines of *Enuma Elish* refer to a time 'when Heaven and Earth had not been named'. It is important to understand that this does not mean that Heaven and Earth did not exist. Rather, it means that the Heaven and Earth of the current Universe had not yet been created by the interaction of the Heaven and Earth of the old Universe.

In the lines that follow, the Heaven of the old Universe is named Apsu-Tiamat. The text describes how the waters of Apsu and Tiamat are mingled together (line 4), and how the gods are formed inside their joint body (line 8). These gods are named Lahmu, Lahamu, Anshar, Kishar, Anu and Ea (they are known collectively as the Anunnaki).

The Epic describes the gods causing a tremendous noise in the heavenly abode and upsetting the belly of Tiamat as they surge back and forth within her (lines 21-28). Apsu then decides to destroy the gods in order to put an end to their noise, but Ea, catching wind of the plan, makes a pre-emptive strike; he puts Apsu to sleep and then slays him, whereupon he establishes his dwelling place upon Apsu (lines 65-77). The meaning of this – we know from other texts – is that Apsu fell from Heaven and became an ocean of the Underworld, i.e. a subterranean sea. Hence the fact that Ea (alias Enki) was the ruler of this subterranean sea (cf the 'drawing of lots' passage in the *Epic of Atra-Hasis*).

The Epic now alludes to a sacred marriage between Ea and Damkina, the latter almost certainly a personification of Mother Earth (their union is thus a sacred marriage of Heaven and Earth, resulting from the fall of the sky). The result of this union is the birth inside Damkina (the Earth) of the young god Marduk, who is described in supernatural terms: 'flashing the look of his eyes...when his lips moved, fire blazed forth... his members were gigantic, he was surpassing in height' (lines 78-100).

The Epic now switches its focus to Tiamat and her brood of gods in Heaven. These gods accuse Tiamat of having stood idly by when Apsu was vanquished.

The gods of Tiamat plot a war of vengeance, announcing that they will descend from Heaven into the Underworld and prevail over Ea and the Anunnaki. Tiamat agrees with this action and produces from within herself a brood of evil gods and appoints Marduk their chief. The text refers to her, rather aptly, as Mother Hubur, literally 'Mother of Noise'.

In the Underworld, the Anunnaki-gods hear of the impending attack, and seek a hero who will ascend into Heaven to make a precipitative strike against Tiamat and her demons. The stage is set for Marduk to step forward as the hero of the Epic, demanding that he be made king of the gods if he can vanquish the enemy.

The remainder of the Epic is dominated by the war between Marduk and Tiamat and her army, with Tablets II and III building up the suspense towards the dramatic climax.

In Tablet IV, lines 19-32, the Anunnaki put Marduk's powers to the test by having him destroy a constellation and then bring it back into existence (this act encapsulates the essential physical-metaphysical duality of the exploded planet religion). Marduk passes the test, collects his arms, and ascends into Heaven to do battle.

To cut a long story short, he vanquishes Tiamat with an arrow into her interior, and casts her lifeless body down into the Underworld, interring it beneath a mountain. In addition, he rounds up Kingu and the other demons, binds them in fetters, and confines them in the Underworld for eternity.

Marduk then creates the new Universe.

First, he splits Tiamat's fallen body into two parts. With one half of her body, he creates the visible heavens; the other half he secures in the Underworld with a bolt, so that her waters cannot escape. Having done this, Marduk measures the fallen body of Apsu and creates an invisible Heaven, Esharra, in its image. He then organises the constellations (this part of the text is not altogether clear) and appoints the orbit of the Moon. Finally, in Tablet VI, Marduk creates mankind from the blood of Kingu, and sets the Anunnaki free from the Underworld by splitting off their spiritual doubles, the Igigi, whom he raises to Heaven to live in Esharra for ever.

The Epic ends with the celebration of Marduk's act of creation and the listing of his fifty victorious titles.

Further Comment on Alternative Interpretations

Several points now need to be made to clarify our understanding of the Epic.

Firstly, there is no basis whatsoever for supposing that Apsu was the Sun, as Zecharia Sitchin has suggested. In fact, the text describes how Apsu was vanquished by Ea and cast down from Heaven to Earth. Anyone who is familiar with the ancient Mesopotamian texts should know that Apsu was the name for the subterranean sea.

Secondly, there is no basis whatsoever for supposing that the gods produced by Apsu were planets of the solar system, as Sitchin suggested. Yes, these gods were produced *from within* Apsu himself (Tablet I, lines 3 and 9; the Epic describes the gods running around in Apsu-Tiamat's insides). But Apsu was not the Sun, but a celestial body which fell from Heaven into the Underworld, i.e. an exploded planet (hence the cataclysmic imagery in the text). There is no basis, therefore, for supposing that Lahmu and Lahamu were Mars and Venus, or that Anshar and Kishar were Saturn and Jupiter, or that Anu and Ea were Uranus and Neptune, as Sitchin suggests. These are all completely false premises.

Thirdly, Marduk did not appear from the cosmic abyss, as Sitchin suggested, but was born from the interior of the Earth – a mode of birth that is well-attested in the myths of the Greek gods. This is evident from lines 73-84 of the Epic, which describe Marduk's mother and father as Damkina and Ea (incidentally, the Assyrian version of the Epic suggests that Marduk's mother and father were Lahmu and Lahamu).

But Ea, we are told, resided in a 'sacred chamber', otherwise known as 'the chamber of fates' (lines 75 and 79). Where was this chamber and dwelling place of Ea? We know from line 71 that it was 'established upon the Apsu'. Where was the Apsu? It was the Underworld of the Earth, for it had earlier been cast down from Heaven (lines 60-70). In summary, then, Marduk was created in the heart of the holy Apsu (line 82), which was the Underworld of the Earth, and from there he soared up into the heavens to do battle against the planet of Tiamat. (This type of cosmic battle myth is well-attested in the myths of ancient Egypt and Greece.)

Fourthly, there is no basis whatsoever for suggesting (as Sitchin did) that Marduk encountered the other planets of the solar system en route to his battle with Tiamat. These other 'planets' (Ea and Anu) were in fact the gods which had emanated from the interior of the exploded planet Apsu.

Fifthly, the battle between Marduk and Tiamat was not a collision between two planetary systems. Yes, Tiamat was envisioned as a physical planet, but Marduk was envisioned as a metaphysical avenger-god who rose up from the Earth to Heaven. The result of the battle was the death of Tiamat, which is to be understood as a second planetary explosion (following the explosion of Apsu recorded earlier in the Epic).

Sixthly, it is incorrect to imagine (as Sitchin did) a break in the battle, pending a future orbital return of Marduk. What the Epic actually says is that 'Valiant Marduk...turned back to Tiamat' (Tablet IV, line 128). This could be read in many different ways, but in any event Marduk did **not** take the form of a physical planet with a conventional orbit.

Seventhly, where ancient texts referred to Marduk as travelling between the locations AN.UR and E.NUN, it must be understood that these were not the perigee and apogee of an orbiting planet. On the contrary, AN.UR was simply the Earth, whilst E.NUN was simply the Deep, i.e. Heaven. By the same token, when Marduk saw 'all the quarters of the universe', this meant that his realm spanned the twin planets of Heaven and Earth, for the Sumerian term for 'Universe' was simply AN.KI, meaning 'Heaven and Earth'. (Virtually all of the activities of the gods in Sumerian myths occurred between these two planets, which were at the heart of the exploded planet mythos.)

Summary

In summary, *Enuma Elish* describes two linked planetary explosions and their role in the creation of the Universe. It does **not** describe a planetary collision. It does **not** describe Marduk as an intruder planet. And it does **not** describe a race of ancient astronauts descending from Marduk to Earth (nowhere does any text state that the gods came down to Earth 'from Marduk'; on the contrary the gods came down to Earth from the destroyed celestial body Apsu-Tiamat). For further information on Enuma Elish and the exploded planet hypothesis, Read Alford' superb books 'When the Gods Came Down' and 'The Atlantis Secret'. (Source:Translation: Kenneth Sublett, Piney.com, Hohenwald, Tennessee)

Enuma Elish, the Babylonian Creation Epic Tablet I

When Marduk heard the speech of the gods,
He made up his mind to perform miracles.
He spoke his utterance to Ea,
And communicated to him the plan that he was considering.

Let me put blood together, and make bones too.
Let me set up primeval man: Man shall be his name.
Let me create a primeval man.
The work of the gods shall be imposed on him, and so they shall be at leisure.

Let me change the ways of the gods miraculously,
So they are gathered as one yet divided in two.
Ea answered him and spoke a word to him,
Told him his plan for the leisure of the gods.

Let one who is hostile to them be surrendered up,
Let him be destroyed, and let people be created from him.
Let the great gods assemble,
Let the culprit be given up, and let them convict him.

Marduk assembled the great gods,
Gave them instructions pleasantly, gave orders.
The gods paid attention to what he said.
The king addressed his words to the Anunnaki,
Your election of me shall be firm and foremost.
I shall declare the laws, the edicts within my power.
Whosoever started the war,
And incited Tiamat, and gathered an army,
Let the one who started the war be given up to me,
And he shall bear the penalty for his crime, that you may dwell in peace.

The Igigi, the great gods, answered him,
Their lord Lugal-dimmer-ankia, counsellor of the gods,

It was Qingu who started the war,
He who incited Tiamat and gathered an army!

They bound him and held him in front of Ea,
Imposed the penalty on him and cut off his blood.
He created mankind from his blood,
Imposed the toil of the gods on man and released the gods from it.

When Ea the wise had created mankind,
Had imposed the toil of the gods on them,
That deed is impossible to describe,
For Nudimmud performed it with the miracles of Marduk.

Then Marduk the king divided the gods,
The Anunnaki, all of them, above and below.
He assigned his decrees to Anu to guard,
Established three hundred as a guard in the sky;
Did the same again when he designed the conventions of earth,
And made the six hundred dwell in both heaven and earth.

When he had directed all the decrees,
Had divided lots for the Anunnaki, of heaven and of earth,
The Anunnaki made their voices heard
And addressed Marduk their lord,
Now, O Lord, that you have set us free,
What are our favours from you?
We would like to make a shrine with its own name.
We would like our night's resting place to be in your private quarters, and to rest there.

Let us found a shrine, a sanctuary there.
Whenever we arrive, let us rest within it.
When Marduk heard this,
His face lit up greatly, like daylight.
Create Babylon, whose construction you requested!
Let its mud bricks be moulded, and build high the shrine!'

The Anunnaki began shovelling.
For a whole year they made bricks for it.
When the second year arrived,

They had raised the top of Esagila in front of the Apsu;
They had built a high ziggurat for the Apsu.
They founded a dwelling for Anu, Ellil, and Ea likewise.

In ascendancy he settled himself in front of them,
And his horns' look down at the base of Esharra.
When they had done the work on Esagila,
And the Anunnaki, all of them, had fashioned their individual shrines,
The three hundred Igigi of heaven and the Anunnaki of the Apsu assembled.

The Lord invited the gods his fathers to attend a banquet
In the great sanctuary which he and created as his dwelling.
Indeed, Bab-ili is your home too!
Sing for joy there, dwell in happiness!
The great gods sat down there,
And set out the beer mugs; they attended the banquet.

When they had made merry within,
They themselves made a taqribtu-offering in splendid Esagila.
All the decrees and designs were fixed.
All the gods divided the stations of heaven and earth.
The fifty great gods were present, and
The gods fixed the seven destinies for the cult.

The Lord received the bow, and set his weapon down in front of them.
The gods his fathers looked at the net which he had made,
Looked at the bow, how miraculous her construction,
And his fathers praised the deeds that he had done.
Anu raised the bow and spoke in the assembly of gods,
He kissed the bow. May she go far!
He gave to the bow her names, saying,
May Long and Far be the first, and Victorious the second;
Her third name shall be Bowstar, for she shall shine in the sky.

He fixed her position among the gods her companions.
When Anu had decreed the destiny of the bow,

He set down her royal throne. You are highest of the gods!
And Anu made her sit in the assembly of gods.
The great gods assembled
And made Marduk's destiny highest; they themselves did obeisance.

They swore an oath for themselves,
And swore on water and oil, touched their throats.
Thus they granted that he should exercise the kingship of the gods
And confirmed for him mastery of the gods of heaven and earth.

Anshar gave him another name: Asarluhi.
At the mention of his name we shall bow down!
The gods are to pay heed to what he says:
His command is to have priority above and below.
The son who avenged us shall be the highest!
His rule shall have priority; let him have no rival!

Let him act as shepherd over the black-headed people, his creation.
Let his way be proclaimed in future days, never forgotten.
He shall establish great nindabu-offerings for his fathers.
He shall take care of them, he shall look after their shrines.
He shall let them smell the qutrinnu-offering, and make their chant joyful.

Let him breathe on earth as freely as he always does in heaven.
Let him designate the black-headed people to revere him,
That mankind may be mindful of him, and name him as their god.
Let their (interceding) goddess pay attention when he opens his mouth.
Let nindabu-offerings be brought to their god and their goddess.
Let them never be forgotten! Let them cleave to their god.
Let them keep their country preeminent, and always build shrines.

Though the black-headed people share out the gods,
As for us, no matter by which name we call him, he shall be our god.
Come, let us call him by his fifty names!
His ways shall be proclaimed, and his deeds likewise! Marduk

Whose father Anu designated him at the moment of his birth, To be in charge of
pasturage and watering places, to enrich their stalls,
Who overwhelmed the riotous ones with his flood-weapon?

And saved the gods his fathers from hardship.
Let the son, majesty of the gods be his name!
In his bright light may they walk forever more:

The people whom he created, the form of life that breathes.
He imposed the work of the gods on them so that they might rest.

Creation and abolition, forgiveness and punishment,
Such are at his disposal, so let them look to him.

Marukka…he is the god who created them.
He pleases the Anunnaki and gives rest to the Igigi

Marutukku…he is the help of country, city, and his people.
Him shall the people revere forever.

Mershakushu---fierce yet considerate, furious yet merciful.
Generous is his heart, controlled are his emotions.

Lugal-Dimmer-Ankia…his name which we gave him in our assembly.
We made his command higher than the gods his fathers'.
He is indeed Bel of the gods of heaven and earth, all of them,
The king at whose instruction the gods are awed above and below.

Nari-Lugal-Dimmer-Ankia is a name that we have given him as director of the gods,
Who founded our dwellings in heaven and earth out of difficulties,
And who shared out the stations for the Igigi and Anunnaki.
At his names may the gods tremble and quake in their dwellings.

Asarluhi first is his name which his father Anu gave him,
He shall be the light of the gods, strong leader,
Who like his name is the protecting spirit of god and country.
He spared our dwellings in the great battle despite difficulties.
Second, they called him Asarluhi as Namtila, the god who gives life,
Who restored all the damaged gods as if they were his own creation.
Bel, who revives dead gods with his pure incantation,
Who destroys those who oppose him but…the enemy.
Asarluhi third as Namru, whose name was given thus,
The pure god who purifies our path.

Anshar, Lahmu, and Lahamu called his three names;
They pronounced them to the gods their sons,
'We have given him each of these three names.
Now you, pronounce his names as we did!
The gods rejoiced, and obeyed their command.
In Ubshu-ukkinakku they deliberated their counsel.
Let us elevate the name of the son, the warrior,
Our champion who looks after us!
They sat in their assembly and began to call out the destinies,
Pronounced his name in all their rites.

Tablet II

Tiamat assembled her creatures
And collected battle-units against the gods her offspring.
Tiamat did even more evil for posterity than Apsu.
It was reported to Ea that she had prepared for war.
Ea listened to that report,
And was dumbfounded and sat in silence.

When he had pondered and his fury subsided,
He made his way to Anshar his father;
Came before Anshar, the father who begot him
And began to repeat to him everything that Tiamat had planned.
Father, Tiamat who bore us is rejecting us!

She has convened an assembly and is raging out of control.
The gods have turned to her, all of them,
Even those whom you begot have gone over to her side,
Have crowded round and rallied beside Tiamat.
Fierce, scheming restlessly night and day,
Working up to war, growling and raging,
They have convened a council and created conflict.

Mother Hubur, who fashions all things,
Contributed an unfaceable weapon: she bore giant snakes,
Sharp of tooth and unsparing of fang.
She filled their bodies with venom instead of blood.
She cloaked ferocious dragons with fearsome rays
And made them bear mantles of radiance, made them godlike,
(chanting this imprecation)

Whoever looks upon them shall collapse in utter terror!

Their bodies shall rear up continually and never turn away!
She stationed a horned serpent, a mushussu-dragon, and a lahmu-hero,
An ugallu-demon, a rabid dog, and a scorpion-man,
Aggressive umu-demons, a fish-man, and a bull-man
Bearing merciless weapons, fearless in battle.

Her orders were so powerful, they could not be disobeyed.
In addition she created eleven more likewise.
Over the gods her offspring who had convened a council for her
She promoted Qingu and made him greatest among them,
Conferred upon him leadership of the army, command of the assembly,
Raising the weapon to signal engagement, mustering combat-troops,
Overall command of the whole battle force.

And she set him upon a throne.
I have cast the spell for you and made you greatest in the gods' assembly!
I have put into your power rule over all the gods!
You shall be the greatest, for you are my only lover!
Your commands shall always prevail over all the Anukki!
Then she gave him the Tablet of Destinies and made him clasp it to his breast.

Your utterance shall never be altered! Your word shall be law!
When Qingu was promoted and had received the Anu-power
And had decreed destinies for the gods his sons, he said,
"What issues forth from your mouths shall quench Fire!
Your accumulated venom shall paralyze the powerful
Anshar listened, and the report was very disturbing.

He twisted his fingers and bit his lip;
His liver was inflamed, his belly would not rest.
His roar to Ea his son was quite weak.
You must be the one who declares war!
Keep brandishing what you have made as arms for yourself!
You are the hero, you slew Apsu.

Where else (will we find) someone to face Tiamat when she rages uncontrollably?
Good sense
Of the gods Nudimmud
....

Ea made his voice heard,
You are the unfathomable fixer of fates!
The power to create and to destroy is yours!

O Anshar, you are the unfathomable fixer of fates!
The power to create and to destroy is yours!
The which you order immediately
(5 lines very fragmentary)
Anshar listened and the speech pleased him.
His heart prompted him to speak to Ea,
Your courage like a god
Rise up against Tiamat!'
(Gap of up to 25 lines)

He (Anshar) addressed Anu his son saying,
This is the kasusu-weapon of warriors.
Its strength is mighty, its attack unfaceable.
Go against Tiamat and stand your ground!
Let her anger abate, let her fury be quelled.
If she will not listen to your word,
Speak our words to her, that she may be calmed.

He listened to the speech of his father Anshar,
And took the road to her and made his way straight to her.
Anu set out. He was trying to find out the strategy of Tiamat.
And he turned back.
He entered the presence of Anshar the father who begot him
He addressed him,
Too great for me.

(Short gap)
She laid the…of her hand on top of me.
Anshar was speechless, and stared at the ground;
He gnashed his teeth.And shook his head in despair at Ea.
Now, the Igigi assembled, all the Anukki.

They sat silently for a while, tight-lipped.
Finally they spoke.
Will no other god come forward? Is fate fixed?
Will no one go out to face Tiamat with...
Then Ea from his secret dwelling called

The perfect one of Anshar, father of the great gods,
Whose heart is perfect like a fellow-citizen or countryman,
The mighty heir who was to be his father's champion,
Who rushes fearlessly into battle: Marduk the Hero!

 Begin 20 lines
He (Ea) told him his innermost design, saying,
O Marduk, take my advice, listen to your father!
You are the son who sets his heart at rest!
Approach Anshar, drawing near to him,
And make your voice heard, stand your ground: he will be calmed by the sight of you.'

The Lord rejoiced at the word of his father,
And he approached and stood before Anshar.
Anshar looked at him, and his heart was filled with joy.
He kissed him on the lips, put away his trepidation.
Then Marduk addressed him, saying:
Father, don't stay so silent, open your lips,
Let me go, and let me fulfil your heart's desire.

Anshar, don't stay so silent, open your lips,
Let me go, and let me fulfil your heart's desire.
Anshar replied
What kind of man has ordered you out to his war?
My son, don't you realize that it is Tiamat, of womankind, who will advance against you with arms?

Marduk answered
Father, my creator, rejoice and be glad!
You shall soon set your foot upon the back of Tiamat!
Anshar, my creator, rejoice and be glad,
You shall soon set your foot upon the neck of Tiamat.

Anshar replied
Then go, son, knowing all wisdom!
Quell Tiamat with your pure spell!
Set forth immediately in the storm chariot;
Let its be not driven out, but turn them back!
The Lord rejoiced at the word of his father;
His heart was glad and he addressed his father,
Lord of the gods, fate of the great gods,

If indeed I am to be your champion,
If I am to defeat Tiamat and save your lives,
Convene the council, name a special fate,
Sit joyfully together in Ubshu-ukkinakku:

My own utterance shall fix fate instead of you!
Whatever I create shall never be altered!
The decree of my lips shall never be revoked, never changed!
Written according to a copy from Assur.

Tablet III

Anshar made his voice heard
And addressed his speech to Kakka his vizier,
O Kakka, vizier who pleases me!
I shall send you to Lahmu and Lahamu.

You know how to probe, you are skilled in speaking.
Have the gods my fathers brought before me;
Let all the gods be brought to me.

Let there be conversation, let them sit at a banquet,
Let them eat grain, let them drink choice wine,
And then let them decree a destiny for Marduk their champion.

Set off, Kakka, go and stand before them, and
Everything that I am about to tell you, repeat to them,
Anshar your son has sent me,
He has told me to report his heart's message,
To say, Tiamat who bore us is rejecting us!

She has convened a council and is raging out of control.
The gods have turned to her, all of them,
Even those whom you begot have gone over to her side,
Have crowded round and rallied beside Tiamat.

They are fierce, scheming restlessly night and day,
They are working up to war, growling and raging,
They convened a council and created conflict.

Mother Hubur, who fashions all things,
Contributed an unfaceable weapon: she bore giant snakes,
Sharp of tooth and unsparing of fang.
She filled their bodies with venom instead of blood.

She cloaked ferocious dragons with fearsome rays
And made them bear mantles of radiance, made them godlike,
(Chanting this imprecation)
Whoever looks upon them shall collapse in utter terror!
Their bodies shall rear up continually and never turn away!

She stationed a horned serpent, a mushussu-dragon, and a Lahmu-hero,
An Ugallu-demon, a rabid dog, and a scorpion-man,
Aggressive umu-demons, a fish-man, and a bull-man
Bearing merciless weapons, fearless in battle.

Her orders were so powerful, they could not be disobeyed.
In addition she created eleven more likewise.
Over the gods her offspring who had convened a council for her.

She promoted Qingu and made him greatest among them,
Conferred upon him leadership of the army, command of the assembly,
Raising the weapon to signal engagement, to rise up for combat,
Overall command of the whole battle force.

And she set him upon a throne.
I have cast the spell for you and made you greatest in the gods' assembly!
I have put into your power rule over all the gods!
You shall be the greatest, for you are my only lover!
Your commands shall always prevail over all the Anunnaki!

Then she gave him the Tablet of Destinies and made him clasp it to his breast.
Your utterance shall never be altered! Your word shall be law!
When Qingu was promoted and had received the Anu-power
And had decreed destinies for the gods his sons, (he said),
What issues forth from your mouths shall quench Fire!

Your accumulated venom shall paralyze the powerful!
I sent Anu, but he was unable to face her.
Nudimmud (Ea) panicked and turned back.

Then Marduk, sage of the gods, your **son**, came forward.
He wanted of his own free will to confront Tiamat.
He addressed his words to me,

If indeed I am to be your champion,
To defeat Tiamat and save your lives,
Convene the council, name a special fate,
Sit joyfully together in Ubshu-ukkinakku:
And let me, my own utterance, fix fate instead of you!
Whatever I create shall never be altered!
The decree of my lips shall never be revoked, never changed!

Hurry and decree your destiny for him quickly,
So that he may go and face your formidable enemy!
Kakka set off and went on his way,
And before Lahmu and Lahamu the gods his fathers
Prostrated himself and kissed the earth in front of them,
Then straightened up and stood and spoke to them,

Anshar your son has sent me.
He has told me to report his personal message,
To say, Tiamat who bore us is rejecting us!
She has convened a council and is raging out of control.
The gods have turned to her, all of them,
Even those whom you begot have gone over to her side,
Have crowded round and rallied beside Tiamat.

Fierce, scheming restlessly night and day,
Working up to war, growling and raging,
They have convened a council and created conflict.
Mother Hubur, who fashions all things,
Contributed an unfaceable weapon: she bore giant snakes,
Sharp of tooth and unsparing of fang.
She filled their bodies with venom instead of blood.
She cloaked ferocious dragons with fearsome rays
And made them bear mantles of radiance, made them godlike,
(Chanting this imprecation)

Whoever looks upon them shall collapse in utter terror!
Their bodies shall rear up continually and never turn away!

374

She stationed a horned serpent, a mushussu-dragon, and a lahmu-hero,
An ugallu-demon, a rabid dog, and a scorpion-man,
Aggressive umu-demons, a fish-man, and a bull-man
Bearing merciless weapons, fearless in battle.
Her orders were so powerful, they could not be disobeyed.

In addition she created eleven more likewise.
Over the gods her offspring who had convened a council for her
She promoted Qingu and made him greatest among them,
Conferred upon him leadership of the army, command of the assembly,
Raising the weapon to signal engagement, to rise up for combat,
Overall command of the whole battle force.

And she set him upon a throne.

I have cast the spell for you and made you greatest in the gods' assembly!
I have put into your power rule over all the gods!
You shall be the greatest, for you are my only lover!
Your commands shall always prevail over all the Anunnaki!
Then she gave him the Tablet of Destinies and made him clasp it to his breast.
Your utterance shall never be altered! Your word shall be law!
When Qingu was promoted and had received the Anu-power
And had decreed destinies for the gods his sons, (he said),
"What issues forth from your mouths shall quench Fire!
Your accumulated venom shall paralyze the powerful!
I sent Anu, but he was unable to face her.
Nudimmud panicked and turned back.
Then Marduk, sage of the gods, your son, came forward.
He wanted of his own free will to confront Tiamat.
He addressed his words to me,
If indeed I am to be your champion,
To defeat Tiamat and save your lives,
Convene the council, name a special fate,
Sit joyfully together in Ubshu-ukkinakku:
And let me, my own utterance, fix fate instead of you!
Whatever I create shall never be altered!
The decree of my lips shall never be revoked, never changed!
Hurry and decree your destinies for him quickly,
So that he may go and face your formidable enemy!
Lahmu and Lahamu listened and cried aloud.
All the Igigi groaned dreadfully,

How terrible! Until he (Anshar) decided to report to us,
We did not even know what Tiamat was doing.
They milled around and then came,
All the great gods who fix the fates,
Entered into Anshar's presence and were filled with joy.
Each kissed the other: in the assembly.
There was conversation, they sat at the banquet,
Ate grain, drank choice wine,
Let sweet beer trickle through their drinking straws.
Their bodies swelled as they drank the liquor;
They became very carefree, they were merry,
And they decreed destiny for Marduk their champion.

Tablet IV

They founded a princely shrine for him.

And he took up residence as ruler before his fathers,
(Who proclaimed)
You are honoured among the great gods.
Your destiny is unequalled, your word (has the power of) Anu!
O Marduk, you are honoured among the great gods.

Your destiny is unequalled, your word (has the power of) Anu!
From this day onwards your command shall not be altered.
Yours is the power to exalt and abase.
May your utterance be law, your word never be falsified.
None of the gods shall transgress your limits.
May endowment, required for the gods' shrines
Wherever they have temples, be established for your place.
O Marduk, you are our champion!

We hereby give you sovereignty over the whole universe.
Sit in the assembly and your word shall be pre-eminent!
May your weapons never miss (the mark), may they smash your enemies!
O lord, spare the life of him who trusts in you,
But drain the life of the god who has espoused evil!

They set up in their midst one constellation,

And then they addressed Marduk their son,
May your decree, O lord, impress the gods!
Command to destroy and to recreate, and let it be so!
Speak and let the constellation vanish!
Speak to it again and let the constellation reappear.

He spoke, and at his word the constellation vanished.
He spoke to it again and the constellation was recreated.
When the gods his fathers saw how effective his utterance was,
They rejoiced, they proclaimed: Marduk is King!
They invested him with sceptre, throne, and staff-of-office.
They gave him an unfaceable weapon to crush the foe.
Go, and cut off the life of Tiamat!

Let the winds bear her blood to us as good news!'
The gods his fathers thus decreed the destiny of the lord
And set him on the path of peace and obedience.
He fashioned a bow, designated it as his weapon,
Feathered the arrow, set it in the string.
He lifted up a mace and carried it in his right hand,
Slung the bow and quiver at his side,
Put lightning in front of him,
His body was filled with an ever-blazing flame.
He made a net to encircle Tiamat within it,
Marshalled the four winds so that no part of her could escape:
South Wind, North Wind, East Wind, West Wind,
The gift of his father Anu, he kept them close to the net at his side.
He created the imhullu-wind (evil wind), the tempest, the whirlwind,
The Four Winds, the Seven Winds, the tornado, the unfaceable facing wind.

He released the winds which he had created, seven of them.
They advanced behind him to make turmoil inside Tiamat.
The lord raised the flood-weapon, his great weapon,
And mounted the frightful, unfaceable storm-chariot.
He had yoked to it a team of four and had harnessed to its side
Slayer, Pitiless, Racer, and Flyer;
Their lips were drawn back, their teeth carried poison.
They know not exhaustion, they can only devastate.
He stationed on his right Fiercesome Fight and Conflict,
On the left Battle to knock down every contender.
Clothed in a cloak of awesome armour,

His head was crowned with a terrible radiance.
The Lord set out and took the road,
And set his face towards Tiamat who raged out of control.
In his lips he gripped a spell,
In his hand he grasped a herb to counter poison.

Then they thronged about him, the gods thronged about him;
The gods his fathers thronged about him, the gods thronged about him.
The Lord drew near and looked into the middle of Tiamat:
He was trying to find out the strategy of Qingu her lover.
As he looked, his mind became confused,
His will crumbled and his actions were muddled.

As for the gods his helpers, who marched at his side,
When they saw the warrior, the leader, their looks were strained.
Tiamat cast her spell. She did not even turn her neck.
In her lips she was holding falsehood, lies, (wheedling),
How powerful is your attacking force, O lord of the gods!
The whole assembly of them has gathered to your place!
But he ignored her brandishments.

The Lord lifted up the flood-weapon, his great weapon
And sent a message to Tiamat who feigned goodwill, saying:
Why are you so friendly on the surface
When your depths conspire to muster a battle force?
Just because the sons were noisy and disrespectful to their fathers,
Should you, who gave them birth, reject compassion?
You named Qingu as your lover,
You appointed him to **rites** of Anu-power, wrongfully his.
You sought out evil for Anshar, king of the gods,

So you have compounded your wickedness against the gods my fathers!
Let your host prepare! Let them gird themselves with your weapons!
Stand forth, and you and I shall do single combat!
When Tiamat heard this,
She went wild, she lost her temper.
Tiamat screamed aloud in a passion,
Her lower parts shook together from the depths.
She recited the incantation and kept casting her spell.

Meanwhile the gods of battle were sharpening their weapons.
Face to face they came, Tiamat and Marduk, sage of the gods.
They engaged in combat, they closed for battle.
The Lord spread his net and made it encircle her,

To her face he dispatched the imhullu-wind so that she could not close her lips.
Fierce winds distended her belly;
Her insides were constipated and she stretched her mouth wide.
He shot an arrow which pierced her belly,
Split her down the middle and split her heart,
Vanquished her and extinguished her life.

He threw down the corpse and stood on top of her.
When he had slain Tiamat, the leader,
He broke up her regiments; her assembly was scattered.
Then the gods her helpers, who had marched at her side,
Began to tremble, panicked, and turned tail.

Although he allowed them to come out and spared their lives,

They were surrounded, they could not flee.
Then he tied them up and smashed their weapons.
They were thrown into the net and sat there ensnared.
They cowered back, filled with woe.
They had to bear his punishment, confined to prison.

And as for the dozens of creatures, covered in fearsome rays,
The gang of demons who all marched on her right,
He fixed them with nose-ropes and tied their arms.
He trampled their battle-filth beneath him.
As for Qingu, who had once been the greatest among them,
He defeated him and counted him among the dead gods,

Wrested from him the Tablet of Destinies, wrongfully his,
Sealed it with his own seal and pressed it to his breast.
When he had defeated and killed his enemies
And had proclaimed the submissive foe his slave,
And had set up the triumphal cry of Anshar over all the enemy,
And had achieved the desire of Nudimmud, Marduk the warrior
Strengthened his hold over the captive gods,
And to Tiamat, whom he had ensnared, he turned back.

The Lord trampled the lower part of Tiamat,
With his unsparing mace smashed her skull,
Severed the arteries of her blood,
And made the North Wind carry it off as good news.
His fathers saw it and were jubilant: they rejoiced,
Arranged to greet him with presents, greetings gifts.

The Lord rested, and inspected her corpse.
He divided the monstrous shape and created marvels from it.
He sliced her in half like a fish for drying:
Half of her he put up to roof the sky,
Drew a bolt across and made a guard hold it.
Her waters he arranged so that they could not escape.
He crossed the heavens and sought out a shrine;
He levelled Apsu, dwelling of Nudimmud.
The Lord measured the dimensions of Apsu
And the large temple (Eshgalla), which he built in its image, was Esharra:
In the great shrine Esharra, which he had created as the sky,
He founded cult centres for Anu, Ellil, and Ea.

The Psalmist in poetic language noted that:

Thou didst divide the sea by thy strength: thou brakest the heads of the dragons in the waters. Psalm 74:13

Thou brakest the heads of leviathan in pieces, and gavest him to be meat to the people inhabiting the wilderness. Psalm 74:14

Thou didst cleave the fountain and the flood: thou driedst up mighty rivers. Psalm 74:15

The day is thine, the night also is thine: thou hast prepared the light and the sun. Psalm 74:16
[146 lines. Fourth tablet. Not complete. Written according to a tablet whose lines were cancelled. Nabu-belshu (son of) Na'id-Marduk, son of a smith, wrote it for the life of himself And the life of his house, and deposited (it) in Ezida.]

He fashioned stands for the great gods.
As for the stars, he set up constellations corresponding to them.
He designated the **year** and marked out its divisions,
Apportioned three stars each to the twelve months
When he had made plans of the days of the year,
He founded the stand of Neberu to mark out their courses,
So that none of them could go wrong or stray.

He fixed the stand of Ellil and Ea together with it,
Opened up gates in both **ribs**,
Made strong bolts to left and right,
With her liver he located the Zenith;
He made the crescent moon appear, entrusted night to it,
And designated it the jewel of night to mark out the days.

Go forth every month without fail in a corona,
At the beginning of the month, to glow over the land.
You shine with horns to mark out six days;
On the seventh day the crown is half.
The fifteenth day shall always be the mid-point, the half of each month.
When Shamash looks at you from the horizon,
Gradually shed your visibility and begin to wane.
Always bring the day of disappearance close to the path of Shamash,
And on the thirteenth day, the year is always equalized, for Shamash is responsible for
the year.

A sign shall appear: Sweep along its path.
Then always approach the…and judge the case.
The Bowstar to kill and rob.
(15 lines broken)
At the New Year's Festival
Year
May
The bolt of the exit
From the days
The watches of night and day

The spittle of Tiamat
Marduk

He put into groups and made clouds scud.
Raising winds, making rain,
Making fog billow, by collecting her poison,
He assigned for himself and let his own hand control it.
He placed her head, heaped up
Opened up springs: water gushed out.
He opened the Euphrates and the Tigris from her eyes,
Closed her nostrils,

He piled up clear-cut mountains from her udder,
Bored waterholes to drain off the catchwater.
He laid her tail across, tied it fast as the cosmic bond ,
And the Apsu beneath his feet.
He set her thigh to make fast the sky,
With half of her he made a roof; he fixed the earth.
He the work, made the insides of Tiamat surge,
Spread his net, made it extend completely.
He…heaven and earth
Their knots, to coil

When he had designed its cult, created its rites,
He threw down the reins and made Ea take them.
The Tablet of Destinies, which Qingu had appropriated, he fetched
And took it and presented it for a first reading to Anu.
The gods of battle whom he had ensnared were disentangled;
He led them as captives into the presence of his fathers.

And as for the eleven creatures that Tiamat had created, he,
Smashed their weapons, tied them at his feet,
Made images of them and had them set up at the door of Apsu.
Let this be a sign that will never in future be forgotten!'
The gods looked, and their hearts were full of joy at him.

Lahmu and Lahamu and all his fathers
Embraced him, and Anshar the king proclaimed that there should be a reception for him.
Anu, Enlil, and Ea each presented him with gifts.

Damkina his mother exclaimed with joy at him;
She made him beam insidehis fine house.
He (Marduk) appointed Usmu, who had brought his greetings present as good news,
To be vizier of the Apsu, to take care of shrines.

The Igigi assembled, and all of them did obeisance to him.
The Anunnaki, each and every one, kissed his feet.
The whole assembly collected together to prostrate themselves.
They stood, they bowed, Yes, King indeed!'
His fathers took their fill of his manliness,
They took off his clothes which were enveloped in the dust of combat.
The gods were attentive to him.

With cypress they sprinkled his body.
He put on a princely garment,
A royal aura, a splendid crown.
He took up a mace and grasped it in his right hand.
His left hand.

He set a mushussu-dragon at his feet,
Placed upon
Slung the staff of peace and obedience at his side.
When the mantle of radiance
And his net was holding fearful Apsu,
A bull
In the inner chamber of his throne

In his cellar
The gods, all that existed,
Lahmu and Lahamu
Made their voices heard and spoke to the Igigi,
Previously Marduk was just our beloved son
But now he is your king. Take heed of his command.'

Next they spoke and proclaimed in unison,
Lugal-Dimmer-Ankia is his name. Trust in him!
When they gave kingship to Marduk,
They spoke an oration for him, for blessing and obedience.

Henceforth you shall be the provider of shrines for us.
Whatever you command, we shall perform ourselves.

Marduk made his voice heard and spoke,
Addressed his words to the gods his fathers,
Over the Apsu, the sea-green dwelling,
In front of Esharra, which I created for you,
Where I strengthened the ground beneath it for a shrine,
I shall make my house to be a luxurious dwelling for myself
And shall found his cult centre within it,
And I shall establish my private quarters, and confirm my kingship.

Whenever you come up from the Apsu for an assembly,
Your night's resting place shall live in it, receiving you all.
I hereby name it Babylon, home of the great gods.
We shall make it the centre of religion.
The gods his fathers listened to this command of his,

Who has your…
More than you by yourself have created?
Babylon, whose name you have just pronounced,
Found there our night's resting place forever!
Let them bring our regular offerings.

Whatever our work that we …
There his toil.
They rejoiced
The gods them
Who knows them light
He made his voice heard, his command
them

They did obeisance to him and the gods spoke to him,
They addressed their lord Lugal-dimmer-ankia,
Previously the Lord was [our beloved] son.
But now he is our king. We shall take heed of his command.
Gave long life

The mantle of radiance, the mace, and staff.
all the lore of sages.
We.

(Palace of Asssurbanipal, king of the world, king of Assyria.)

Tablet VI

When Marduk heard the speech of the gods,
He made up his mind to perform miracles.
He spoke his utterance to Ea,
And communicated to him the plan that he was considering.

Let me put blood together, and make bones too.
Let me set up primeval man: Man shall be his name.
Let me create a primeval man.
The work of the gods shall be imposed on him, and so they shall be at leisure.

Let me change the ways of the gods miraculously,
So they are gathered as one yet divided in two.
Ea answered him and spoke a word to him,
Told him his plan for the leisure of the gods.

Let one who is hostile to them be surrendered up,
Let him be destroyed, and let people be created from him.
Let the great gods assemble,
Let the culprit be given up, and let them convict him.

Marduk assembled the great gods,
Gave them instructions pleasantly, gave orders.
The gods paid attention to what he said.
The king addressed his words to the Anunnaki,
Your election of me shall be firm and foremost.
I shall declare the laws, the edicts within my power.
Whosoever started the war,
And incited Tiamat, and gathered an army,

385

Let the one who started the war be given up to me,
And he shall bear the penalty for his crime, that you may dwell in peace.

The Igigi, the great gods, answered him,
Their lord Lugal-dimmer-ankia, counsellor of the gods,
It was Qingu who started the war,
He who incited Tiamat and gathered an army!

They bound him and held him in front of Ea,
Imposed the penalty on him and cut off his blood.
He created mankind from his blood,
Imposed the toil of the gods on man and released the gods from it.

When Ea the wise had created mankind,
Had imposed the toil of the gods on them -
That deed is impossible to describe,
For Nudimmud performed it with the miracles of Marduk.

Then Marduk the king divided the gods,
The Anunnaki, all of them, above and below.
He assigned his decrees to Anu to guard,
Established three hundred as a guard in the sky;
Did the same again when he designed the conventions of earth,
And made the six hundred dwell in both heaven and earth.

When he had directed all the decrees,
Had divided lots for the Anunnaki, of heaven and of earth,
The Anunnaki made their voices heard
And addressed Marduk their lord,
Now, O Lord, that you have set us free,
What are our favours from you?
We would like to make a shrine with its own name.
We would like our night's resting place to be in your private quarters, and to rest there.

Let us found a shrine, a sanctuary there.
Whenever we arrive, let us rest within it.
When Marduk heard this,
His face lit up greatly, like daylight.

Create Babylon, whose construction you requested!
Let its mud bricks be moulded, and build high the shrine!

The Anunnaki began shovelling.
For a whole year they made bricks for it.
When the second year arrived,
They had raised the top of Esagila in front of the Apsu;
They had built a high ziggurat for the Apsu.
They founded a dwelling for Anu, Ellil, and Ea likewise.

In ascendancy he settled himself in front of them,
And his horns' look down at the base of Esharra.
When they had done the work on Esagila,
And the Anunnaki, all of them, had fashioned their individual shrines,
The three hundred Igigi of heaven and the Anunnaki of the Apsu assembled.

The Lord invited the gods his fathers to attend a banquet
In the great sanctuary which he and created as his dwelling.
Indeed, Bab-ili is your home too!
Sing for joy there, dwell in happiness!
The great gods sat down there,
And set out the beer mugs; they attended the banquet.

When they had made merry within,
They themselves made a taqribtu-offering in splendid Esagila.
All the decrees and designs were fixed.
All the gods divided the stations of heaven and earth.
The fifty great gods were present, and
The gods fixed the seven destinies for the cult.

The Lord received the bow, and set his weapon down in front of them.
The gods his fathers looked at the net which he had made,
Looked at the bow, how miraculous her construction,
And his fathers praised the deeds that he had done.
Anu raised (the bow) and spoke in the assembly of gods,
He kissed the bow. May she go far!
He gave to the bow her names, saying,
May Long and Far be the first, and Victorious the second;
Her third name shall be **Bowstar**, for she shall shine in the sky.

He fixed her position among the gods her companions.
When Anu had decreed the destiny of the bow,
He set down her royal throne. You are highest of the gods!'
And Anu made her sit in the assembly of gods.
The great gods assembled
And made Marduk's destiny highest; they themselves did obeisance.
They swore an oath for themselves,
And swore on water and oil, touched their throats.
Thus they granted that he should exercise the kingship of the gods
And confirmed for him mastery of the gods of heaven and earth.

Anshar gave him another name: Asarluhi.
At the mention of his name we shall bow down!
The gods are to pay heed to what he says:
His command is to have priority above and below.
The son who avenged us shall be the highest!
His rule shall have priority; let him have no rival!

Let him act as shepherd over the black-headed people, his creation.
Let his way be proclaimed in future days, never forgotten.
He shall establish great nindabu-offerings for his fathers.
He shall take care of them, he shall look after their shrines.
He shall let them smell the qutrinnu-offering, and make their chant joyful.

Let him breathe on earth as freely as he always does in heaven.
Let him designate the black-headed people to revere him,
That mankind may be mindful of him, and name him as their god.
Let their(interceding goddess pay attention when he opens his mouth.
Let nindabu-offerings be brought to their god and their goddess.
Let them never be forgotten! Let them cleave to their god.
Let them keep their country preeminent, and always build shrines.

Though the black-headed people share out the gods,
As for us, no matter by which name we call him, he shall be our god.
Come, let us call him by his fifty names!
His ways shall be proclaimed, and his deeds likewise!
Marduk

Whose father Anu designated him at the moment of his birth, To be in charge of pasturage and watering places, to enrich their stalls,
Who overwhelmed the riotous ones with his flood-weapon?

388

And saved the gods his fathers from hardship.
Let the son, majesty of the gods be his name!
In his bright light may they walk forever more:
The people whom he created, the form of life that breathes.
He imposed the work of the gods on them so that they might rest.

Creation and abolition, forgiveness and punishment.
Such are at his disposal, so let them look to him.

Marukka---he is the god who created them.
He pleases the Anunnaki and gives rest to the Igigi

Marutukku---he is the help of country, city, and his people.
Him shall the people revere forever.

Mershakushu---fierce yet considerate, furious yet merciful.
Generous is his heart, controlled are his emotions.

LugaL-Dimmer-Ankia…his name which we gave him in our assembly.
We made his command higher than the gods his fathers'.
He is indeed Bel of the gods of heaven and earth, all of them,
The king at whose instruction the gods are awed above and below.

Nari-Lugal-Dimmer-Ankia is a name that we have given him as director of the gods,
Who founded our dwellings in heaven and earth out of difficulties,
And who shared out the stations for the Igigi and Anunnaki.
At his names may the gods tremble and quake in their dwellings.

Asarluhi (first) is his name which his father Anu gave him,
He shall be the light of the gods, strong leader,
Who like his name is the protecting spirit of god and country.
He spared our dwellings in the great battle despite difficulties.
Second, they called him Asarluhi as Namtila, the god who gives life,
Who restored all the damaged gods as if they were his own creation.
Bel, who revives dead gods with his pure incantation,
Who destroys those who oppose him but…the enemy.
Asarluhi third as Namru, whose name was given…thus,
The pure god who purifies our path.

Anshar, Lahmu, and Lahamu called his three names;
They pronounced them to the gods their sons,
'We have given him each of these three names.
Now you, pronounce his names as we did!
The gods rejoiced, and obeyed their command.
In Ubshu-Ukkinakku they deliberated their counsel.
Let us elevate the name of the son, the warrior,
Our champion who looks after us!
They sat in their assembly and began to call out the destinies,
Pronounced his name in all their rites.

Tablet VII

Asare, bestower of ploughland, who fixes its boundaries,
Creator of grain and linseed, producer of vegetation.

Asar-Alim, whose weighty counsel in the Chamber of Council is most valued;
The gods, even those who know no fear, pay heed to him.
Asar-Alim-Nuna, the honoured one, the light of the father who begot him,
Who directs the orders of Anu, Ellil, Ea, and Damkina.
He indeed is their provider, who allocates their incomes,
Whose farmland makes a surplus for the country.

He is Tutu, first as creator of their renewal.

He shall purify their shrines, that they may stay at rest.
He shall invent an incantation, that the gods may be at peace.
Even if they should rise up in anger, he shall turn them back.

He shall be pre-eminent in the assembly of the gods his fathers;
None among the gods shall rival him.

He is Tutu, second as Zi-Ukkina, the inspiration of his people,
Who fixed pure skies for the gods,
Who set their ways and marked out their stations.
May he not be forgotten by teeming humanity, may they uphold his work.

Thirdly, they named him Tutu and Ziku, upholder of purification,
The god of sweet breath, lord of obedience and consent,
Producer of riches and abundance, who maintains a surplus,
Who turns whatever is scant into plenty.
Even in the worst hardship we can smell his sweet breath!
May they speak in worship and sing his praises!

Fourthly, let the people glorify Tutu as Agaku,
Lord of the pure incantation, who revives the dying,
Who showed mercy even to the captured gods,
Who removed the yoke imposed upon the gods his enemies,
Who created mankind to set them free,
The merciful one who has the power to give life!
His words shall be firm; they shall never be forgotten
In the mouth of the black-headed people whom he created with his own hands.

Fifthly, let their mouths show forth Tutu as Tuku, whose spell is pure,
Who uprooted all the wicked with his pure incantation.He is Shazu, aware of the gods
intentions, who can see emotions,
Who does not allow evil-doers to escape him,
Establisher of the gods' assembly, gratifier of their wishes,
Who makes the arrogant **kneel** beneath his wide canopy.
Director of justice, who plucks out crooked speech,
In whose place lies can be distinguished from truth.

Secondly, let them worship Shazu as Zisi, silencer of the aggressor,
Expeller of deathly silence from the bodies of the gods his fathers.

Thirdly, he is Shazu as Suhrim, uprooter of all the foe by force of arms,
Dispelling their plots, scattering them to the winds,
Extinguishing all the wicked, wherever they may be.
May the gods always proclaim the triumph in the assembly!

Fourthly, he is Shazu as Suhgurim, responsible for the obedience of the gods his fathers.
Uprooter of the foe, destroyer of their offspring,
Dispeller of their works, who left no trace of them.
Let his name be proclaimed and spoken in the land.

Fifthly, let future generations consider Shazu as Zahrim,

Destroyer of all enemies, every one of them arrogant,
Who brought all the refugee gods into shrines:
Let this be established as his name.

Sixthly, let them all praise Shazu as Zahgurim too,
Who destroyed all the foe by himself in battle.
He is Enbilulu, the lord, their enricher;
Their deity is mighty, responsible for sacrificial omens,
Who looks after pasturage and watering places, establishes them for the land,
Who opens up wells and apportions the waters of abundance.

Secondly, let them address Enbilulu as Epadun, lord of the countryside and…
Canal-controller of heaven and earth, establisher of the furrow,
Who maintains pure ploughland in the countryside,
Who directs ditches and canals and marks out the furrows.

Thirdly, let them praise Enbilulu as Gugal "canal-controller" of the gods' irrigated land.
Lord of abundance and the luxuriance of great grain-piles.
Responsible for riches, who gives surplus to homes,
Giver of cereals, producer of grain.

Fourthly, he is Enbilulu as Hegal "Abundance", who heaps up a surplus for people,
Who brings rain of abundance over the broad earth, and makes vegetation grow profusely.
He is Sirsir, who piled a mountain over Tiamat,
And took as booty the corpse of Tiamat, by his force of arms.
Governor of the land, their righteous shepherd,
Whose gifts are cultivation, garden plots and ploughland,
Who waded into the broad Sea-Tiamat in his fury:
Like a bridge he spanned her battlefield.

Secondly, they maned Sirsir as Malah "Boatman" may she, Tiamat,
Be his barque forever, and he her sailor.
He is Gil, who amasses mighty heaps and mounds of grain.
Producer of cereals and flocks, giver of the land's seed.

He is Gilima, who established the cosmic bond of the gods, who created stability;
The ring that encompasses them, who prepares good things,

He is Agilima, the lofty, who pulled the crown from the wicked,
And built the earth above the water, established the upper regions.

He is Zulum who designated fields for the gods, and divided up what he had created.
Bestower of incomes and food offerings, supplier of shrines.
He is Mummu, fashioner of heaven and earth, director of…
The god who purifies heaven and earth, secondly as Zulum-Ummu
Whom no other god equals for strength.
Gish-Numun-AB, creator of all people, maker of the world's quarters,
Destroyer of Tiamat's gods, maker of people in their entirety.

Lugal-AB-Dubur, the king who scattered Tiamat's brood and snatched her weapon,
Who made a firm base in the van and the rear.

Pagal-Guena, leader of all lords, whose might is supreme,
Who is greatest of the gods his brothers, prince of them all.

Lugal-Durmah, king, bond of gods, lord of the cosmic bond,
Who is greatest in the royal abode, highest of the gods by far.

Aranuna, counsellor of Ea, creator of the gods his fathers,
Whom no god equals in his princely way.

Dumu-Duku, whose pure dwelling is marked out for him on the holy mound,
Dumu-duku, without whom rules cannot be decided, Lugal-Duku.

Lugal-Shanna, king whose might is supreme among the gods.
Lord, might of Anu, who is pre-eminent as the namesake of Anshar.Iruga, who took them all captive from inside Tiamat,
Who unites all wisdom, and is broad of understanding.

Irqingu, who took Qingu captive as foe in battle,
Who administers decrees for everything, who confirms supremacy.

Kinma, director of the gods, giver of counsel,
At whose name the gods themselves quake in fear as in a tempest.

As E-Sizkur, he shall sit highest in the house of prayer,
And the gods shall bring their presents before him,
As long as he accepts revenues from them.
None may perform miracles without him.
No other god shall designate the revenues of the black-headed people, his own creation,
Without him, nor decisions about their lifetimes.

Gibil, who establishes the…of weapons,
Who performed miracles in the battle with Tiamat.
Profound in wisdom, skilled in understanding,
So profound, that none of the gods can comprehend.

Addu shall be his name: let him cover all the sky,
And may his fine noise rumble over the earth.
May he shed water from the clouds,
And give sustenance to the people below.

Asharu, who like his name is responsible for the gods of destinies:
He does indeed take charge over every single person.

Neberu: he does indeed hold the crossings of heaven and earth.
Neither up nor down shall they cross over; they must wait on him.
Neberu is the star which is bright in the sky.
He controls the crossroads; they must look to him,
Saying: He who kept crossing inside Tiamat without respite,
Shall have Neberu as his name, grasping her middle.
May he establish the paths of the heavenly stars,
And may he shepherd all the gods like sheep.
Let him defeat Tiamat, constrict her breath and shorten her life,
So that for future people, till time grows old,
She shall be far removed, not kept here, distant forever,
Because he created a place, he fashioned Dannina.

Enkurkur, father Ellil named him.
Ea heard that name, by which the Igigi all called him,
And was delighted, saying,
He whose fathers have given him such a splendid name
Shall have the name Ea, just like me.
He shall have mastery over the arrangement of all my rites,
And shall direct every one of my decrees.
With **fifty** epithets the great gods
Called his fifty names, making his way supreme.
May they always be cherished, and may the older explain to the younger.
Let the wise and learned consult together,
Let the father repeat them and teach them to the son.

Let the ear of shepherd and herdsman be open,
Let him not be negligent to Marduk, the Ellil of the gods.
May his country be made fertile, and himself be safe and sound.
His word is firm, his command cannot alter;
No god can change his utterance.

When he is angry, he does not turn his neck aside;
In his rage and fury no god dare confront him.
His thoughts are deep, his emotions profound;
Criminals and wrongdoers pass before him.

He the scribe wrote down secret instruction which older men had recited in his presence,
And set it down for future men to read.
May the peoples of Marduk whom the Igigi gods created
Weave the tale and call upon his name
In remembrance of the song of Marduk
Who defeated Tiamat and took the kingship.

***   ***   ***

INDEX

Made in the USA